Jeremy Dalton has been at the very forefront of immersive technologies over the past decade and is a global thought leader on its potential impact on our society. This brilliant book encompasses his deep knowledge, personal unique insights and extensive experience to contextualize the potential benefits of XR for business.
**Professor Shafi Ahmed, Advisor in Digital Health Transformation and Innovation, Department of Health Abu Dhabi and Faculty Member, Harvard Medical School**

If you're looking for an easily digestible but comprehensive guide to the commercial benefits of immersive technologies, and how to execute those projects well, you'll find this in Jeremy Dalton's *Reality Check*. Having myself built a global VR/AR business over the past five years, providing immersive content solutions to many of the world's leading brands and enterprises, I am yet to come across a guide that takes a vast range of use cases and practical challenges and distils them as neatly as *Reality Check*. I have no doubt that it will become the handbook for both the experienced and the as yet uninitiated reader.
**Damian Collier, Founder and Chief Executive Officer, Blend Media**

This is the most comprehensive evidence-based review of using immersive technologies in a business context that I have read. Jeremy Dalton encompasses all the different variations and uses of XR giving a pragmatic and informative review of each, the pros and cons and even some top tips. If you are already on your XR journey or looking to start then this is a must-read. Jeremy Dalton has cut through all the hype and clickbait and given a practitioner's view of the industry with fantastic use cases that can only aid you in your thinking and development needs.
**Marco Faccini FLPI, Chief Executive Officer, Silkroad Edtech and Non-Executive Director, Digitalnauts**

Jeremy Dalton has gone and done what the XR sector has needed for a long time: created an incredibly informative, easy to read, accessible and valuable guide to XR technology. Only someone with his level of insight, knowledge and passion for the sector could deliver such a clear and succinct summary of what you need to know when working in AR and VR and brings people into the conversation rather than isolate them. A must-read for those who wish to know more about this evolutionary technology and how it can enhance and add value to business, and our lives, now and into the future.

**Fiona Kilkelly, Founder of Immerse UK and Chairperson of Eirmersive**

*Reality Check* is the roadmap that industry urgently needs. Immersive technologies will change all corners of the commercial world, and every leader needs to understand how and why this technology will transform their business. Jeremy Dalton has produced the guide to our 'virtual' future that should be essential reading for anyone who cares about technology and the future of the global economy.

**Mark Mon-Williams, Director of the Centre for Immersive Technologies, University of Leeds, and Turing Fellow, Alan Turing Institute, London**

Jeremy cannot only see into different realities, he can also see into the future with his timely and comprehensive guide to the available technologies that enable you to transform consuming digital information in our new normal. Amazing insights. Start reading now and check you don't stop until the real end!

**Professor Eddie Obeng, Founder, The Virtual Business School and Inventor, QUBE-SuperReality**

*Reality Check* is a great read, written by one of the world's leading immersive technology experts. The book works if you know very little about AR/VR technology or if you are already active in its deployment and business use. Full of cases studies of actual implementations, clear explanations of the jargon used in the industry and covering both the business and deployment benefits and challenges. *Reality Check* is a must-read for everyone interested in understanding how XR will help their business!

**Mark Sage, Executive Director, Augmented Reality for Enterprise Alliance (AREA)**

# Reality Check

*How immersive technologies
can transform your business*

*Jeremy Dalton*

**KoganPage**

**Publisher's note**

Every possible effort has been made to ensure that the information contained in this book is accurate at the time of going to press, and the publishers and authors cannot accept responsibility for any errors or omissions, however caused. No responsibility for loss or damage occasioned to any person acting, or refraining from action, as a result of the material in this publication can be accepted by the editor, the publisher or the authors. The views expressed in this book are the author's and do not necessarily reflect those of any other entity.

First published in Great Britain and the United States in 2021 by Kogan Page Limited

| 2nd Floor, 45 Gee Street | 122 W 27th St, 10th Floor | 4737/23 Ansari Road |
| London | New York, NY 10001 | Daryaganj |
| EC1V 3RS | USA | New Delhi 110002 |
| United Kingdom | | India |
| www.koganpage.com | | |

© Jeremy Dalton 2021

The right of Jeremy Dalton to be identified as the author of this work has been asserted by him in accordance with the Copyright, Designs and Patents Act 1988.

Kogan Page books are printed on paper from sustainable forests.

**ISBNs**
Hardback    978 1 78966 636 6
Paperback   978 1 78966 633 5
Ebook       978 1 78966 634 2

**British Library Cataloguing-in-Publication Data**

A CIP record for this book is available from the British Library.

**Library of Congress Control Number**

2020950157

Typeset by Hong Kong FIVE Workshop, Hong Kong
Print production managed by Jellyfish
Printed and bound by CPI Group (UK) Ltd, Croydon CR0 4YY

*To everyone in the virtual reality and augmented reality industry who show us how magical these technologies can be.*

# CONTENTS

# ACKNOWLEDGEMENTS

To my partner, Alicia, for her enduring encouragement during the many early mornings, late evenings and weekends I spent writing this book.

To my brother, Daniel, for his patience and honest suggestions during his reading and re-reading of my 'almost finished' and 'pretty much there – just a little bit more to go' drafts.

To my parents for their unwavering enthusiasm and faith in everything I do (whether warranted or not).

To my friends for promising to purchase this book regardless of their interests. In particular, Ashank, Babu, Jas, Prem, Rani, Tanay and Varun for their long-standing friendship.

To my team and my colleagues in PwC whom I am proud to work with. In particular, Louise Liu as well as Andrea Mower, Daniel Eckert, Jon Andrews, Lyndsey DePalma, Matthew Goldsmith and Phil Mennie for their contributions and support.

To my editor, Géraldine Collard, for encouraging me to write this book and for applying just the right amount of pressure to ensure I completed it in good time!

To Alex Rühl for contributing her experience and expertise to the introductory 360 video guide in this book.

To the numerous organizations whose case studies feature in the book for being so helpful in contributing details and images to help bring these applications to life for readers.

To everyone I spoke to in the virtual reality and augmented reality community globally for being generous with their time, their stories and their positivity. In particular, Alvin Wang Graylin, Anthony Steed, Ben Resnick, Brianna Benson, Charles King, Dave Haynes, Dominik Pötsch, Gregory Hough, Joe Michaels, Julian Rocholl, Kadine James, Mike Campbell, Oval Liu, Paschal McGuire, Si Brown, Steve Dann and Tipatat Chennavasin. I expect we will share lots of exciting news in the years to come.

# 01

# Loading...

## A book on virtual reality and augmented reality technology?

One of the questions I am regularly asked when discussing this book with others is: 'Why write a book about an emerging technology?' The implication behind the question is twofold:

1 Books are a dying medium and we should encourage the use of succeeding platforms.
2 This book will soon be out of date.

On the first point, despite what many think, the market for books continues to show growth year on year. On a more practical and unsophisticated note, many people simply enjoy reading books to obtain information. For me to ignore that and blindly impose a technology where it does not fit would go against one of the very tenets I mention in this book: technology is not the solution to every problem.

On the second point, some of this information will date – that is the nature of most topics thanks to the progress of humanity – but the underlying reasons for adopting virtual reality and augmented reality will remain. While the case studies detailed in this book may grow older with time, the lessons learnt from them will persist and the value they bring to businesses will only grow stronger.

Emerging technologies are particularly vulnerable to rapid obsolescence, but just as the hesitant smartphone buyer waits perpetually for the next phone on the horizon, sometimes you need to place a stake in the ground and make the purchase. That's what I've done here (writing, that is, not purchasing, although the new iPhone is looking rather attractive, I must admit...).

## Who is this book for?

This is primarily aimed at those of you who may have heard of virtual reality (VR), augmented reality (AR), mixed reality (MR), spatial computing or the gamut of other terms used to describe immersive technologies that fall under the umbrella term extended reality (XR) and want to know more about:

- what XR is (and isn't);
- how it's applicable to business;
- how different organizations have been using it;
- the practical aspects and challenges of implementing it;
- common myths and perceptions associated with the technology and why they're wrong.

You might be considering implementing XR solutions in your business, or you may simply be curious.

## My approach

Many AR and VR applications – for example, training applications – are shared across multiple industries and it would be awfully dull of me to repeat each of these in every single industry as I go along. Therefore, I have organized my commentary not by industry but by application. I then expand on the reason behind XR's value in these areas using industry examples for case studies and discussion. Sometimes, I will dive deeper into a certain industry to illustrate a point, but the language won't be technical and I have reduced the number of acronyms to a bare minimum. This application-first approach will allow you to make a connection to your own business and hopefully even inspire new ideas.

Where it is possible for both VR and AR to be used as a solution for a particular application, I will default to talking about the more applicable technology of the two.

Many believe that VR and AR technology will converge in the future, and they are already doing so to some extent with devices that are capable of displaying both types of experiences. This may well be true, but even then they will continue to serve different purposes, so I have separated them where relevant and combined them (under the umbrella term XR) where there is shared commentary to make.

If you ever find yourself feeling bewildered at the use of a certain technical term, please feel free to peruse the glossary at the back of this book.

## Summary and objectives

Virtual reality and augmented reality are two emerging technologies mired in a swamp of confusion, complexity and contradictions. Many people might think that these technologies are new, not ready for business, or even that they don't have any business applications. This is understandable given that what we hear most in the media about VR and AR are stories designed to catch our attention – they are entertaining, amusing, outrageous and therefore mostly relevant to the consumer world.

In any case, it is rarely newsworthy to hear of an organization that uses AR to increase sales, VR to enhance its training programmes, or either technology to hold sustainable and cost-efficient workshops. Unfortunately, the side effect of seeing only one side of what these technologies are capable of leads to an inevitable shift in public opinion. VR and AR risk being seen as purely entertainment devices, a minuscule market, a passing fad, too immature to hold any real value, or all of the above.

What we don't hear a lot about are organizations like Ford, a century-old automotive manufacturer, that has been using VR since the year 2000 to optimize ergonomics in its manufacturing process;[1] Walmart, the biggest employer in the world, deploying more than 17,000 VR headsets to enhance employee training;[2] Coca-Cola using AR to sell more coolers and reduce the level of returns;[3] the UK National Health Service using AR to allow healthcare workers to visit patients remotely – the list goes on.

Analyst firm IDC predicts worldwide spending on XR solutions will reach $31 billion by 2023, most of which is expected to come from commercial (ie non-consumer) sectors such as retail, banking, manufacturing, education and utilities.[4] PwC's economic impact analysis predicts that XR will provide a $1.5 trillion boost to the global economy by 2030, primarily through productivity increases as a result of new and improved ways of working and learning.[5]

But regardless of the exciting predictions, XR is already being used every day by organizations around the world. It is this story of present-day practical applications in business that I would like to focus on in this book.

## Definitions

VR and AR do not exist as single points; rather, they encompass a spectrum of devices, content and technologies. They can be experienced in different ways on different hardware at different levels of fidelity and functionality. Figure 1.1 illustrates the differences between reality, augmented reality and virtual reality and provides a good base for the main terms you'll encounter in this book and elsewhere. If you'd like to explore this world in more detail, please see the glossary at the end of the book.

FIGURE 1.1

Clockwise from top left: Illustrating the differences between reality (1), augmented reality (2, 3) and virtual reality (4). Thanks to Emanuel Tomozei for the images.

### Reality

Let's start with what we know: the physical world. The top left image in Figure 1.1 shows a picture taken with a regular camera of a physical room with a laptop on a table.

### Augmented reality

Suppose you're wearing a pair of smart glasses or holding out your phone with the camera on to get the view in the second image in Figure 1.1. You're in the same physical room and in addition you have an overlay of information about the laptop. When you start to bring digital elements – information, objects, images, videos – into the physical world, this is the realm of augmented reality.

### Augmented reality (sometimes subcategorized as mixed reality)

The third image shows another form of AR (sometimes subcategorized as mixed reality). Once more, this is the same physical environment but the physical laptop has been replaced by a digital 3D model which behaves like a physical object – it appears to sit on the table, and if I were to move around the virtual laptop it would remain in its position, just like any physical object, and I would be able to see it from different angles. To achieve this, your AR device needs to be able to understand the surfaces of your physical environment. This type of AR, where digital elements can be anchored to points in the physical environment, is sometimes colloquially referred to as 'mixed reality'. In contrast, the digital informational text box in the second image in Figure 1.1 is simply overlaid on the physical world. You can think of this scenario as two intersecting planes: one is the image of the physical environment and the second is the digital information – put one on top of the other and you have the most basic of AR experiences.

### Virtual reality

When your entire world is digital, you have entered virtual reality. In the final image, the entire room has been digitally recreated, meaning everything in this image is computer-generated.

If these terms are already too confusing, take solace in knowing that below are the three key definitions I will be using most often in this book:

- **Virtual reality:** immerses users in a fully digital environment through a headset or surrounding display. This environment can be computer-generated or recorded from the physical world.
- **Augmented reality:** presents digital information, objects or media in the physical world through a mobile device or headset. These elements can appear as flat graphics or can behave as a seemingly real 3D object.
- **Extended reality:** represents the spectrum of technologies from the part-digital world of augmented reality to the fully immersive experience of

virtual reality. Sometimes the terms immersive technology or spatial computing are also used.

I've outlined these definitions here so we are all on the same page, so to speak, when I use them. While definitions are important for clear and accurate communication, at the end of the day, what the technology is called is less important than what it can do.

## Notes

1  https://www.forbes.com/sites/leoking/2014/05/03/ford-where-virtual-reality-is-already-manufacturing-reality/#14b2d766e4db (archived at https://perma.cc/9ZR5-QBH2)

2  https://corporate.walmart.com/newsroom/innovation/20180920/how-vr-is-transforming-the-way-we-train-associates (archived at https://perma.cc/9PY7-C438)

3  https://www.augment.com/customer-stories/coca-cola/ (archived at https://perma.cc/QCV7-J3E4)

4  https://www.idc.com/getdoc.jsp?containerId=prAP46164620 (archived at https://perma.cc/XP8A-22D5)

5  https://www.pwc.com/seeingisbelieving (archived at https://perma.cc/SA6E-JSTX)

# 02

# Why XR means business

The value of XR in business stems from the unique attributes of each technology.

## Strengths of virtual reality

Virtual reality's power comes from its ability to immerse users in an environment or perspective safely, cost-effectively and in less time than would be possible physically. This is the principal feature of VR that differentiates it from other technologies. It achieves this by:

- **Creating an emotional connection.** Successfully immersed users react to the virtual world in the same way that they would to similar circumstances in the real world. Place a user on a stage in an auditorium in front of a virtual audience of 1,000 people and they may feel anxious. Put a user on the receiving end of a verbally abusive rant and they might feel upset. Suspend them 100 metres above the ground to perform maintenance on a cell tower and it could cause them to panic. In other words, VR is capable of evoking a true-to-life sense of pressure, anxiety, awkwardness, empathy and a range of other emotions relevant to different workplace situations.

- **Providing a distraction-free environment.** How many times have you witnessed a colleague multitasking in a meeting, attempting to pay attention while transfixed by their mobile phone? Have you ever been on a video call, muted your microphone and minimized the window to work on other tasks? The modern world is full of tempting distractions across a range of devices. When you are engrossed in a completely virtual environment both visually and audibly, there are no application windows to open or close and it is much harder to quickly check a notification on your mobile phone without deliberately disconnecting from the experience and jumping between the virtual and the physical environment – possible, but a process that carries more work, which acts as a natural disincentive.

- **Removing the constraints of the physical world.** While being an effective immersion tool, VR also doesn't limit you to what is physically possible. You can collaborate with colleagues in a virtual workshop without having to physically travel; spawn an unlimited number of screens without worrying about the logistics of transporting, setting up and powering them; and walk through a refurbished version of an office without having to buy any materials. 3D models can be resized to better examine them at a human scale: molecular structures can be enlarged while towering buildings can be downscaled. VR also makes it possible to revisit a past scenario or simulate a future one in an impactful way. What would you do as the pilot of US Airways Flight 1549 after its engines had lost power? How could you simulate a scientific research mission on Mars?

## Strengths of augmented reality

Augmented reality's power comes from its ability to connect to, make sense of and display information on the physical objects and environments around us in a user-friendly way. To expand on this, AR technology:

- **Communicates relevant information conveniently.** This information is displayed intuitively in context with the physical environment and objects. At a glance, a technician can view the current temperature and tempo of a machine they're looking at, receive instructions on how to safely take it apart and be visually guided to the next machine in the maintenance queue; a retailer can give customers the ability to view products remotely without any specialist hardware; a field worker can call for assistance remotely and within seconds a senior colleague on the other side of the world can see everything they're seeing and highlight which compartments to open, buttons to press and screws to remove.

- **Reveals the invisible.** Not everything can be seen with the naked eye – from the network of pipes under our cities to the highways of veins beneath our skin, we live in a world of hidden machinery, and AR can help bring this information to the surface.

DID YOU KNOW?

AR is being used in healthcare right now to reveal the location of a patient's veins. Haemoglobin in blood absorbs infrared light, reducing the amount that is reflected back. The AccuVein is a handheld device that takes advantage of this phenomenon to identify veins and project a visual map of them against the surface of the skin. Measuring against the centerline of a vein, it has an accuracy of less than the width of a human hair, resulting in clinicians being 3.5 times more likely to successfully insert a needle on their first attempt.

- **Performs hands-free.** Having both hands available is a requirement in many scenarios, from performing surgical procedures on patients to mechanical procedures on machinery. The key benefits are being able to save time, reduce risk and eliminate errors that come from having to refer to documentation or instructions that are away from your place of work or are inconvenient to access. You may be a mechanic examining the undercarriage of a vehicle – having to stop, take out your smartphone or printed materials, refer to a complex set of instructions, commit them to memory, return to the task and successfully apply the information is a series of steps that is time-consuming, prone to error and potentially dangerous if you are working in a hazardous environment. In some cases, it may not even be possible – if you are working in half a metre of mud servicing a broken-down tractor, it isn't practical to get out a tablet. And even where not absolutely necessary, implementing hands-free AR technology can lead to improved productivity.

DHL: HANDS-FREE AR FOR 'VISION PICKING' IN WAREHOUSE OPERATIONS

DHL is a global logistics company founded in 1969 that delivers about 1.6 million parcels to more than 220 countries around the world. It has over 380,000 employees, some of whom work in warehouse operations.

DHL, in collaboration with one of its customers, Ricoh, ran a pilot programme to use AR for order picking at a warehouse in Bergen op Zoom in the Netherlands. Ten order pickers were equipped with AR headsets. Over the course of three weeks, they picked more than 20,000 items using the technology, completing 9,000 orders.

Outside of this pilot programme, picking was done in the regular way with a handheld scanner and paper lists. By taking a hands-free and paper-free approach through AR, DHL was able to increase productivity, save time and reduce errors. This is particularly relevant when many pickers are temporary workers who usually need to undergo costly training to be able to perform reliably and efficiently. The easy-to-understand system of presenting relevant information at the right time using AR helps to manage this.

> Picking accounts for 55–65 per cent of warehouse operations costs, creating a significant opportunity for cost savings by implementing AR technology.[1]

DHL worked with vendor Ubimax to deploy an AR application that was bespoke to the task and environment. This was loaded onto AR smart glasses which the order pickers wore. To log in, each picker simply looked at an identification card which contained a QR code specific to them. The camera on the smart glasses scanned the code and logged them in. From there, the picker could begin their day, scanning barcodes on available trolleys to receive information in their field of view on how to process them. Some of this information included how many items they needed to pick, their aisle and shelf position, the location of their next pick order, and the total progress made. Once they found the product, another scan verified that it was correct and highlighted the trolley compartment where the picker needed to place the item.

Pickers rated the solution highly, citing it as easy to use and validating it as an effective picking tool. Following the success of the pilot programme, DHL deployed 440 AR smart glasses to freight hubs in Brussels and Los Angeles.[2]

DHL is seeing an average increase in efficiency of 15 per cent as a result of using AR technology for order picking as well as increased accuracy rates. Onboarding and training times have also been halved as a result of the intuitiveness of the system.[3]

## What outcomes can XR drive in business?

XR technologies can benefit businesses across all industries in a number of areas. Below is a summary of outcomes that you can expect to see when XR is implemented in the right way. The importance and applicability of these will vary depending on the sector, business and team.

*Learning and development*

- Faster training.
- Improved learner confidence.
- Improved learner focus.
- Improved retention of information.
- Increased emotional engagement.
- Reduced reliance on human trainers.
- Greater cost efficiencies in deployment.
- Reduced upkeep of physical training locations.
- Increased portability of training.
- Less disruption to operations for on-site training.
- Improved learner insight through unique data capture.
- Improved ability to deliver high-risk training safely and effectively.
- Improved company culture.

*Operations*

- Reduced complexity of operations.
- Reduced costs.
- Time saved.
- Reduced travel and associated carbon emissions/improved sustainability.
- Improved remote collaboration.
- More efficient and effective remote assistance.

*Health and safety*

- Decreased number of accidents.
- Decreased accident-related costs.

*Design*

- Faster speed to market.
- Reduced time and cost of creating physical prototypes.
- Greater alignment of design vision.

*Sales and marketing*

- New revenue channels.
- Improved customer engagement.
- Increased understanding of consumer behaviours.

## Notes

1 https://www.dhl.com/content/dam/downloads/g0/about_us/logistics_insights/
  csi_augmented_reality_report_290414.pdf (archived at https://perma.cc/
  NH67-WPBR)
2 https://edelivery.net/2019/05/dhl-deploys-new-google-glass-advanced-ar-picking/
  (archived at https://perma.cc/E9AW-V9JX)
3 https://thearea.org/ar-news/dhl-supply-chain-makes-smart-glasses-new-standard-
  in-logistics/ (archived at https://perma.cc/8HU4-98E3)

# 03

# Learning and development

Training employees is not only a matter of operational competency and efficiency, it is a pathway to a happier workforce, increased employee retention, greater revenue and a reduction in wasteful costs.

Employees in the modern workplace value development and upskilling opportunities. An average of 78 per cent of employees of all ages rate 'professional or career growth and development opportunities' as important to them.[1] Dissatisfied employees leave organizations and $11 billion is lost each year due to employee turnover.[2] Meanwhile, organizations that can engage employees successfully attract 2.5 times more revenue than competitors with poor engagement levels.[3] This reveals an aligned motivation between employees and organizations and represents an opportunity to benefit both parties by deploying engaging learning and development programmes.

Training to date has been delivered in many different ways through many different mediums. Instruction manuals, videos, e-learning modules, classroom training and on-the-job-training all form part of the learning and development toolkit. And now VR is also part of that toolkit.

VR is being used by organizations to train employees on how to:

- operate new machines and equipment;
- execute a new process successfully and efficiently;
- build empathy towards customers and colleagues;
- deliver difficult messages;
- negotiate confidently;
- communicate and present effectively;
- convert more sales faster;
- improve customer service;

- manage difficult customers;
- develop leadership skills;
- deal with emergencies.

Better trained employees in these areas will perform their job more effectively and require less supervision and coaching. They will progress faster and perform more successfully in future roles. And they will be better equipped to respond to challenging situations. VR can be used to deliver realistic scenarios on the above topics without the cost or inconvenience of having to recreate those scenarios through role play or by ring fencing company resources.

Classroom training and e-learning are the two main methods currently used to deliver training to a wide audience. Classroom training offers opportunities for discussions, hands-on interactions and role-play activities, which can be very effective in delivering information on how to perform a task or respond in a relevant situation. However, classroom-based training is not always accessible to everyone and is difficult to scale due to the logistical and cost issues associated with training a large and geographically dispersed number of people.

E-learning meanwhile is very scalable as it can be delivered through an employee's laptop or smartphone, and can be accessed on demand. It is also cost-effective to deliver at scale as a result of lower variable costs. However, clicking or tapping on a screen is not the most inspiring or physically representative way of learning many skills and can lead to a lack of focus and a tick-box attitude.

VR represents a balanced learning solution that gives you the best of all worlds as it is:

- reasonably priced compared with classroom training at scale;
- more effective than e-learning in many cases, especially for training on practical and soft skills;
- accessible to users around the world more easily than classroom training;
- more flexible than classroom training as it is available on demand.

The choices individuals make in VR are more reflective of the choices they would make in the physical world. This is because a well-developed virtual scenario is far closer to its physical equivalent than an e-learning module or classroom lecture. As a result, VR could be even more effective than the classroom for certain learning objectives.

DID YOU KNOW?

A study conducted by the University of Maryland found that users remember information better if it is presented to them in VR rather than on a computer screen. Researchers concluded that using VR headsets resulted in an 8.8 per cent improvement in recall accuracy.[4]

Like all tools, VR is only as effective as the person that wields it. Poorly designed experiences or ineffective applications of the technology can be damaging to a learning objective. Knowing when to adopt immersive learning is as valuable as knowing when not to. Keep the strengths of VR in mind when assessing possibilities and ensure you design an experience that plays to those strengths.

## Soft skills

The term 'soft skills' started to proliferate in the early 1990s but it originated from a US Army training manual back in 1972 to contrast with the knowledge of how to work 'hard' machines ('hard skills'). Thus, the distinction was made between skills that require technical knowledge and those that were more closely related to personality traits, behaviours and interactions that with increased proficiency lead to more positive outcomes. They are also often applicable to many roles and industries.

Examples within the soft skills domain include:

- communication:
  - customer service;
  - negotiation;
  - sales;
  - feedback;
- teamwork;
- leadership;
- empathy;
- conflict management;
- stress management;

- problem solving;
- decision making;
- situational awareness;
- creativity;
- adaptability;
- work ethic.

Businesses benefit from employees that develop their soft skills in a number of ways:

- greater customer satisfaction;
- greater employee satisfaction;
- increased sales;
- improved productivity;
- higher employee retention.

The importance of soft skills to business is being recognized more and more. More than 1,000 global leaders from 28 countries took part in the Future of Work Global Research Study and half of the leaders surveyed were from organizations with over 500 employees. Soft skills dominated the 'most valued skills'. This is echoed by reports from many other organizations, including the World Economic Forum.[5,6]

Between VR and AR, VR is the most effective of the two technologies for the majority of soft skills training because it has a greater emotional impact on the user. Being put on stage in front of a crowd of hundreds blankly staring at you as you attempt to deliver a pitch on the company's latest initiative while a timer counts down unforgivingly is a daunting process. But all the emotions that form during such an encounter – the discomfort, anxiety, fear – are possible only if you genuinely feel that you are on stage and not in your living room at home or at your desk at work.

VODAFONE: PRACTISING PRESENTATION SKILLS IN VR

Vodafone is a British multinational telecommunications company founded in 1982 and headquartered in London, UK. With mobile, broadband and TV offerings, the company has significant operations in Asia, Africa, Europe and Oceania.

VirtualSpeech was hired to digitally rebuild the Pavilion, one of Vodafone's large conference rooms, and to make it available for communications training on demand as a VR experience.[7] This would allow Vodafone employees to practise their public speaking skills virtually before delivering their speech at the real Pavilion in front of a live audience.

Within six weeks, VirtualSpeech had visited the site, taken a panoramic photo for reference and rebuilt the Pavilion in 3D for use in VR, complete with a virtual audience (Figure 3.1).

FIGURE 3.1

Top: a photo taken at the Vodafone UK Pavilion. Bottom: the 3D recreation of the Pavilion, with interactive slides, timer, speech analysis data and a virtual audience.

In addition to presenting a recreation of the space, the experience allowed users to:

- upload their own presentation slides and notes;
- upload audio-recorded questions to be asked by the audience at the end of the presentation.

During the presentation, the user is given live feedback. If they are speaking too softly, they will be prompted with a notification suggesting they speak more loudly.

After the event is complete, the user is presented with an evaluation on their speech performance, including metrics such as pace, volume, tone, use of hesitation words, listenability and eye contact with different parts of the audience.

Performance analytics, feedback data and even entire recorded speeches can be saved in the app and an online learning management system which both learners and managers can view to understand areas of strength and improvement. With this knowledge, learners can hone their skills and attempt additional training with increased knowledge and confidence.

Feedback from Vodafone employees was positive: the average time spent by each employee in the VR training experience was 36 minutes and 91 per cent of respondents said they would like to see more VR training at Vodafone.

## Diversity and inclusion

Diversity and inclusion (D&I) in business are two distinct but equally important and intertwined concepts. Diversity means creating a workplace which employs a mix of people that is reflective of wider society. The Society for Human Resource Management defines inclusion as 'the achievement of a work environment in which all individuals are treated fairly and respectfully, have equal access to opportunities and resources, and can contribute fully to the organization's success'.[8]

> Verna Myers, a diversity and inclusion consultant, described the difference between the two concepts succinctly and memorably as: 'Diversity is being invited to the party; inclusion is being asked to dance.'

Balanced representation and fair treatment of employees are not only ethical objectives but also contribute to business objectives as supported by studies from multiple, independent sources:

- increased sales revenue;[9,10]
- increased profitability;[11,12]
- more customers;[13]
- greater sales of innovative products and services;[14,15]

- growth in market share and expansion into new markets;[16]
- enhanced ability to attract and retain talent;[17,18,19]
- lower project costs;[20]
- improved company reputation and brand.[21]

To leverage these benefits requires a change in mindset, a greater understanding of the challenges of minority groups, and impactful action to change the status quo. In other words, leaders and the wider workforce need to step into the shoes of others.

As you probably will have figured out by now, virtual reality is a great conduit technology to achieve this. VR is often described as the 'ultimate empathy machine' for the impact it can have: users feel a greater connection to the characters they are embodying and this can lead to a reduction in unconscious bias.

Jeremy Bailenson and Mel Slater are two researchers from Stanford University and the University of Barcelona respectively who have contributed significant research on VR generating empathy where users embody an avatar that is not their own. Some of these studies have yielded positive outcomes as far back as 2006.

In a more recent example from a paper published in July 2020, Bailenson collaborated with academics from the Zucker School of Medicine and Northwell Health to study the impact of a 20-minute VR racism experience.[22] One hundred and twelve faculty and staff members experienced the VR module, which was one component of a larger professional development programme; 76 participants completed a post-workshop survey where:

- 94.7 per cent agreed that VR was an effective tool for enhancing empathy;
- 90.8 per cent felt engaged in the VR experience;
- 85.5 per cent felt the session enhanced their empathy for racial minorities;
- 67.1 per cent said that their approach to communication would change.

This self-reported evidence is also supplemented by objective, directly measured evidence of VR's impact on racial bias. Slater and his team conducted a study where white people were embodied in black avatars and asked to participate in a virtual tai chi class. Participants wore a full-body motion-capture suit which allowed the movements of their whole body to be tracked and replicated in VR. A racial Implicit Association Test (IAT) was given to participants the week before and after their VR experience. Only 10 minutes of being embodied in a black avatar once was enough to observe a reduction in implicit racial bias a week after the event.[23]

> Implicit Association Tests measure the strength of a subconscious connection in someone's mind between a concept (eg black people, young people) and a positive or negative evaluation (eg joyous, detest). They can be used to investigate unconscious bias in a number of areas, including age, race, gender, sexuality and religion.[24]

VR invites empathy not only from a racial perspective but more broadly. A Stanford-developed VR experience called 'Becoming Homeless' was given to 560 people aged 15 to 88 from at least 8 ethnic backgrounds. They were guided through an interactive narrative in which they lose their job and have to sell personal items to pay rent. In the end, they are evicted, seeking shelter on a public bus while desperately trying to protect their few remaining belongings from being stolen.[25] The experience was built for VR but some participants were provided with a 2D version or a text narrative as an alternative to compare against. After the experience, among other measures of empathy, participants were asked to sign a petition in support of affordable housing. Those who went through the VR experience were approximately 20 per cent more likely to sign the petition than those who experienced the 2D or text versions.[26]

VR is capable not only of creating empathy but also of encouraging action to be taken afterwards. 'Clouds over Sidra' is a mini-documentary produced in partnership with the United Nations and Samsung.[27] Filmed in 360 video, it follows a day in the life of a 12-year-old Syrian refugee at the Za'atri Refugee Camp in Jordan. It premiered at the World Economic Forum in Davos, Switzerland in January 2015 and was later screened at a high-level donor meeting. This event raised $3.8 billion – almost 70 per cent more than expected – and brought in donations at twice the normal rate.

VR in D&I is being used to tackle not only unconscious bias relating to race but also gender, sexual orientation, disability, pregnancy and personality type.

> 'Being open to diversity is not just something to learn. It's something you "feel". So, how do you get people to understand that feeling? Tell stories? Sure. For people who will listen, listening to others is a great place to start. Even better is to get people to "feel" it. And that's virtual reality.' – Rhonda Brighton-Hall, CEO, mwah.[28]

PWC: TESTING THE EFFECTIVENESS OF VR FOR SOFT SKILLS TRAINING

PwC, in collaboration with Cleanbox, Oculus and Talespin, released one of the largest studies globally to measure the effectiveness of VR for soft skills training versus classroom and e-learning methods.[29] To accomplish this, PwC developed a VR soft skills training course around inclusive leadership which was delivered to participants using 72 VR headsets across 12 different locations.

A classroom and e-learning course on the topic was already available – the scenarios in these courses were kept and adapted to VR through a collaboration between PwC's Emerging Technology Group and its Learning and Development Innovation Team. To take advantage of VR's strengths, instead of considering the scenario from an outsider's perspective, learners had the opportunity to be directly involved in it, participating in conversations with virtual colleagues on who to hire, staff and credit for success on various projects. In total, the VR course took almost three months to design.

After deploying the training and collecting data on its performance, PwC found that VR learners are:

- Trained up to four times faster than with other methods. The same material that was delivered in 2 hours in a classroom (or 45 minutes in an e-learn) took only 30 minutes in VR. Even if you consider the extra time needed for first-time users to familiarize themselves with the equipment, VR learning is still four times faster than its classroom equivalent.

- Up to 275 per cent more confident in applying what they learnt following their training. This represents a 40 per cent improvement over classroom learners and a 35 per cent improvement over e-learners.

- More emotionally connected to the learning content – 3.75 times more than classroom learners and 2.3 times more than e-learners. Three-quarters of surveyed learners also reported that they had a wake-up call moment as they realized they were not as inclusive as they thought they were.

- More focused – up to 4 times more than their e-learning peers and 1.5 times more than classroom learners. VR commands a learner's vision and attention, removing notifications, the ability to multitask and access to a distracting device like a smartphone.

Additionally, the study determined that VR learning can be more cost-effective at scale. Although the VR content initially required up to 48 per cent greater investment than similar e-learning or classroom courses, it very quickly achieved cost parity per learner. At 375 learners, the cost of VR training per learner was equivalent to that of classroom training. At 3,000 learners, VR was 52 per cent more cost-effective than classroom training.

## Practical skills

Using XR to learn how to perform technical 'hard skills' associated with a job can deliver time, cost and other efficiencies for organizations by digitally recreating different training environments, assets and procedures in VR or by providing step-by-step instructions overlaid on the environment and assets around you through AR.

By allowing employees to practise in simulated circumstances they are able to become familiar with an environment and the actions they need to perform. This will eventually become a reflex when they come across the same situation in the physical world. As a bonus, it is also a fun and engaging way to conduct training on tasks that may be seen by some employees as mundane despite how important they are.

VR simulations or AR instructions are both ways of digitizing large amounts of information about an environment or process into an application which can be loaded by any user with the right hardware. Given how portable a lot of XR equipment is, this technology can make effective training accessible anywhere in the world at a lower cost than trying to replicate the process with a physical simulator.

AMERICAN AIRLINES: PRACTISING CABIN CREW PROCEDURES IN VR

American Airlines (AA), based out of Fort Worth, Texas, is the world's largest airline by fleet size, comprising 874 aircraft across more than 10 different models and configurations from suppliers Airbus and Boeing.

Training cabin crew on such a large range of aircraft is challenging, particularly as the different aircraft are not always easily accessible when required. And even when they are, there can be a lot of pressure on trainees to practise quickly so others can have their turn and the training group can complete in time.

AA wanted a better way to train flight attendants that allowed them to learn at their own pace but one that also improved throughput without compromising on the accuracy of the procedures. They turned to virtual reality as a way of achieving this while increasing student confidence and ability prior to using a physical simulator.[30]

In 2017, AA became the first airline in the world to adopt VR for cabin crew training. In collaboration with Quantified Design, AA built a 12-room VR training lab allowing 12 students to simultaneously practise self-guided training on door operations, emergency equipment locations and pre-flight-check requirements. By increasing the number of students able to be trained at the same time, the total amount of training time was reduced.

At the entrance of the lab was an instructor station with 14 screens giving the trainer the names of the trainees, an external video feed of them in each room and their individual first-person views in the virtual environment. AA employed tethered headsets which needed to be connected to a computer system. Normally, this would limit the user's ability to walk unrestricted; however, they also used backpack PCs which connected to the headsets, creating a system that allowed the trainees to move freely. The trainees' hands were tracked without the need for controllers, allowing them to physically pull handles, open doors and create muscle memory of these actions as a result.

Unlike the traditional system of queuing up to use a physical plane, in VR students are able to make mistakes in a safe environment without the anxiety of instructors or other students looking on from behind them. If the trainee flight attendants had made a mistake, such as accidentally deploying an emergency slide, the training could be reset or taken back one step at the click of a button.

## DID YOU KNOW?

The accidental deployment of a physical emergency slide, in addition to being a serious hazard, can cost an airline up to $30,000 to recheck, repair and repack. If a flight is cancelled as a result, the cost can spike to $200,000.[31,32]

To test the VR system's effectiveness, a group of 50 trainees were studied based on their performance and self-reported perceived ability to perform tasks. The results showed that the percentage of students:

- confident in reporting a high ability to perform increased from 20 per cent before the training to 68 per cent afterwards;

- required to repeat procedures on a physical simulator dropped from 25 per cent to 2 per cent;
- performing error-free increased from 34 per cent to 82 per cent.

The VR training system resulted in a reduced need to use physical trainers (and therefore instructors) as there were fewer procedures that needed to be repeated. It also led to a cost saving for new hires of over $600,000 a year – excluding the secondary effect of reducing inadvertent slide deployments or retaining flight attendants for longer.

All in all, the study showed that only 20 minutes of VR training per user was enough to have a significant impact.

## Health and safety

Health and safety issues are a particular concern for organizations as the consequences of adverse related events can be highly damaging. Notwithstanding the loss of human life, such events can result in direct and indirect costs, including the following.

### Direct costs

- Legal costs as a result of litigation.
- Regulatory fines.
- Compensation payments to injured claimants.
- Medical care for injured parties (immediate and ongoing).
- Delays to projects.
- Replacement or repair for damaged equipment.
- Decreased productivity.
- Loss of labour.
- Increased insurance premiums.
- Loss of business.

### Indirect costs

- Lowered company morale.
- Negative publicity.
- Decrease in reputation.

DID YOU KNOW?

The International Labour Organization estimates there to be 380,500 fatal occupational accidents and 374 million non-fatal occupational accidents per year.[33]

Virtual reality simulations allow trainees to practise tasks in a realistic manner that could be dangerous for novices to undertake physically. Without VR, the risk is usually mitigated through lots of theory, a physical mock-up and shadowing of more senior employees; however, a physical mock-up is often not portable or fully functional, coaching requires time from both members of staff, and using working equipment disrupts operations. Any mistakes trainees make may also take the equipment out of service.

DID YOU KNOW?

Human error contributes to 17 per cent of unplanned downtime according to a study by GE Digital, which surveyed decision makers across a number of sectors, including energy and utilities, healthcare, logistics and transport, manufacturing, oil and gas, and telecommunications.[34]

FORD: REDUCING PRODUCTION LINE INJURY THROUGH VIRTUAL MANUFACTURING

The Ford Motor Company is a global automotive manufacturer founded in 1903 and headquartered in Michigan, USA. It produces about 5.5 million vehicles each year and employs approximately 190,000 people worldwide.

Since 2000, Ford has been using virtual software tools to optimize the comfort and safety of its 'industrial athletes', a term used to describe its assembly line employees due to the physical nature of their role.[35,36]

When a new vehicle is being designed, the assembly process needs to be considered, tested and optimized, otherwise workers can end up with injuries, or in some cases a task can become impossible because a previous step made a component inaccessible.

Instead of using a physical mock-up of the vehicle, which can be costly, time-consuming and disruptive to operations, Ford uses a virtual environment to study the ergonomics of the assembly process. A worker puts on a VR headset, which immerses them in the future workstation of a vehicle. Their movements are tracked using a 23-camera motion-capture system, which is used to analyse the feasibility and proficiency with which they can carry out different tasks.

From 2003 to 2015, through the use of this technology and other ergonomics initiatives, Ford reduced the injury rate of its more than 50,000 industrial athletes by 70 per cent.

FIGURE 3.2

A Ford employee uses a VR headset to simulate the process of attaching a transmission to an engine. Photo credit: Ford Motor Company

Health and safety is not only about being able to operate machinery competently. Sometimes emergencies happen and the ability to follow the right protocol calmly while under extreme stress is the only way out of these situations. This raises the same challenges we've discussed: it is difficult and disruptive to effectively replicate an emergency, and requires a lot of time, money and resources to be allocated to what is usually a one-off event. In many cases, it is also more dangerous than simulating the scenario in virtual reality.

VR gives us the best of all worlds: the ability to create a believable, engaging and easily repeatable emergency but without the associated danger of the real thing.

---

### SHELL: EMERGENCY RESPONSE VR TRAINING AND ASSESSMENT

Shell is a British–Dutch oil and gas company that was founded in 1907 and is headquartered in The Hague, Netherlands. It has about 86,000 employees in more than 70 countries.

Shell wanted a safe, practical and cost-effective way to accurately recreate an accidental overspill scenario on a storage tanker that leads to a fire. In this case, e-learning is not powerful enough to provoke the intense emotions that users feel in such an event.

Shell teamed up with Immerse to simulate the scenario using VR, giving trainees the opportunity to physically apply their knowledge and skills to overcome the emergency as they would be expected to do in the real world.[37]

The trainee in VR can be joined by an assessor inside the VR experience or through a desktop, web-based interface. The assessor has the ability to control different aspects of the scenario such as when the fire starts. This results in more dynamic and variable training where the trainee is not given any advance warning or instructions and is kept on their toes throughout.

With an alarm blaring in the background, water sprinklers raining down and the user battling a raging fire near a massive container of petrol, the experience is intense enough – visually and audibly – to ensure the trainee is able to conduct the appropriate procedures under stressful conditions.

As a result of implementing this training in VR, Shell has benefited from being able to:

- recreate high-risk training scenarios effectively, safely and consistently;
- run a larger number of trainees through the overspill scenario;
- capture objective and trackable data.

  'It is faster, cheaper, more challenging and more fun than other types of learning – and it is also deeper... Today's immersive learning is compelling because it is better.' – Jorrit Van Der Togt, Executive VP of HR Strategy & Learning, Shell

IN SUMMARY

- VR is a powerful technology which can deliver effective soft skills and practical skills training when designed correctly.

- VR learners can be more confident in applying what they learnt, more emotionally connected to the learning content, more focused and take less time to learn than classroom and e-learners.

- While there is a significant upfront cost to delivering a VR training programme, for a large number of learners it can be more cost-effective than classroom or e-learning training.

- VR offers the best of all worlds: the ability to create a believable, engaging and easily repeatable scenario but without the associated cost, disruption or danger of the real thing.

## Remote assistance

Machines can be incredibly complex, or at least appear so to the untrained. Appropriate training that covers every possible task can be time-consuming, if not unfeasible to deliver before an employee starts work. Hence, a lot of training is conducted on the job under the direct supervision of a more senior team member with the right experience. This relies on those senior team members being present when their colleagues encounter a new or challenging task, but this is costly, labour-intensive and ultimately an inefficient method for a large workforce.

Being able to regularly and successfully coach workers through novel issues is not only a matter of operational importance but is key to successfully training the next generation of employees. This is becoming an increasingly important issue with ageing workforces, a high turnover of technicians and a decreasing supply of young people entering the market.

Augmented reality can help with knowledge sharing by allowing off-site experts to see what their colleagues in the field see and to advise them via video chat, by sharing relevant documents and through annotating the physical environment to highlight specific areas and instructions – all hands-free. For example, a remote expert might identify the model of a machine by examining it through the video feed, send a PDF diagram of the correct procedure to perform and circle a particular panel that should not be removed. All of this information will remain in view of the on-site worker while they perform the necessary actions.

Twenty-five per cent of high-performing service management organizations surveyed used AR for knowledge-sharing purposes compared with 17 per cent of others. Organizations using AR to service equipment benefited over non-AR users through an average:[38]

- 11 per cent increase in customer retention;
- 8 per cent increase in customer satisfaction;
- 3.4 per cent increase in revenue;
- 6.3 per cent decrease in time spent on administrative functions.

---

### BECTON DICKINSON: REMOTELY SUPPORTING COLLEAGUES THROUGH AR

Becton Dickinson (BD) is a US-headquartered business with approximately 70,000 employees that manufactures and sells medical technology.

BD faced challenges related to remotely located expertise. One of its facilities in Tijuana, Mexico was responsible for manufacturing healthcare products for hospitals, but the machinery involved was complex and the troubleshooting experts who had specialist knowledge of this machinery were located in San Diego, USA. The return journey time between these two cities is an hour under normal conditions, which includes navigating a border crossing, but with regular troubleshooting requirements, the wait time soon adds up, which impacts operations and profitability.

To enhance its ability to provide assistance remotely and effectively, BD turned to augmented reality.[39] By giving workers AR headsets and software that allows for sharing of video and audio as well as annotation and typing within the worker's field of view, they could create a powerful two-way communication channel with the troubleshooting team. Experts from this team would be able to see what the workers were looking at, diagnose the issue and provide instructions for a solution remotely. Even on a noisy machine floor, communication is clear and any voice instructions are understood through the system's sensitive voice-recognition function. Each support session can be saved and referred to later for training purposes or to repeat a similar procedure.

As a result of the AR implementation, BD increased the speed at which machines were repaired by 60 per cent and reduced travel costs as repairs could be successfully performed without having the experts travel over the border to Mexico. In turn, this benefited the workers, who felt empowered, knowing they were able to call upon an expert quickly and efficiently, as well as the remote experts whose work–life balance was improved through reduced travel requirements.

The advantages of using AR for remote assistance are not limited only to the industrial sector. Any job role requiring regular input from an expert can benefit. Customer service teams can be enhanced to better help consumers set up, configure and troubleshoot their devices; insurance companies can run more efficient claims-processing procedures; and hospitals can conduct virtual ward rounds to maintain patient oversight while reducing exposure to infectious diseases.

## NATIONAL HEALTH SERVICE (NHS): VISITING PATIENTS VIRTUALLY THROUGH AR

Imperial College Healthcare NHS Trust was formed in October 2007 in partnership with Imperial College London, one of the top 10 universities in the world. The organization is one of the largest of its kind in the UK, operating 5 hospitals in London with 11,000 staff and handling more than 1 million patients each year.

Dr James Kinross, a consultant surgeon and senior lecturer at Imperial College, having witnessed 29 people working in close proximity during the Covid-19 pandemic, realized a new way of working would be required. The solution came in the form of an AR headset provided by Microsoft.[40] Instead of having multiple doctors and nurses travelling between patients with a computer in tow, a single physician wearing the headset took on this duty. They were able to remotely communicate with team members via voice and video and share a single view of the patients through the camera embedded in the front of the headset.

These remote ward rounds reduced the number of clinical staff exposed to Covid-19 and, as a result, the amount of personal protective equipment (PPE) needed. The headset is controlled through voice, eye gaze or by making gestures in the air which the device recognizes and actions, reducing the physical contact that would be necessary when using a desktop computer. As a result, less cleaning is required and the risk of transmitting the virus is lowered.

Preliminary findings from the adoption of this technology indicate:

- staff required per ward round were reduced by between 66 per cent and 83 per cent, a saving of 50.4–55.4 hours of ward staff time per week;
- 106–420 fewer sets of PPE were used per ward per week;
- there was a 30 per cent reduction in the time needed to conduct ward rounds.

Additionally, staff felt the use of AR improved communication for the sickest patients, likely from the one-to-one connection between the single physician and the patient while simultaneously linking in with a team behind the scenes and also being able to see and interact with the patient's information in their field of view.

Patients are used to seeing clinical staff with a full suite of PPE, including visors, masks and gloves, so the addition of an AR headset came across as natural. Children did not find the device intimidating and parents and adult patients welcomed the use of innovative technology, particularly when linked to the reduced exposure to the virus.

# Notes

1  https://www.gallup.com/workplace/236438/millennials-jobs-development-opportunities.aspx (archived at https://perma.cc/J7C3-XTQ3)

2  https://www.inc.com/bryan-adams/this-avoidable-situation-is-costing-us-businesses-11-billion-every-single-year.html (archived at https://perma.cc/QNE7-JA32)

3  https://www.qualtrics.com/blog/employee-experience-stats/ (archived at https://perma.cc/HF2Q-J37K)

4  https://umdrightnow.umd.edu/news/people-recall-information-better-through-virtual-reality-says-new-umd-study (archived at https://perma.cc/GH7W-99GL)

5  https://www.weforum.org/agenda/2019/02/these-4-trends-are-shaping-the-future-of-your-job (archived at https://perma.cc/K484-ESH2)

6  https://www.futurecareerreadiness.com/wp-content/uploads/2019/11/OIGP_Future-of-Work-Report_2019_Harmonics-Reduced.pdf (archived at https://perma.cc/7GZC-R7NY)

7  https://virtualspeech.com/resources/case-study/vodafone-case-study (archived at https://perma.cc/7K8C-NL3V)

8  SHRM (2008) SHRM's Definition of Diversity, Alexandria, VA: Society for Human Resource Management

9  https://www.asanet.org/sites/default/files/savvy/images/journals/docs/pdf/asr/Apr09ASRFeature.pdf (archived at https://perma.cc/T4GH-XNVY)

10  https://www.mckinsey.com/~/media/McKinsey/Business%20Functions/Organization/Our%20Insights/Why%20diversity%20matters/Why%20diversity%20matters.ashx (archived at https://perma.cc/M9BU-9JNR)

11  https://www.asanet.org/sites/default/files/savvy/images/journals/docs/pdf/asr/Apr09ASRFeature.pdf (archived at https://perma.cc/T4GH-XNVY)

12  https://www.mckinsey.com/business-functions/organization/our-insights/why-diversity-matters (archived at https://perma.cc/J6UK-8YQS)

13  https://www.asanet.org/sites/default/files/savvy/images/journals/docs/pdf/asr/Apr09ASRFeature.pdf (archived at https://perma.cc/T4GH-XNVY)

14  https://www.bcg.com/en-us/publications/2017/people-organization-leadership-talent-innovation-through-diversity-mix-that-matters (archived at https://perma.cc/9Z8S-5Y7P)

15  https://diversityproject.com/sites/default/files/resources/Pwc-Diversity%20Project%20-%20Divesity%20is%20the%20Solution.pdf (archived at https://perma.cc/N3WZ-UH4J)

16  https://hbr.org/2013/12/how-diversity-can-drive-innovation (archived at https://perma.cc/5CMW-WNQ9)

17  https://diversityproject.com/sites/default/files/resources/Pwc-Diversity%20Project%20-%20Divesity%20is%20the%20Solution.pdf (archived at https://perma.cc/N3WZ-UH4J)

18  https://images.forbes.com/forbesinsights/StudyPDFs/Innovation_Through_Diversity.pdf (archived at https://perma.cc/XE8B-9YF3)

19  https://thedeamergroup.com/workplace-diversity-inclusion-employee-retention/ (archived at https://perma.cc/G2Y9-W2VW)

20  https://diversityproject.com/sites/default/files/resources/Pwc-Diversity%20Project%20-%20Divesity%20is%20the%20Solution.pdf (archived at https://perma.cc/N3WZ-UH4J)

21  https://diversityproject.com/sites/default/files/resources/Pwc-Diversity%20Project%20-%20Divesity%20is%20the%20Solution.pdf (archived at https://perma.cc/N3WZ-UH4J)

22  https://vhil.stanford.edu/mm/2020/07/roswell-am-cultivating.pdf (archived at https://perma.cc/Y8CV-458V)

23  https://www.ncbi.nlm.nih.gov/pmc/articles/PMC5126081/ (archived at https://perma.cc/W674-Q7LS)

24  https://implicit.harvard.edu/implicit/ (archived at https://perma.cc/A3NR-S6TZ)

25  https://news.stanford.edu/2018/10/17/virtual-reality-can-help-make-people-empathetic/ (archived at https://perma.cc/6DN9-56QC)

26  https://journals.plos.org/plosone/article/file?id=10.1371/journal.pone.0204494&type=printable (archived at https://perma.cc/SBN6-NGRU)

27  http://unvr.sdgactioncampaign.org/cloudsoversidra/#.X2zR32hKhPZ (archived at https://perma.cc/7GPW-6VVK)

28  https://mwah.live/blog/the-reality-of-inclusion (archived at https://perma.cc/B97H-4WQL)

29  https://www.pwc.com/us/vlearning (archived at https://perma.cc/EJN9-XXQZ)

30  https://www.wats-event.com/wp-content/uploads/2019/05/Jones_Lowe.pdf (archived at https://perma.cc/V5RZ-YUB8)

31  https://www.businessinsider.com/united-airlines-flight-attendant-emergency-slide-not-employed-2016-4?r=US&IR=T (archived at https://perma.cc/TK8T-TUQA)

32  https://ljs-aviation.com/wp-content/uploads/2019/02/LJS_Brochure.pdf (archived at https://perma.cc/J72S-FQF6)

33  https://www.ioshmagazine.com/global-work-deaths-total-278-million-year (archived at https://perma.cc/JPV3-XSNU)

34  https://lp.servicemax.com/rs/020-PCR-876/images/1-Unplanned-Downtime_Infographic-final2.pdf (archived at https://perma.cc/E4G9-XR35)

35  https://www.assemblymag.com/articles/86145-ergonomics-ford-simulates (archived at https://perma.cc/K3BC-9HB3)

36  https://media.ford.com/content/fordmedia/fna/us/en/news/2015/07/16/ford-reduces-production-line-injury-rate-by-70-percent.html (archived at https://perma.cc/MX55-TK5F)

37  https://immerse.io/case_study/shell-health-and-safety-emergency-response-training/ (archived at https://perma.cc/L8GH-NRBS)

38  https://www.ptc.com/-/media/Files/PDFs/Augmented-Reality/ar-for-service-aberdeen/Aberdeen-How-Best-in-Class-Use-AR-for-Service-Management.pdf (archived at https://perma.cc/LT6S-QG9K)

39  https://www.ubimax.com/case-study/becton-dickinson-2019 (archived at https://perma.cc/7UQ7-KRN4)

40  https://cloudblogs.microsoft.com/industry-blog/en-gb/health/2020/07/03/measuring-patient-and-clinical-effectiveness/ (archived at https://perma.cc/7533-MMSZ)

# 04

# Operations

## Collaboration, conferences and remote working

Our world is becoming increasingly connected: as of July 2020, almost 4.6 billion people (around 60 per cent of the worldwide population) were active internet users, approximately double that of 2010.[1] We are generating more income from products and services: global GDP in 2019 was $85 trillion, up by nearly 30 per cent since 2010.[2] And this is all happening while we work remotely more and more. From 2010 to 2020, the number of people working at least once a week from home grew by nearly 400 per cent.[3]

These trends are creating a mounting demand for effective remote working solutions. Video conferencing has responded as one of the tools that workers can employ. It is convenient, familiar, and supports both mobile and desktop devices. It is a low-hassle solution that works well for remote catch-ups, updates, presentations and other forms of information exchange meetings.

When deeper collaboration is required, or when the updates include three-dimensional information, XR represents a powerful solution. Primarily driven by VR (for now), users are able to summon a virtual environment, complete with all the collaboration infrastructure and functionality you would expect in the physical world – whiteboards, screens, sticky notes – as well as some that would only be possible in the virtual world – life-size 3D models, instant control over attendee location. This makes it ideal for creative workshops, idea generation sessions and design reviews.

Research conducted by University College Dublin in collaboration with the Bank of Ireland and VR meeting software MeetingRoom.io shows the strengths of VR over video conferencing for collaboration purposes. One hundred participants were recruited to experience both a VR meeting and a video conference call in different orders. The study found that participants in the VR meeting felt more immersed and closer to each other and so could conduct a more focused meeting – so much so that some participants had to be reminded that they were in a bank with others around who could hear them![4]

## AF GRUPPEN: COLLABORATING IN VR ON A NORWEGIAN FREEWAY PROJECT

AF Gruppen is the third largest construction and civil engineering company in Norway. Headquartered in Oslo, it has 3,100 employees and operates in China, Norway, Sweden and the United Kingdom.

One of AF Gruppen's projects involved constructing a new four-lane freeway connecting the west of the city of Kristiansand to the east of the town of Mandal in Norway.[5] This 19-kilometre stretch of road involves integrating 47 different structures, including 5 double-track tunnels and 8 double-track bridges, and is expected to be completed in autumn 2022. The project is worth 4.7 billion NOK ($480 million).

As you can imagine, this is an incredibly complicated and technically challenging project with hundreds of (and soon expected to be more than 1,000) building information modelling (BIM) files, which provide detailed information on the geometry, components and other data relating to various structures.

Throughout the project, construction will progress with sections of the road and adjoining structures in various stages of completion. Accurate and swift communication about this evolving state is of paramount importance to ensure the project timeline is met. Site managers, leaders, engineers, BIM specialists and other stakeholders regularly meet to discuss progress and plans for future stages. These design review sessions tend to precede the related construction by 3–4 weeks to ensure everything is in place by the time construction is ready to begin on that particular phase.

To aid these collaborative sessions, and to visualize the construction in a powerful way, AF Gruppen uses virtual reality technology. On the hardware front, the company employs four headsets: three at the project office in Kristiansand where there are 400 employees, and one at the headquarters in Oslo where the designers are based. The software the company uses, which allows it to import its 3D designs into a VR environment and collaborate with multiple stakeholders, is built by a company called Dimension10, based in Oslo.

From February 2019 to December 2019, Rune Huse Karlstad, BIM Manager and XR Leader at AF Anlegg (the civil engineering division of AF Gruppen) analysed the impact of using VR technology to conduct design reviews in collaboration with the Center for Integrated Facility Engineering (CIFE) at Stanford University. He analysed eight VR design review meetings involving 16 stakeholders during that time and tracked metrics from users via a survey after each meeting in line with the Virtual Design and Construction (VDC) framework developed by CIFE, reporting results and iterating plans monthly.

The majority of users (56 per cent) reported having a low level of experience of VR prior to these meetings (as determined by a rating of less than 5 out of 10). To manage this, 15-minute training sessions with individuals or pairs were run at Dimension10 to teach users the basics. A one-page document and an instructional video were also provided as a reference guide to help users navigate within VR and learn how to start a meeting.

Some users had not even used a tablet before as their role did not require it, but despite that many found the VR system to be intuitive, engaging and fun, enthusiastically contributing comments and feedback based on what they were seeing. In total, 62.5 per cent of users found it easy to start and open the VR session and three-quarters of users were able to locate and load the necessary BIM files for each VR review meeting, showing that you do not need to have extensive experience in VR to take advantage of the technology. For the remaining users who found it challenging, a VR technician was on hand during each meeting to assist as well as to take relevant screenshots and record the meeting for future reference.

As is normal during design reviews in the construction industry, potential issues were identified and resolved. Seventy-five per cent of users agreed that VR helped them to understand these issues better. For 12.5 per cent of users, there were no issues to discuss, leaving only a minority of 12.5 per cent who did not see the value of VR in this instance. Depending on the complexity of the feedback received in each meeting, any changes could take the designers anywhere from one hour to three days to implement, allowing stakeholders to return rapidly for a review. Any changes are automatically synchronized across all stakeholders' systems overnight so they always have the latest version.

From a travel perspective, meeting in VR was more sustainable, less time-consuming and less costly than a traditional meeting, which could involve between 8 and 20 people needing to make a return flight from Oslo to Kristiansand. Despite this flight being just under an hour, the disruption in terms of time due to preparation, airport procedures and local transport is at least five times that per person. All factors considered, the financial cost of each trip per person is between $1,000 and $1,500.

To put this all together, for a team of, say, 15 to make this journey would require 75 people hours, cost nearly $20,000 on average and output approximately 3 tonnes of $CO_2$. This is for a single meeting which could last only a few hours. By using VR, the time spent would be contained to the time of the meeting, the financial cost reduced significantly, with a comparatively negligible impact on $CO_2$ levels. Understandably, just over 80 per cent of the users agreed that conducting these design review meetings in VR was effective enough to forgo the need to travel to and from the project office. The remaining 20 per cent of users were based on-site at the project office so the question was not applicable to them. No users disagreed with the statement.

From a return on investment perspective, and from a purely financial standpoint, the cost of the hardware and software employed was recouped after only a handful of meetings.

From April 2019 to November 2019, the number of sessions hosted and the hours spent in VR for such meetings increased from 16 to 34 and 6 to 32 respectively, representing an increase over the period of 113 per cent and 433 per cent respectively. This significant and sustained increase in the use of VR technology for collaborative design sessions was a strong indicator of the benefits that it provides.

The use of VR at AF Gruppen for communication, collaboration and visualization with its clients has been so successful that the internal design team has now adopted the technology for use in its own meetings.

> 'Even though we also use 3D models on standard screens today, VR technology opens up a new dimension that makes it easier for us to see what and where to build' – Rune Huse Karlstad, BIM Manager and XR Leader, AF Anlegg (civil engineering division of AF Gruppen)

Taking the concept to the next level, VR can be used not only for team meetings but also for much larger events such as conferences. As VR transcends the rules of the physical world, venue capacity needn't be an issue, all sorts of audiovisual special effects can be employed and attendees can experience the event from any perspective they want.

## HTC: MOVING A CONFERENCE FROM THE PHYSICAL WORLD TO VIRTUAL REALITY

HTC is a mobile device and VR headset manufacturer and one of the major players in the VR industry. Headquartered in Taiwan, the company employs approximately 5,000 people worldwide.

In March 2020, HTC held its fifth annual XR industry conference entirely in VR, making it the first business event to be replaced by a VR counterpart.[6] Approximately 2,000 people from over 55 countries registered for the event, which was nearly 4 hours long. Speakers included high-profile figures such as HTC's chairwoman, Cher Wang, and Dr Thomas Furness, who has led pioneering research into VR since the 1960s. All speakers had digital avatars specially made to their likeness which represented them on the virtual stage.

FIGURE 4.1

Images from HTC's fifth annual XR industry conference which was held entirely in VR

The virtual environment was custom built and included a number of special effects such as a flypast by three jets to kick off the event and 3D representations of topic areas to keep the audience engaged and assist speakers in communicating their points.

One of the speakers, Alvin Wang Graylin, the China president of HTC's Vive division, commented: 'One of the biggest benefits of XR is the ability to remove the perception of distance and boundaries for users.'

## Data visualization

The ability to collect, visualize, analyse and communicate insights from data is becoming an increasingly important part of any organization.

## The scale of data is unimaginably large

To illustrate the amount of data being generated in the world, consider that each day 294 billion emails are sent, 500 million tweets are posted and 5 billion searches are made.[7] In a single minute, that equates to 188 million emails, 87,500 tweets and 3.8 million search queries.

Email, Twitter and internet search are ubiquitous, of course, but let's consider a more niche subject area – connected cars. These are cars that are part of the internet of things ecosystem – that is, they collect data and make it available to the vehicle's owner and other stakeholders where relevant. This real-time communication channel makes it possible to alert the emergency services in the event of an accident, or the vehicle owner via a smartphone notification when the oil needs changing, or to recommend a new route when a planned route has a large build-up of traffic.

It also means a lot of data: 4 terabytes (4,000 gigabytes) is generated from each connected car daily and by 2023 there will be an estimated 76 million connected cars shipped globally.[8,9] That's more than 300 million terabytes of data just from connected cars, which is only a minuscule part of a much larger picture – expand this out to include other areas and it's easy to see the volume of the data being generated in the world is becoming gargantuan.

Creating actionable insight from data has become so important that the role of the chief data officer (CDO) has risen to prominence: Capital One appointed the first CDO in 2002 and research suggests that the number of hirings for this role has more than quadrupled since 2012.[10]

---

DID YOU KNOW?

A survey conducted in 2018 found that 62.5 per cent of Fortune 1000 senior executives responded that their organization had appointed a chief data officer[11]

## How can XR help?

Given the growing size and importance of data in the world, we will need to develop new and effective methods of collecting, filtering, visualizing, analysing and communicating this data. XR is capable of enhancing the latter stages of this journey because it offers:

- **The ability to process more information.** The large visual real estate of digital elements afforded by a headset in which you can look around in 360 degrees allows for far more data to be displayed and processed.
- **Greater focus.** Being immersed in the data means that outside distractions are minimized and you can concentrate on the data patterns in front of you.
- **Opportunities for collaboration.** Users can work together within the same virtual space that the data is being displayed to communicate thoughts and analyses.
- **Interaction with data that is intuitive.** Instead of using a keyboard and mouse as a proxy for your actions, you can examine the data from different angles naturally by physically moving and reaching out to manipulate it.
- **More efficient communication of spatially connected data.** Data that is linked to an environment can be displayed within that environment, immersing the user in both the data and its context.
- **More effective multidimensional analysis.** To analyse data across multiple dimensions requires a way of communicating those dimensions. Users can walk and look around a three-dimensional space of data in VR. The size, colour and shape of objects in that space can be used to communicate more dimensions. 3D audio and haptics technology (the stimulation of the sense of touch) could also be employed to expand this further – in other words, multiple human senses in addition to sight can be employed in VR to analyse various dimensions of data.

  Note that 'dimensions' in this context refers not only to the visible spatial dimensions (1D, 2D, 3D) but rather the attributes of the data. A 12-dimensional example could be an analysis of homes in a city that includes the type of home (1), the size of home (2), the year it was built (3), the market value (4), the number of inhabitants (5), whether it's under a flight path (6), proximity to public transport (7), proximity to schools (8), rating of its local area (9) and the home's location in terms of longitude (10), latitude (11) and altitude (12).

## CISCO: VISUALIZING ORGANIZATIONAL NETWORKS AND INFORMATION FLOW IN VR

Cisco is a California-based company founded in 1984 that develops, manufactures and sells networking hardware and software solutions.

Cisco's Intelligent Human Network project aims to analyse connections within and between teams, helping to visualize the flow of work not only from a hierarchical perspective but also from the informal networks that we naturally build from being around others in the same organization.[12]

This type of organizational network analysis can provide unique insights, such as identifying brokers who play an important role in bridging the knowledge gap between different parts of the organization. This supports one of Cisco's missions to have more teams performing like its best ones.

Experience designer Chuck Shipman has been working as a lead developer on the Intelligent Human Network project for the last few years. It was originally built as a 2D platform but given the scale and complexity of the data, Cisco's HR team wanted to expand this to VR and demonstrate to leadership the technology's transformative potential to analyse this type of data.

Slanted Theory, specialists in immersive data exploration, was brought in to build the Organizational Network in Virtual Reality (ONVR) application. This prototype enabled Cisco to explore the influential relationships and connections between employees in an immersive data structure.

The details of these relationships provide insight into why certain employees are connected and the benefits they receive and contribute to the network. Relationships were categorized by those who provide:

- information;
- help with decision making;
- problem solving;
- career advice;
- personal support;
- sense of purpose;
- innovative ideas.

This data was collected through a questionnaire that was given to a selection of Cisco employees from 84 locations around the world. The result was a total of 3,353 individuals with 9,500 different types of influential connections between them.

All of this is displayed as a cloud of points and connective lines in 3D space that users can physically explore and interact with naturally. With their hands, they can reach out and grab, rotate, expand or shrink sets of data. And they can do this in collaboration with colleagues, allowing them to explore and communicate thoughts and ideas with each other.

Chuck describes the benefits of analysing this data in VR: 'I can focus. I can slow down. I can absorb. I can see disconnections, bottlenecks and isolation. What's more, everyone is enlisted in the data manipulation and discovery process: their insights are immediately consumed in the same context by everyone else.'

The Institute for the Future (IFTF), an independent, non-profit strategic research organization, was commissioned by Cisco to write a report that draws on its research and interviews with domain experts to analyse the ONVR application and identify other possibilities for using VR tools like this. This information and further details are included within it.[13]

It is important to note that XR is not useful for every data visualization. A simple graph that can be easily understood on a 2D line chart should remain so as it would add little value to visualize it using XR.

Any visualization that is three dimensional or higher may benefit from being explored in XR. Attempting to represent it in 2D is suboptimal as some data can be occluded, it is less natural to explore, and it is more cognitively taxing as your brain needs to perform the conversion from a 2D plane to a 3D object.

'Virtual reality allows us to visualize complex relationships that just aren't possible in 2D. The human intelligence evolved in a 3D world and our ability to see subtle and complex patterns runs very deep in our neurological systems that are designed for navigating a spatialized 3D world' – Toshi Hoo, Emerging Media Lab Director, Institute for the Future[14]

## Exploring data on written reports with AR

A written report is static by nature. Whether printed or in PDF form, it represents a screenshot of information that cannot be changed once a user has downloaded or printed one. It is also impossible to filter, expand or customize the data without leaving the report.

AR can help overcome these constraints by communicating data in an interactive, customizable and engaging way. It can also be used to ensure that any data presented is up to date, so even if a new edition of a report is released, anyone with a prior version will still see the latest data. This is beneficial as in a lot of cases, data in reports can be cut and displayed in different ways but space and focus are limitations that prevent us from presenting every single view. Different stakeholders will have different interests – some will be interested in viewing data from a specific country, from a specific year and so on. If every single angle from the data was covered, however, a report would become much larger, unwieldy and unattractive to readers. AR can help contain all of those views and offer them out on demand without impacting the size of the report.

In PwC's *Seeing Is Believing* report, readers can visualize the magnitude of XR's expected contribution to the global economy in real-world seconds via AR. They can also select different years – 2019, 2025 or 2030 – to see how it changes. The visualization can be accessed through the user's own smartphone without the need to install any software as it runs straight from the web browser using webAR technology.[15]

FIGURE 4.2

A user activates one of the AR experiences in PwC's *Seeing Is Believing* report on their smartphone. Thanks to Randa Dibaje for the photo.

IN SUMMARY

- There is a huge amount of data in the world already and it is getting larger, more complex, and is being generated at a faster pace.

- XR can help users derive insights from data more quickly by enabling users to interact with it more intuitively, examine more of it in a single, focused view, and collaborate with others to share analyses.

- XR is best employed for the visualization of large, multidimensional and spatial data. For simpler data that can be satisfactorily displayed in 2D, XR has limited value.

- AR can enhance reports, giving readers the most up-to-date data and enabling them to explore it in greater depth.

## Environment and asset visualization

XR can help bring to life the details of environments and assets wherever you are in the world so they can be better understood, reviewed and improved. XR has been used this way in a number of areas, including:

- industrial design to design and build products;
- civil engineering to align stakeholders on large-scale projects;
- consumer research to help understand buyer behaviours;
- interior design to explore different room layouts, materials, colours and furniture;
- architecture to align stakeholders on building designs;
- construction to oversee site progress;
- energy and utilities to reveal underground infrastructure;
- retail to market consumer products;
- tourism to market holiday destinations;
- forensic investigations to simulate accidents, crimes and other scenarios;
- city planning to model the effects of urban design proposals;
- building conservation to preserve historical sites;
- journalism to immerse users in a news story.

It has even been used in corporate finance to give potential investors a better understanding of companies and their operations.

---

**LINTBELLS: CLOSING THE DEAL ON A MUSSEL FARM WITH THE HELP OF VR**

Lintbells is a British business of about 65 people specializing in nutritional supplements for pets. The company was established in 2006 in response to a growing market of pet owners looking for innovative health products. Its flagship product is sourced from green-lipped mussels, which can be farmed only in specific locations in New Zealand.

PwC's Mergers and Acquisitions team acted as lead financial advisor to Lintbells, which was seeking investors in the business. The farming and harvesting techniques Lintbells developed to produce mussels with a high content of the active ingredient are critical to its success, so it was important to communicate this to potential buyers. To achieve this, a VR experience was created to take buyers on a boat journey to the offshore mussel farm and show them the harvesting process. The 360 filming for the experience was conducted locally by New Zealand-based company ImmerseMe.[16,17]

Using VR helped to 'transport' buyers to Lintbells' operations in New Zealand in less time, at a lower cost and with fewer carbon emissions.

'By using virtual reality – to give potential investors a thorough understanding of our New Zealand-based operations without flying them there – [PwC] were able to run a faster and more efficient auction process, and still communicate the key success factors of the business, which was crucial for finding the right buyer' – John Howie, CEO & Co-Founder, Lintbells

---

## Design reviews

If virtual reality is capable of making you believe that you are in another environment, it can be used to effectively test changes to that environment. Such tests could be conducted for aesthetic purposes (to assess a new wall-paper at a restaurant, for example) or functional purposes (to simulate and optimize the entryways and exits at a train station). Creative concepts in stores, new layouts in offices and even brand revamps in hotels can be assessed and iterated without having to modify the physical environment. This means no furniture needs to be hauled from one side of the room to the other, no shelves need to be drilled in, no walls need erecting, no tiles have to be ordered, no carpet swatch books need to be organized and no lights need rewiring. It also means that objects which don't even exist yet can be quickly mocked up and tested in the environment.

All of this reduces hassle, creates a massive time saving, and ultimately leads to more aligned, emotionally invested and satisfied stakeholders thanks to the effective communication enabled by XR.

Consider the alternatives to XR for visualizing a new design concept:

- **Oral or textual communication:** physically speaking or writing descriptively about the design.
- **2D plans:** hand-drawn, printed or digital technical drawings.
- **3D visualizations:** hand-drawn, printed or digital concepts of what the end result would look like from a user's perspective, such as architectural renders.
- **Physically redesigned environment:** effectively, building the concept physically.

These methods have been used to varying degrees across a number of industries, including architecture, engineering, construction, mining, manufacturing, real estate, retail, hospitality and interior design – and they all have their pros and cons. Physically redesigning an environment may be a possibility for a smaller project or idea such as modifying the layout of merchandise in a retail store but it is unfeasible for larger projects such as the restructuring of an entire shop to optimize the customer experience and maximize the appeal of high-value stock. Even relatively minor changes such as the rearrangement of existing furniture in a show home often require a significant chunk of time and effort, making it unappealing when there are other visualization tools available.

Speaking or writing about a design is an easy way to communicate an initial vision but cannot carry major projects to completion as it evokes different images for different people. Baltimore-based interior designer Patrick Sutton commented about VR: 'Up until that point, a lot of decisions were made based on the combination of verbal description and trust. If you were not a good communicator or hadn't yet developed a level of trust with your client, that made for real challenges.'[18]

Once a concept gains traction it needs to be supplemented with technical details and effective visualizations. It is possible to do this with a 2D plan which can communicate information including the dimensions and positions of rooms, areas and objects. But it still requires some mental translation to piece together different 2D viewpoints to achieve a clear and accurate visualization.

3D visualizations were a necessary evolution, getting us closer to the physical design vision by lowering the mental load required to translate concept to reality, and with it the possibility of miscommunication. In particular, 3D visualizations presented via digital technology can be dynamic, aiding in the running of simulations such as how queues in a school cafeteria can be managed.

For non-digital, paper-based designs (whether 2D or 3D), it is difficult to make significant changes on the fly, making it a relatively inflexible media format.

So how does VR take the visualization of design concepts to the next level? By immersing users in the environment and allowing them to physically explore it. Through this, not only is every element in the environment capable of being created at a human scale, it is also possible to engage the senses in a more powerful way. For example, you might feel a sense of claustrophobia when exploring an off-plan home due to the low ceilings and small floor area; an aisle which looks okay on paper may turn out to be too narrow once it is populated with a sideboard and thick picture frames and a user attempts to walk along it; the textures and colours of the floor and furniture may clash upon further inspection; doors, once opened, may block access to important areas; the view from the planned bedroom window on the third floor may not provide as grand a vista as the buyer had envisioned. The sense of presence and the natural interactions within VR can lead to quicker identification of scale, ergonomics and aesthetic-related issues like these so they can be resolved before they become expensive mistakes.

Where VR succeeds in giving stakeholders first-hand experience of exploring an unbuilt or modified environment, AR sacrifices immersion for a direct connection to the physical world. By simply pointing your mobile device's camera at an appropriate location, you can create a window into the future in which a planned environment is digitally overlaid onto the physical one. You could summon a new decking, test the scale of a new home extension or even change the exterior colour of your home.

Using AR for visualization can also help reveal otherwise hidden information in a constructed building, such as the location of wall studs, and warn you of impending conflicts if, for example, you're planning to install a light switch where a set of cupboards will soon be.

## Visualization of hidden utilities

The utilities that we take for granted every day – gas, electricity, water, internet – are often delivered to us via a complex network of underground pipes and cables that course through the city like the criss-crossing veins of a living organism. The UK alone has over 1.5 million kilometres of underground utility infrastructure – that is enough to reach the moon and back, twice. Despite its immensity and importance, we rarely consider this world because it is out of sight to us most of the time.[19]

At some point over the last few weeks (maybe even today), you've likely come across some excavation work. This could be to maintain your area's infrastructure, start construction on a new building, repair a damaged pipe, plant some trees, or lay down some new fiber optic cable.

Before such work can be done, any existing pipes or cables need to be identified to avoid colliding with them while digging – these incidents are known as utility strikes and can be extremely damaging from a number of perspectives: workers can be injured or killed, water can be cut off from homes, gas leaks can create hazardous situations, traffic can pile up and business can be disrupted. The full cost of a utility strike that considers both the financial and social costs can reach over \$100,000 in some cases.[20]

---

DID YOU KNOW?

Damage from excavation work is estimated to cost the United States \$6 billion each year.[21]

---

It is clearly important for any organizations involved in activity that could result in a utility strike to accurately know what utility infrastructure lies within their digging zone. To do this, a multitude of tools and data in different forms is put to use. The need to locate underground assets is so significant that a niche industry dedicated to locating utilities exists and is expected to be worth \$7.5 billion by 2023.[22]

But with so many cables and pipes buried underground, sometimes densely packed together and almost always inaccessible, visualizing this intricate network of assets while above ground is a challenging task.

## The status quo

Consider the scenario: you have multiple maps of the same location, each detailing the position and route of different utilities – some are printed, some are PDFs – and most, but not all, have information relating to the depth of those utilities. For those that do, this is represented only by an adjacent number. The mental translation necessary to transform all this information into a single comprehensive view that is accurate and easily understood is taxing, time consuming and prone to error. Additionally, with any non-digital media, workers are handicapped even further as the information is:

- more difficult to share;
- potentially spread across multiple sources to avoid crowding a single diagram;
- static – there is no way to filter or query the data further;
- less durable.

When you consider the hazardous impact of any errors, it's clear that a better system is needed.

## AR's suitability as a solution

Augmented reality as a visualization technology is capable of providing a lot of value here. By overlaying underground cables and pipes on the physical world, AR is capable of making the invisible visible, providing a clear and inarguable picture of the underground utility network.

This picture is a ready-to-go, single consolidated view of the scene which can adapt, flex and contract to meet specific requirements. A number of utilities may be crossing over each other at different depths in an area of interest. If a field worker is specifically interested in working on a cable TV line at a shallower depth to other lines, they can make their 'x-ray vision' of the subterranean world less confusing by filtering the view so only that line will remain. As it is digital, it is easier to share with others than print media, which can be shared only with people nearby. Communication also becomes easier as a crowded diagram may not translate the same way for different people. Because it is easier and quicker to understand, problems can be identified and resolved faster. A clearer understanding of the situation also leads to fewer errors, which means fewer incidents.

## PROMARK-TELECON: STUDYING THE EFFECTIVENESS OF AR FOR UTILITY VISUALIZATION

Promark-Telecon is a Canadian underground infrastructure locating provider headquartered in Montréal with a team of 650 employees.

Together with AR visualization company vGIS, the company conducted a five-month study to investigate the effectiveness of AR technology for utility locating.[23] The study took place in Toronto, which has a diverse mix of new and old infrastructure as well as personal, commercial and industrial buildings. During that period, the Promark study participants recorded the time that it took to perform locate tasks with and without the vGIS AR software.

They analysed a number of factors, including time taken per job, accuracy and safety. In 89 per cent of cases, a time saving of 30 minutes per job on average was recorded. Almost three-quarters of all jobs were completed in half the time or less. As a whole, this resulted in 12–20 hours of time saved per utility locator per month.

A survey given to job participants revealed that 84 per cent of them felt that the AR system had made their role easier. The system also helped to prevent issues in approximately half of all jobs.

FIGURE 4.3

A screenshot of the vGIS AR system displaying underground utilities against the physical environment (bottom). Compare this to the utilities information presented on a 2D diagram (top).

AR integrates information in tune with how we see the physical world. This is why it is more intuitive to understand than a top-down 2D digital diagram. When concepts are more easily understood, they are more easily communicated and less prone to errors.

## Forensic visualization

While VR can be used to visualize structured points of data, it can also be used to visualize environmental data. The legal industry has been using the technology for this purpose to provide both judge and jury with a richer visualization of evidence. This makes sense when the evidence consists of a lot of spatial details, where the environment, its surroundings and characters' interaction within that environment are relevant or moving according to a timeline. Trying to convey this level of detail in an accurate and memorable way is challenging with only words and diagrams.

There are many forms of evidence that can be presented in a courtroom. The usual suspects include verbal communication, sketches, paper diagrams, photographs, videos, digital maps, representative demonstrations, jury visits and CCTV footage. Many of these involve translating a dynamic 3D environment to a static 2D representation. In the process of doing this, a sacrifice is made: some information is lost for the sake of being able to communicate the scene to a group of people.

One of the first cases to make use of a 3D forensic visualization was Stephenson *v* Honda Motors Ltd of America in June 1992. The defendant (Honda) wanted to effectively show that the plaintiff was at fault for a motorcycle accident because they chose to ride on dangerous terrain and that the accident was not Honda's responsibility.[24] To communicate the hazardous terrain to the jury, Honda pushed to be able to reconstruct the environment as a three-dimensional, interactive simulation, arguing that two-dimensional photographs and videos would not be as realistic. This was accepted by the court, which determined that the three-dimensional view was more informative, relevant and valuable as a form of evidence.

DID YOU KNOW?

Computer-built 3D visualizations have been used in courtrooms as far back as 1989 when an animation of the Delta Air Lines Flight 191 crash was created by the US Department of Justice as a visual aid to explain the circumstances of the accident. It cost approximately $260,000 and took nearly two years to produce. The use of the technology in such a situation was so novel back then that it was featured on the cover of the December 1989 issue of the *ABA Journal*.

## UK COURT OF LAW: VR EVIDENCE OF A ROAD TRAFFIC COLLISION

From humble beginnings in animation followed by interactive graphics that are rendered in real time, forensic visualizations advanced to VR headsets. In March 2016, virtual reality evidence was submitted to a UK court of law in an attempt to resolve a dispute involving a road traffic collision that had been ongoing for three years and had racked up costs of nearly $10 million.[25]

A VR recreation of the collision was built by Spearhead Interactive. Unlike the near two-year timeline to produce the 3D animation of Flight 191, this simulation took only four weeks to build.

The attention to detail was comprehensive: the real-world environment was laser-scanned to produce a replica 3D model. The vehicle models were animated, taking into account even the correct speed and rotation of the tyres and accurate views from the mirrors on the vehicles. Furthermore, data from the UK Meteorological Office was integrated into the scene so weather conditions, wind speed, temperature and the position of the sun could be considered in case they had an effect on the collision.

The experience allowed for users to move around the scene and view the incident from a number of key positions, including in drivers' seats and at known witness locations, which could then be used to validate or invalidate statements. One of the few elements that couldn't be determined was whether the vehicles' headlights were used at any point. To allow for the demonstration of different scenarios, the simulation was built with the functionality to turn these on and off for each vehicle.

The experience was created for VR and a desktop version was made available for users to view on a monitor.

Within two weeks of the solicitors receiving the VR evidence, the case was dropped and the civil claim that followed was concluded without issue.

'Whether one likes it or not, in the future the technology used to generate computer games is going to be increasingly used to generate advanced visual evidence presentations in a number of courtroom jurisdictions around the world' – Dr Damian Schofield, Director of Human-Computer Interaction, State University of New York[26]

VR is also assisting with the continued progress of the Nuremberg trials, the military tribunals prosecuting Nazi war criminals involved in the Holocaust. The Bavarian State crime office created a simulation of Auschwitz as it existed in the 1940s. Buildings that no longer exist were recreated from archived blueprints in 3D, so every single structure is accurate in the virtual recreation. Ralf Breker, who led the project, spent five days obtaining laser scans of Auschwitz which could be imported into the visualization. Even the trees as they were back then are accurately positioned based on over 1,000 photos from the time. This level of detail makes it possible to view the camp from the perspective of a suspect in a specific watchtower, and to understand what they were able to see and whether the foliage or buildings blocked certain views. All in all, the project took six months to complete.

All of this information forms a key part of the investigations, one of which was concluded in 2016 when former SS guard Reinhold Hanning was convicted on 170,000 counts of being an accessory to murder. The judge presiding over the case explicitly commented on the value of the visualization, stating that 'the model made it possible to grasp what Reinhold Hanning would have seen from his post at the watchtower'.[27]

'I think that within five to ten years, virtual reality will become a standard tool for police, not just in Germany but all over the world, because it's a way to make scenes of crime accessible even years later' – Ralf Breker, Head of Central Photo Technology and 3D Crime Scene Mapping, Bavarian State Police[28]

---

IN SUMMARY

VR technology can be used in forensics to improve:[29]

- Understanding: complex spatial evidence in three dimensions is more easily understood, processed and remembered when it is experienced as it would be in reality – in three dimensions.
- Efficiency: as the data can be understood quicker, the whole court process can proceed at a faster rate.
- Attentiveness: dynamic objects draw more attention, such as those in 3D visualizations. While immersed in a VR recreation of a civil or criminal scenario, for that moment only that world exists for the user and so their attention is focused.
- Outcomes: with a greater understanding of the evidence and more attention being paid to it, we should expect the outcomes of any trial to be derived from a more accurate and widespread base of information.

---

# Notes

1 https://www.statista.com/statistics/617136/digital-population-worldwide/ (archived at https://perma.cc/J8CX-ZP23)

2 https://data.worldbank.org/indicator/NY.GDP.MKTP.KD (archived at https://perma.cc/9UTH-HG5E)

3 https://www.getapp.com/resources/decade-in-tech/ (archived at https://perma.cc/DZ2V-K44H)

4 https://www.researchgate.net/publication/330832155_Uses_of_Virtual_Reality_for_Communication_in_Financial_Services_A_Case_Study_on_Comparing_Different_Telepresence_Interfaces_Virtual_Reality_Compared_to_Video_Conferencing (archived at https://perma.cc/R48T-LTR6)

5 https://dimension10.com/cases (archived at https://perma.cc/X36V-TGDV)

6 https://engagevr.io/2020/04/v%C2%B2ec-2020-virtual-vive-ecosystem-conference/ (archived at https://perma.cc/H3X4-6QRP)

7 https://www.weforum.org/agenda/2019/04/how-much-data-is-generated-each-day-cf4bddf29f/ (archived at https://perma.cc/5NU9-5ADZ)

8 https://newsroom.intel.com/editorials/self-driving-cars-big-meaning-behind-one-number-4-terabytes/#gs.h5wl1h (archived at https://perma.cc/UW6R-AGKZ)

9   https://www.statista.com/statistics/743400/estimated-connected-car-shipments-globally/ (archived at https://perma.cc/E4PN-BVDU)

10  https://www.zdnet.com/article/what-is-a-chief-data-officer-everything-you-need-to-know-about-the-cdo-role/ (archived at https://perma.cc/M4AH-CY3J)

11  https://www.zdnet.com/article/what-is-a-chief-data-officer-everything-you-need-to-know-about-the-cdo-role/ (archived at https://perma.cc/M4AH-CY3J)

12  https://www.alaira.co.uk/#visualizations (archived at https://perma.cc/5FQX-FVGL)

13  https://www.iftf.org/fileadmin/user_upload/images/More_Projects_Images/Immersive_Human_Networks_Report.pdf (archived at https://perma.cc/LFL3-8NPK)

14  https://www.iftf.org/onvr/ (archived at https://perma.cc/SYR8-7YTQ)

15  https://www.pwc.com/SeeingIsBelieving (archived at https://perma.cc/9U2P-AY9L)

16  https://www.pwc.co.uk/who-we-are/annual-report/stories/2019/transporting-uk-clients-to-new-zealand-at-flick-of-switch.html (archived at https://perma.cc/9EPF-NCNS)

17  https://www.pwc.co.uk/services/deals/publications/advised-lintbells-ltd-on-sale-of-minority-equity-stake-to-inflex.html (archived at https://perma.cc/UK6K-G7J7)

18  https://www.architecturaldigest.com/story/virtual-reality-designer-client-communication-patrick-sutton (archived at https://perma.cc/5E95-RWYA)

19  https://www.localgov.co.uk/Digging-Up-Britain/48762 (archived at https://perma.cc/2TUW-5WSH)

20  http://cdn.linesearchbeforeudig.co.uk/pdfs/LSBUD-UK-Report_2018.pdf (archived at https://perma.cc/QXL5-JLBW)

21  https://www.vgis.io/wp-content/uploads/2019/07/vGIS-Promark-Augmented-Reality-GIS-Locate-Industry-Study.pdf (archived at https://perma.cc/X2W8-A624)

22  https://www.prnewswire.com/news-releases/the-utility-locator-market-is-expected-to-reach-usd-7-50-billion-by-2023-from-usd-5-62-billion-in-2018--at-a-cagr-of-5-94-between-2018-and-2023--300661706.html (archived at https://perma.cc/4TSE-CW36)

23  https://www.vgis.io/wp-content/uploads/2019/07/vGIS-Promark-Augmented-Reality-GIS-Locate-Industry-Study.pdf (archived at https://perma.cc/X2W8-A624)

24  https://ro.ecu.edu.au/cgi/viewcontent.cgi?article=1559&context=ecuworks2013#:~:text=Stephenson%20v.,Honda%20Motors%20Ltd.&text=The%20attorney%20convinced%20a%20California,motorcycle%20(Dunn%2C%202001) (archived at https://perma.cc/M77T-GE2B).

25  https://www.tees.ac.uk/sections/news/pressreleases_story.cfm?story_id=6360 (archived at https://perma.cc/C9KC-LL3S)

26  https://warwick.ac.uk/fac/soc/law/elj/jilt/2009_1/schofield/ (archived at https://perma.cc/6E89-22HS)

27  https://www.bbc.co.uk/news/technology-38026007 (archived at https://perma.cc/Y3W9-KC6Q)

28  https://www.bbc.co.uk/news/technology-38026007 (archived at https://perma.cc/Y3W9-KC6Q)

29  https://www.researchgate.net/profile/Damian_Schofield/publication/258564589_Virtual_Evidence_in_the_Courtroom/links/02e7e529de3ba9dc18000000/Virtual-Evidence-in-the-Courtroom (archived at https://perma.cc/ZPS6-DBPZ)

# 05

# Sales and marketing

## A new sales avenue

There's a concept in psychology and behavioural economics called the endowment effect. It describes the phenomenon that people get attached to and overvalue things they own – and psychological ownership can be as powerful as actual ownership. Studies have shown that users value more highly products that they make, touch and think about.

---

**DID YOU KNOW?**

The idea that consumers would pay more for a product they were involved in making comes from a study led by Michael Norton of Harvard Business School, which found that participants who had assembled their own furniture were willing to pay 63 per cent more for it versus pre-assembled equivalents. It is dubbed 'the IKEA effect'.[1]

---

In a nutshell, the closer a consumer feels to a product, the greater their sense of ownership over it and the more they are willing to pay for it. This holds true even if the product is digital in nature. One study showed that when a 3D image of a product which consumers could rotate with their mouse was presented to them on a screen, it increased feelings of ownership by 18.9 per cent versus a 2D image of the product. Taking this a step further, another study examined AR's sense of presence (that is, how realistic an item shown anchored in a user's environment through AR looked and felt compared to a 2D equivalent). It concluded that AR has a 174 per cent greater sense of presence compared with 2D images.[2] It would be reasonable to expect such realistic depictions of a product in a customer's natural environment to create a greater sense of ownership with that customer. With AR holding the strongest ability of any digital medium to achieve that, its sales potential should not be underestimated.

Interestingly, online shopping is even influenced by the device you use. Using a tablet to browse requires swiping and tapping on products to explore them, involving the use of your fingers directly on the product. In contrast, with a laptop touchpad or mouse, you are more distant from the product, both physically and psychologically. Shopping in this more tactile way through a tablet creates a greater sense of ownership of the product and increases the amount consumers are willing to pay for it.[3]

This raises some interesting connections to XR. Using AR, a product can be 'touched' in a similar way to the tablet in the study above but with an even greater connection as it is displayed accurately in the user's own environment and can still be moved around and rotated within that environment. Therefore, it is not surprising that AR is proving to be a powerful tool for selling. On this basis, as haptics technology improves, we should expect to see XR-enabled sales boosted as a result.

Both VR and AR can help build a more intimate connection between products and customers as they prime customers to think about these products in their lives, fuelling the endowment effect while increasing sales and decreasing returns due to a closer alignment of expectations. They achieve this through the following main scenarios:

- AR can enable customers to digitally 'try on' personal items.
- AR can help showcase products in the customer's environment.
- VR can be used to immerse customers in an environment to aid in a product's sale.

These technologies can even help sell products that are out of stock, haven't been physically built yet or are impractical to transport by bringing them to life for customers in an immersive way using portable XR devices.

Delta Power Solutions, headquartered in Taiwan, sells a modular data centre solution composed of 28 shipping containers – this is obviously not something sales teams can take to conferences and client meetings easily. To mitigate this, they commissioned a VR replica of their data centre solution that they can easily transport to clients wherever they are.[4]

*AR can enable customers to digitally 'try on' personal items*

'Try before you buy' is of particular importance when you are considering personal items such as clothes, shoes, glasses, accessories and makeup. Consider a watch as a potential purchase – how will it look on your wrist? Is it too big, too small, or just right? Will it complement the clothes you wear? Without travelling to a store, relying on a suitable watch being in stock and finding a free salesperson, this exercise requires a heavy dose of (often inaccurate) mental translation and spatial awareness to visualize a 2D watch on a screen in 3D on your wrist. AR offers a way to solve this problem by digitally applying the watch instantly to your wrist wherever you are, using the technology that likely already exists in your pocket. Similar initiatives have been executed by jewellers to allow customers to virtually try on rings, necklaces and sunglasses.

> Tissot gave window shoppers the opportunity to try on different models of watches by raising their wrist to a camera which then displayed the picture back to them on an adjacent screen with their selected watch superimposed. This resulted in an 85 per cent increase in sales.[5]

With AR, products can be made available for sampling:

- without consumers having to travel;
- with zero inventory or logistics costs;
- hygienically.

For very personal items like makeup, AR can actually encourage customers to explore more products even if they are in store with physical samples available thanks to the convenience and accuracy of the technology. Physical cosmetics samples would usually be applied only on a consumer's hand for hygiene reasons, but through AR, samples can be applied directly to the face without worry. Cosmetics brands Benefit, Bobbi Brown, Cover Girl, L'Oréal and Sephora have all used either AR mobile applications or 'magic mirrors' to achieve this.

DID YOU KNOW?

In a study conducted in collaboration with University College London, consumers that used AR in a store virtually tried on an average of 18 makeup products – 'substantially more than they would try using physical tester products'.[6]

---

## POIZON: TRY ON SHOES DIGITALLY WITH AR

POIZON is a Chinese e-commerce company based out of Shanghai and is the world's biggest sneaker trading platform. It started in July 2015 and achieved 'unicorn' status in April 2019.

> In the tech world, a unicorn is a term used to describe a startup that has reached a valuation of more than $1 billion – a rare sight (almost as rare as the mythical creature itself!).

POIZON worked with AR startup Vyking to enable its customers to try on sneakers digitally, saving them time and the inconvenience of visiting a physical store while giving them the confidence to assess how different sneakers would look on them.[7] Moreover, some sneakers are so sought after that it would be impossible to try them on in a store due to low local stock levels – this AR feature lets customers try on more than 2,000 of some of the world's rarest sneakers instantly.

To implement this feature, POIZON built 3D models of thousands of its shoes. These were then integrated with the AR try-on software on the mobile app, giving customers access to the new functionality – the integration took 5–10 days.

On the product detail page of each shoe, the user is prompted to 'try them on in AR'. When the user taps the button, the mobile camera turns on and the shoes appear virtually over the user's feet, tracking them in real time.

As a result of implementing this AR try-on functionality:

● more than 100,000 customers use the feature every day;

● the percentage of those who go on to add an item to their shopping basket after examining it tripled when the AR try-on feature was used;

● each unique customer spent an average of 60 seconds using the AR feature.

When the Covid-19 lockdown period started in early 2020, the application received a surge in traffic and the AR functionality allowed customers to continue engaging with POIZON despite the physical restrictions.

FIGURE 5.1

Screenshots from a smartphone running the POIZON mobile app. On the left, you can see the storefront advertising the AR functionality. The picture on the right shows the AR in action (the shoes in the picture are digital).

## *AR can help showcase products in the customer's environment*

Customers can view physical products through a mobile device or headset, either on their own or assisted by a company's sales representative. A 3D model of the product is placed directly in the customer's home, store, factory – wherever is relevant. AR technology has advanced to the level where these products:

- can detect surfaces such as tables, counters, floors and walls so objects can be placed on them or against them;
- are displayed at a 1:1 scale (their actual life size);

- are locked in position in the environment so a customer can move around them and see them from different angles;
- match the brightness of the environment around them;
- can be customized on the fly.

A number of retailers, including Amazon, Argos, Bang & Olufsen, Currys PC World, Home Depot, IKEA and Wayfair, are using AR to give customers a more realistic and integrated view of their products.

FIGURE 5.2

Left: Screenshot of a stand mixer listing on a retailer's website accessed through the iPhone web browser. Right: Another screenshot taken a moment later after tapping a single button on the website, which opens up the phone's camera to display a life-size 3D model of the mixer on a kitchen counter. 3D model produced by Eyekandy.

## COCA-COLA: SELLING MORE COOLERS WITH AR

The Coca-Cola Company is an American beverage manufacturer founded in 1892 which sells more than 2,800 products in over 200 countries. Headquartered in Atlanta, Georgia, it is the largest beverage manufacturer in the world.

Its sales teams face a variety of challenges when engaging customers about its beverage coolers as there are a lot of options available involving different designs and sizes and it is not straightforward to picture how these will look in the customer's space. If they don't meet the customer's requirements when they arrive, it can result in delays and dissatisfaction.

To limit this, Coca-Cola's sales teams have adopted AR technology through supplier Augment to help customers better visualize the different options available to find the ideal size and look for a cooler to match their space.[8] The salesperson uses their smartphone or tablet to select different cooler styles, colours and sizes, which appear in the customer's environment through the device's camera.

FIGURE 5.3

A business developer at Coca-Cola Hellenic runs through cooler options with a bar owner in Bulgaria, using AR to place 3D digital versions of various Coca-Cola coolers in the bar.

The solution is integrated with Salesforce, a customer relationship management platform, so the sales representative always has access to the latest 3D cooler models, which are stored on the platform. Once they know what the customer's interests are, they can send this information back to the customer's record in Salesforce in the form of screenshots and other notes directly from the mobile application.

As a result, when the time comes for installation, the installers have accurate information detailing the exact model, design and location of the cooler so the customer doesn't need to be asked again.

Augment has seen sales increase by up to 27 per cent as a result of implementing AR in this way.[9]

AR sales solutions are not limited to mobile devices. Using headset-based AR, sales executives from German industrial engineering company thyssenkrupp were able to measure, assess and give customers a quote for a stairlift solution that was bespoke to their home and its potential obstacles. Customers were also able to see the recommended stairlift in their home through AR. As a result, delivery time for the product was reduced from 40–70 days to just 14 days.[10]

## VR can be used to immerse customers in an environment to aid in a product's sale

While AR is a powerful tool to sell products, VR can be equally impactful by creating a dedicated showroom for the customer to focus on. The product could be the environment itself (in the case of a new kitchen) or an object within the environment (such as a superyacht in a virtual marina). VR has already been used as a sales tool for real estate, cars, household renovations, school and university places, holidays and more.

Ruach Designs is a small, family-run kitchen design business based on the outskirts of London. Its team of 11 uses virtual reality to help its customers envisage their dream kitchen.[11]

## XR enhances product customization and premiums

Approximately one out of every three consumers wants to be able to buy customized products and services and would even pay a 20 per cent premium to do so.[12] However, it is not possible to physically show consumers every model and variation of a product as there usually isn't enough space to store or display all of the items. Some products like cars have thousands of possible combinations of extras to choose from. And some customizations are so bespoke that it wouldn't make sense to stock them.

As you've seen from the numerous examples in this section, XR allows consumers to explore and visualize a full range of products without having to worry about the limitations of the physical world. This helps drive increased sales with minimal variable costs once the solution has been implemented.

## A new research tool

Understanding what consumers value and what drives their purchasing decisions is key to marketing and selling products optimally. The first challenge is obtaining data that can scale easily. The second is creating the right stimulus for market research participants. The product could be anything from a pair of differently designed vacuum cleaners to an entire aisle of products in a store. How can you give that experience to participants in a representative way?

- You could send them the items, but that would incur a lot of cost very quickly, not to mention the complexity of dealing with the logistics of dispatching and ensuring the safe return of the items from the participants. This is also not appropriate for analysing marketing displays.

- You could recruit participants within travelling distance of a central research location. However, this may limit the number and diversity of the participants and is slow to conduct as there are only so many people who can be processed in a day. If the research location is an operational site such as a store, it can also be disruptive to the business as well as costly and, in the case of marketing displays, time-consuming to produce multiple physical versions.

- You could use XR. AR can be used to digitally bring products into a participant's home instantly through their mobile phone. VR can be used to immerse participants in a store or outdoor environment to test marketing. In both cases, this opens up participation from anyone globally, is scalable and doesn't disrupt business operations.

You may be wondering how VR can be used with participants that don't have headsets. In 2014, Google revealed a VR headset design made of cardboard which runs off a user's smartphone. Others adapted it so it could be flat packed and transported easily. They cost a few dollars to produce (when ordered in large quantities) so there is no need to worry about returns. While quite basic, and unsuitable for most corporate scenarios, it is a low-cost, scalable way of using VR with a large number of people that works well for market research requirements.

## O2 UK: OPTIMIZING IN-STORE MARKETING DISPLAYS WITH VR DATA

O2 is the second largest mobile network operator in the UK with 34 million customers. Founded in 1985 by British Telecom, it is currently owned by Telefónica and headquartered in Slough.

In preparation for a wider launch throughout the UK, O2 tested a new set of smart home products in three stores; however, consumer awareness, footfall and sales were underperforming.[13] Prior to the wider launch, O2 wanted to test the effectiveness of different displays to see which one consumers would respond best to.

The company teamed up with immersive research specialist Gorilla in the room, which recorded a 360 video of one of the pilot stores and digitally replaced the in-store smart home display with variants to produce a total of five 360 videos. Meanwhile, research consultancy Populus recruited a panel of 400 people who were open to smart home technology. The panel was split into groups of five and each group was shown one of the five different in-store displays.

FIGURE 5.4

A 360 video of one of the in-store displays together with five variants which were digitally inserted to create five separate 360 videos. Photo credit: Gorilla in the room Limited..

The VR experience was integrated into the qualitative online survey that participants were asked to complete on their phones. When they clicked on a unique link within the survey they were instructed to place their phone into their headset. This activated the VR experience and they were free to look around the virtual store. Using VR at scale with such a large number of remote participants was achieved through the use of cardboard VR headsets, which were sent to all participants in advance of them completing the survey.

Participants were immersed in what felt like a physical O2 store, which led to a number of benefits:

- Participants were 68 per cent more engaged compared with similar but non-immersive studies.
- The data that was collected more accurately reflected actual O2 sales figures – traditional research produced data that was overstated by 50 per cent.
- The data provided O2 with a clear direction on the best-performing displays that would improve awareness, footfall and sales.

The Market Research Society, the world's largest professional body for market research, awarded the solution in official acknowledgement of its effectiveness in immersive research.

'AR and VR will be indispensable in research in a few years' – Ian Bramley, Deputy Managing Director, Populus

## A new marketing medium

Consumers constantly crave new and exciting experiences, especially ones that they can record, share and discuss with their networks. XR aligns with this goal by enabling such experiences and has been used by brands in a number of ways, including to:

- communicate corporate culture, product information and initiatives;
- act as a launch event platform for a new product release;
- attract consumers to stores.

VR is a powerful storytelling medium, which is why casual footwear company TOMS used VR to take customers on a journey through a TOMS Giving Trip to Peru, helping them to see first hand the work the company is doing to improve education and health programmes. Following a successful retail test, the VR experience was rolled out to more than 30 stores worldwide.[14]

XR has been used to engage the media and customers during product launches. Jaguar used VR to launch its first electric vehicle, giving 300 high-profile guests a virtual tour of the car.[15] ASICS sent journalists VR headsets pre-installed with an experience to market a new line of running shoes.[16]

---

### ONEPLUS: THE WORLD'S FIRST PRODUCT LAUNCH IN AR

OnePlus is a smartphone manufacturer founded in 2013 in Shenzhen, China, and employs approximately 3,000 people.

OnePlus had previously launched its new phones in an exclusive VR experience but was limited by the number of customers who owned VR headsets. To tackle this, the company turned to Blippar to create an AR experience to make the launch event of the OnePlus Nord accessible to smartphone users worldwide from the comfort of their own home. This took place in July 2020 and was the world's first product launch in AR.[17]

Three hundred thousand people downloaded the mobile app, which gave them access to the AR launch experience. This was a social, connected event in which guests could create their own avatar, see one another, and participate in the event by conveying comments and reactions.

Through AR, a miniature stage appeared in every user's physical environment and Carl Pei, one of the cofounders of OnePlus, kicked off the event. A 3D model of the new OnePlus phone appeared, allowing users to see it in different colours from whatever angle they desired. An exploded view of the phone offered deeper insight into the components and inner workings of the device, and a number of its features were highlighted. The experience was interactive too – towards the end, users were invited to guess the price of the phone by tapping a number into the application. Price bubbles floated behind Carl indicating the guesses of other users at the event.

The launch event was also streamed live on YouTube but this offered only a fixed perspective to users which couldn't be changed, unlike the AR view which was fully flexible and allowed users the freedom to explore the phone virtually.

More than 620,000 guests attended the event simultaneously and the phone's launch broke multiple records, including the highest open sales day in OnePlus history and the most pre-ordered product on Amazon India.

## *Attracting consumers to stores with AR*

In a beautiful example of the physical and virtual working together, AR games have been used to drive consumers to a physical location by rewarding players with an in-game or in-store bonus. This could be extra currency or points in the game which can be spent on in-game items, discount coupons that can be used when purchasing items in store, or access to rare, sought-after products that are made available only to those who engage with the experience. Some businesses may incorporate such features into their own app as Foot Locker did with 'The Hunt', an AR scavenger hunt game that kicked off at the start of the NBA season. Users were guided to a series of locations to unlock clues, which resulted in them being given the chance to purchase speciality footwear.[18]

However, you don't have to build your own application as there are benefits to partnering with an existing vendor. Niantic, creator of Pokémon GO, offers sponsored locations to businesses of all sizes. This makes users aware of your business's location and encourages them to visit to obtain in-game bonuses. Special events can even be scheduled to coincide with quieter hours to drive visitors at the right times to fill gaps during the day. Large companies like AT&T, McDonald's, Sprint and Starbucks have partnered in this way with Niantic.

---

DID YOU KNOW?

Niantic drove 500 million visitors to sponsored locations through Pokémon GO.[19]

---

The usefulness of engaging with an AR vendor relies on alignment between your business's target market and the typical user demographics of the vendor's application. This could change over time and differ from country to country, but the results may surprise you: despite video gaming being stereotypically seen as a male-dominated pursuit, of the 82 per cent of Pokémon GO players who visited a business while playing the game, 84 per cent were women.[20]

# A new advertising channel

Advertising is usually seen online, on TV, in magazines or on public displays – anywhere there is a chance of catching the eye of consumers. Consequently, given the amount of time spent within it, the digital world is becoming an increasingly important place for advertisers too – and with it, XR.

> Digital advertising spend in 2020 reached $341 billion worldwide compared with $379 billion spent on traditional ads. In the USA, digital ad spend has already surpassed traditional ad spend.[21]

## *Advertising within XR environments*

Advertising can be presented within XR experiences in a non-intrusive way by creating ad space that is expected and customary – in VR this could be a billboard in a virtual city, perimeter ads at a virtual football stadium, or a branded box of pizza on the table in a virtual home. From an AR perspective, a consumer may be trying to navigate to a location using their mobile phone and, while following the augmented overlaid directions, comes across a digital vending machine advertising a brand's beverages. Or they might be playing an augmented reality game at home which, as part of its ad revenue model, superimposes a 3D digital laptop onto the table in their living room that they can click on for further information and purchasing options.

It is product placement on a large scale in immersive environments. Software developers can include placeholders in their application for advertisements, which brands can then bid on depending on their product and its alignment to the application's users. Powerful metrics can be logged and analysed. Ad views as well as the duration of views and more complex consumer behaviours can be tracked, all made possible by analysing each user's gaze in VR or their mobile device's view in AR.

UBER: ADVERTISING IN VR APPLICATIONS

As part of Uber's $500m 'Doors Are Always Opening' advertisement campaign, the largest in its history, it ran a four-week ad placement campaign with Admix.[22] The aim was to refresh perceptions of the brand, generate optimism about the future, and connect to consumers on an inspiring and emotional level. Uber was therefore looking at innovative ways of engaging with its US audience, which is where it came across the idea of advertising in VR, a relatively untapped medium.

Following confirmation of the campaign, the ads were live in less than a week using Uber's existing banners and video assets. Relevant digital environments for Uber were prioritized, including driving simulation, flight simulation and social space applications. These applications hosted almost 1 million monthly active users, so the daily cap on spend that Uber stipulated was met every day of the campaign.

Overall, Uber reached 165,000 unique users during the campaign and those users spent a collective 19 hours looking at its brand through advertisements placed in the virtual worlds.

National Geographic, State Farm and Universal are examples of other companies that have already placed advertisements in VR applications.

## *Integration with existing advertising channels*

In addition to being a new channel for advertising, XR can be used within existing advertising. This is mostly relevant to AR due to the convenience and widespread nature of mobile devices among consumers.

With a single tap, supported ads on social media, websites and applications can activate the mobile device's camera and enable a company's products to be visualized or tried on, as mentioned in earlier examples.

Luxury fashion brand Michael Kors integrated AR within Facebook ads, allowing consumers to customize, visualize and share their look with different Michael Kors sunglasses. The two-week campaign resulted in a 14 per cent increase in purchases.[23]

## IN SUMMARY

- XR can help consumers develop a better understanding and a stronger connection to a company's products. Closing this gap between buyer and seller is key to increasing sales and decreasing costs through returns as a result of a misalignment of expectations.

- AR enables consumers to try out tangible products in their environment and try out personal products on themselves while VR can help consumers try out products that are primarily environment-based.

- Consumer behaviours can be better understood by employing XR, which allows for a wider selection of participants to be given more immersive, representative experiences during consumer research projects.

- Exciting, new marketing experiences can be created using XR to communicate information to consumers and even attract them to physical stores.

- XR expands potential within existing advertising while also acting as an entirely new advertising channel.

# Notes

1   https://www.hbs.edu/faculty/Publication%20Files/11-091.pdf (archived at https://perma.cc/X8ED-5TJB)

2   https://gorillaitr.com/project/174-more-realistic-compared-to-2d-stimulus/ (archived at https://perma.cc/4T8E-6XAP)

3   https://onlinelibrary.wiley.com/doi/abs/10.1016/j.jcps.2013.10.003 (archived at https://perma.cc/58AM-PGR9)

4   https://www.glitchstudios.co/portfolio_page/delta-modular-data-center-vr/ (archived at https://perma.cc/47AB-4ADY)

5   https://thinkmobiles.com/blog/augmented-reality-jewelry/ (archived at https://perma.cc/9PWA-M8TV)

6   https://medium.com/@Holition/applying-augmented-reality-to-beauty-retail-134490acf1ad (archived at https://perma.cc/855N-E8R7)

7   https://footwearnews.com/2020/business/retail/expivi-vyking-3d-ar-virtual-technology-ecommerce-1202967739/ (archived at https://perma.cc/NS8N-7H2A)

8   https://www.augment.com/portfolio-items/coca-cola/ (archived at https://perma.cc/2D6K-7TDV)

9   https://www.augment.com/customer-stories/fnac-darty/ (archived at https://perma.cc/7USW-CSAA)

10  https://www.thyssenkrupp.com/en/newsroom/press-releases/thyssenkrupp-elevator-rolls-out-hololinc---world-s-first-industry-4-0-solution-to-transform-measurement-and-delivery-in-the-stairlift-industry-10834.html (archived at https://perma.cc/4EEC-LKBT)

11  https://ruachdesigns.co.uk/general/try-before-you-buy-virtual-reality-vr-kitchen-design/ (archived at https://perma.cc/D4UM-KJTP)

12  https://www2.deloitte.com/content/dam/Deloitte/ch/Documents/consumer-business/ch-en-consumer-business-made-to-order-consumer-review.pdf (archived at https://perma.cc/V958-V9MW)

13  https://gorillaitr.com/project/o2-retail-vr-market-research-case-study/ (archived at https://perma.cc/2663-B4M2)

14  https://www.fastcompany.com/3059526/why-toms-shoes-and-att-are-taking-a-virtual-reality-trip-to-colombia (archived at https://perma.cc/8ZQB-JW46)

15  https://media.jaguar.com/news/2016/11/jaguar-electrifies-i-pace-concept-car (archived at https://perma.cc/8FKW-72KG)

16  https://corp.asics.com/en/press/article/2020-03-31 (archived at https://perma.cc/5Q85-NFVP)

17  https://forums.oneplus.com/threads/how-to-experience-oneplus-nord-on-july-21.1259500/ (archived at https://perma.cc/9TWF-NKLA)

18  https://www.campaignlive.co.uk/article/foot-locker-leans-ar-scavenger-hunt-sneaker-launch/1496892 (archived at https://perma.cc/WA6T-5ASJ)

19  https://www.adweek.com/digital/pokemon-go-has-now-driven-500-million-visits-to-sponsored-locations/ (archived at https://perma.cc/64GT-GJZX)

20  https://www.inc.com/larry-kim/9-need-to-know-facts-on-how-pokemon-go-players-engage-with-businesses.html (archived at https://perma.cc/KF9S-CHZP)

21  https://jacoblevideoproduction.com/digital-ads-have-surpassed-tv-ads-for-the-first-time-ever/ (archived at https://perma.cc/WFS3-3HWC)

22  https://admixplay.com/uber/ (archived at https://perma.cc/3XNB-G6S6)

23  https://www.facebook.com/business/success/4-michael-kors (archived at https://perma.cc/4T43-K269)

# 06

# Five phases of XR implementation

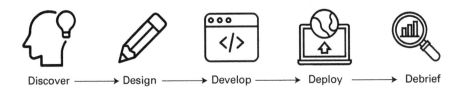

Discover ⟶ Design ⟶ Develop ⟶ Deploy ⟶ Debrief

There are five phases on every XR project, each with a different objective, outlined below. These are chronological but may overlap. Ensuring you give some thought to each of these phases will put your XR project in the best position for success.

## Discover

*Research, identify and communicate the value of XR*

What are VR and AR? What can these technologies deliver? What organizations are using them and to achieve what outcome? What developments are on the horizon? Are they feasible for your organization? Considering all of this, is there an intersection with problems you're facing or opportunities that you're missing?

The discovery phase is all about understanding the value of XR and communicating that value to relevant stakeholders, such as potential project sponsors, helping them to determine what is possible and how this knowledge could be effectively targeted towards organizational issues and opportunities.

# Design

*Plan each aspect of the solution*

Once the relevant stakeholders understand and support XR as a potential solution, the next step is outlining a high-level project plan to cover how the solution will be built, deployed and analysed. This will include:

- budget;
- timeline;
- scope – including content type and functionality;
- success criteria and metrics;
- data collection methods (for analysing solution performance);
- resourcing;
- hardware selection;
- deployment model – including hardware quantity and location.

The plan doesn't need to be detailed. The objective here is not to create a complete and final set of documentation, it is to apply some thought to all aspects of the implementation. By doing this, you will avoid potential issues down the line. In some cases, this exercise will lead you to abandon the project altogether, which should be viewed positively: the earlier an inadequate project is stopped, the less costly the lesson is.

# Develop

*Build and test the software*

This is the most well-known of the five phases. It comprises building the software behind the solution, including testing, bug fixing and iterating as necessary. It also includes the creation of assets such as 3D models and 360 media along with any animation, editing or other work that needs to be performed on them.

The result is software or media that is ready to run on an XR device.

# Deploy

## *Launch the programme with your end users*

The deployment of an XR solution comes in many shapes and sizes influenced by the plan developed during the design stage. By now, you'll have working software, a selection of predefined hardware and staff assigned. You'll need to bring this all together to ensure the end users have the best experience possible.

Don't forget to collect any relevant data to use as feedback to understand how the solution is performing.

# Debrief

## *Analyse the data collected*

Having gathered relevant data during the deployment of the XR solution, this phase is dedicated to analysing that data so that results can be obtained, their impact assessed and any improvements (or a change in direction) actioned.

As with all projects, and in particular with projects relating to the implementation of emerging technologies, you will face a number of challenges on the way. I've attempted to outline the key ones over the next few chapters, especially where distinctly related to XR. I have provided guidance on how to overcome (or at least mitigate) these challenges where possible, but there isn't always an answer – at this stage, you will have to be comfortable that some issues may remain. Some may be critical to the success of your project while others may be irrelevant. Consider these issues in context with the objective you are trying to achieve – this will help determine whether they are deal breakers or not.

# 07

# Discovery challenges

## Educating yourself and others on the potential of XR

The XR industry moves at a rapid pace. Stay up to date by researching XR solutions and industry developments through books, online news, networking, conferences, or via your own dedicated research team if resources permit. Keep experiencing the latest the technology has to offer by maintaining relationships with XR vendors. The more you know about what is possible with XR, the better equipped you will be to handle conversations, suggest solutions and build a case with stakeholders for the adoption of XR.

### Promoting XR to others requires presentation and demonstration

As you'll see in Chapter 11, there are a number of misconceptions surrounding XR that prevent organizations from even beginning to consider the potential applications to their business. Additionally, unlike many other emerging technologies, XR is primarily a sensory, experiential or visualization tool – this makes it difficult to articulate in an accurate and effective way. Reading about and listening to presentations on the topic will only get you so far in terms of understanding these technologies. To complete that winding trail requires first-hand experience of a range of content on various devices.

### Demonstrate relevant experiences

To give others that first-hand experience will involve demonstrating the technology to them. When engaging stakeholders on a potential XR project, the closer a demonstration application is to the one you are trying to sell, the fewer mental hoops they need to jump through and the better the chances are of a positive response.

There are three main attributes to consider in demonstration applications:

- **Use case:** what area the solution is targeted at (eg soft skills training, asset design, collaboration).

- **Industry:** what group of companies it is targeted at (eg real estate, healthcare, oil and gas).

- **Quality:** the strength of the experience as a whole, which takes into account the user experience and the effectiveness of the content.

Ideally, the application you demonstrate will be of a high standard and directly relevant to the stakeholder's use case and industry of interest. If not, then aim to connect it through a similar use case (eg visualization of assets) but from a different industry. Any more distant than this and you risk the stakeholder not being able (or willing) to make the connection in their mind.

## Take inspiration from other areas

While it makes sense to explore content most relevant to any immediate opportunities, it is also worth diversifying your knowledge by looking outside of your immediate area of focus as you may see something that others miss and the experience could stimulate ideas on your current or future projects.

If you are in the business of operating cranes, for example, you might immediately look to experience a high-end virtual reality lifting simulator on a tethered headset as a potentially powerful training solution for your organization. This is a valid exercise, but what if you could achieve similar results on a cheaper, more portable headset? What if a demonstration of a VR application that analyses consumer behaviour in a retail environment stirs some thoughts around how you could collect and track useful data within the crane simulation environment?

The XR industry is progressing at such a blistering pace that the production-ready industry and application-specific experiences that you have today may not take advantage of the recent advancements in the technology.

Having to play catch-up with technology can be an uncomfortable feeling, but this often stems from the wrong mindset: positioning yourself as a reactive party who is constantly having to respond to technological developments can create a sense of helplessness and become overwhelming, whereas proactively researching, exploring and testing new technologies instils a sense of confidence and control over this rapidly developing environment.

## Avoid using XR as an event filler

You may receive inquiries to demonstrate XR technologies during optional periods of an event – registration, break, lunch, drinks, and networking sessions. Many of these requests are from well-meaning individuals motivated to show off emerging technologies at their events or to use them as a filler to engage attendees while they nibble on cheese and biscuits. XR is an appealing target as it is often very visual, novel and fun. Unfortunately, from the perspective of any demonstrator of XR who is interested in communicating its value, the two objectives are not aligned.

While these invitations may seem like temptingly convenient opportunities to demonstrate XR to a large number of people, the reality is that it is generally not a good use of time and resources as attendees are far too busy eating, drinking and talking to pay much attention to the technology.

Not only is interest from attendees generally poor at these sessions, but it also doesn't put the technology in the best light as it reinforces the stereotype that XR is 'just for fun' and makes it even more challenging to sell as a business tool. Even if you are in the business of fun (perhaps you are thinking of setting up a VR arcade), running demos at lunchtime without any other context signals to attendees that it is undeserving of a main slot in the event's agenda.

> Note that this scenario is different to exhibitions or other demonstration-specific sessions (such as rotations where groups cycle between various presentations). In these cases, the primary aim for attendees is to use, understand and connect the technology's relevance to their business issues or opportunities. During a registration or break time, the attendees' comfort or hunger are the primary concerns – the technology and its potential are secondary.

If you find yourself with such an invitation, I advise negotiating a main slot in the agenda to at least articulate the value of the technology, garner increased interest and provide context to any demonstrations. This is sometimes challenging, but with the right communication you can get your point across while maintaining a good relationship with the person who made the request.

## Avoid a problem–solution mismatch

When organizations engage with an emerging technology simply because it is an emerging technology, this often ends with a lacklustre result, either because it fails to solve any problem or because it requires more effort to solve the problem than the status quo. These vanity projects are sometimes the result of a leader looking to create a fresh image, or pressure from senior leaders to be more innovative without suitable accompanying guidance. In any case, excitement about such initiatives usually starts quite high and then wanes as the realization dawns that there is no substance behind the solution.

There are two paths that lead to XR solutions being considered in an organization: one starts with a problem, the other with an opportunity. Problems are more commonly understood: they represent issues having a negative impact on business that already exist, and as a result are a constant thorn in the organization's side. Opportunities, meanwhile, are problems in the making. They represent improvements, efficiencies and transformations that organizations have yet to explore and undertake. Generally, these are driven by technological innovations (like XR) or simply new ways of doing things.

Opportunities are not urgent until competitive forces make them so. As competing organizations take advantage of these new methods and innovations, it becomes possible for them to operate more efficiently, attract greater talent, and sell products and services more cheaply. Eventually, these actions collectively will enable the competition to push ahead and widen the gap between their company and yours.

Whether a current or future problem, there will be a number of solutions to consider. Some of these may be based on XR technologies. Once you've identified a list of potential solutions, they will need to be filtered for feasibility and suitability. Feasibility refers to how practical they are to implement in your particular organization and takes into account the total cost to implement and the skill set and availability of any people required to build, manage and deploy the technology. Suitability refers to how well the solution meets the criteria for success (in other words, how valuable it is as a solution).

Take a problem-centric approach, not a tech-centric one. Always ask yourself: is this addressing a problem or opportunity? Will it be more effective than the current solution? There is, of course, no way to know for certain, but if the answer to the former is 'yes' and the latter 'possibly', that is a good enough starting point to continue investing more time in exploring the possibilities.

> I have cautioned against as many XR initiatives as I have encouraged. One of my favourite anecdotes is from a project that started off as an immersive training programme. This is one of VR's strongest and most well-known applications so naturally I enquired further. It soon became apparent that the project stakeholders intended for it to be part of a large rollout of a customer relationship management (CRM) platform throughout their organization and they wanted to have an equally impressive training plan to match the grandeur of this event. VR is a wow-inducing technology so they naturally gravitated towards it. The issue is that for technical training of a 2D web-based application like the CRM system, there are more effective solutions out there and VR would simply not add enough value to warrant the investment, so I advised them as such and suggested alternative solutions.

Implementing an unsuitable solution does no one any favours in the long run. The organization relying on the technology will be burnt, and may carry an inaccurate perception of the technology into the future; the reputation of the team building the technology will be damaged; and the end users (whether customers or employees) will be underwhelmed.

## A closed mindset is closed to potential opportunities

Sometimes, there isn't an obvious problem but an opportunity for improvement. Often, businesses are unable to take advantage of these opportunities because they are too busy firefighting operational issues. This indicates a resource problem and a ticking time bomb in terms of disruption. Eventually, other organizations that have understood the importance of capitalizing on technologies and trends on the horizon will take steps forward. They will explore, experiment and engage with XR and other technologies. The importance of this will not be immediately obvious as the effect on the competition will initially be negligible. However, as these technologies progress and those businesses have built up the experience of using them and benefiting from them, the claws of competitive advantage will start to dig in. These businesses will be the ones best placed to reduce their costs, open up new revenue channels and create more efficient operations. Slowly, this advantage will become apparent as it permeates through the organization to land on the bottom line.

History is littered with examples of companies that failed to engage with technological opportunities. Western Union, founded in 1851, was primarily a telegraph company that by 1900 operated 1 million miles of telegraph lines and undersea cables. Its core business came under threat from the invention of the telephone, which eventually led to the divestment of Western Union's telegraph infrastructure and the focus on financial services, including money transfers.[1]

In 1876, Alexander Graham Bell patented the telephone (or the 'talking telegraph' as he initially called it). He offered it to Western Union for $100,000, but William Orton, the President of Western Union at the time, rejected it, saying, 'After careful consideration of your invention, while it is a very interesting novelty, we have come to the conclusion that it has no commercial possibilities... What use could this company make of an electrical toy?' What followed was the slow demise of the telegraph, the rise in the use of the telephone and many years of Orton unsuccessfully challenging Bell's patents.[2] This attitude has parallels in the current age with many people unable to see XR beyond its use as a fun, video-gaming technology.

In 2007, Steve Ballmer, CEO of Microsoft, responded to the challenge of the iPhone with an incredulous chuckle. 'Five hundred dollars? Fully subsidized? With a plan? That is the most expensive phone in the world. And it doesn't appeal to business customers because it doesn't have a keyboard, which makes it not a very good email machine.'[3] Millions of iPhones have sold successfully above the $1,000 mark and keyboards on smartphones are almost non-existent these days, having been replaced by touch-screen technology. Steve's response illustrates the difficulty of predicting new user interfaces with the digital world, some of which, like voice recognition, are already being used in XR applications and others of which, such as hand and controller tracking, are growing in maturity.

In one of the most famous examples of dismissing upcoming technology, Blockbuster spokesperson Karen Raskopf commented about video-on-demand (VOD) services like Netflix: 'VOD is further off than we thought it was. We keep monitoring all this stuff, and when it looks like a sustainable profitable model, we can get into these things.'[4] At its peak in 2004, Blockbuster had more than 9,000 stores worldwide; now, the only nostalgic reminder of Blockbuster's operations lies in a single store in Oregon, USA.[5]

For those who may be tempted to brush off Blockbuster's claim of monitoring VOD technology as mere lip service, did you know that Blockbuster and Enron Broadband Services (EBS) were in partnership talks starting in 1999 to create a VOD business? The deal being proposed involved EBS doing the lion's share of the work to get the VOD infrastructure up and running, after which Blockbuster and EBS would share in the revenues of the operation. Despite this seemingly advantageous deal for Blockbuster, the company remained sceptical about the promise of VOD. It was also proving time-consuming to negotiate VOD agreements with the major film corporations. In the end, Blockbuster decided not to progress the deal any further and to concentrate on its original brick-and-mortar business model.[6] Netflix approached Blockbuster in 2000 and its partnership proposal was met with a similar rejection.[7]

As the saying goes, hindsight is 20/20, so we cannot be too harsh or judgemental in our retrospective assessment of these actions. However, the lesson we can take is one of an improved mindset: in a similar vein to the emerging technologies above, if we are open to the opportunities XR technologies can offer, inquisitive about their potential, and consciously challenge our beliefs regardless of the extensive experience in our specialist areas, then we are open to taking advantage of the potential of XR in our business.

---

IN SUMMARY

- When considering XR as a potential solution, always test the connection to the technology's strengths. If no such connection exists or it is tenuous, then it may not be the best solution to pursue. Engaging with XR purely for the novelty of it will harm all stakeholders in the long run.

- The opportunities of today are the problems of tomorrow. Concentrate on solving a business problem and keep that in mind throughout the project's duration.

- Avoid using XR at events when not part of the core agenda of those events.

- If XR is being considered as a potential solution, it should offer more value than alternatives (both technological and non-technological) or the incumbent solution.

---

## Hardware considerations and selection

There are numerous XR headsets on the market and the number is growing every day. Each has its own set of attributes. Below I've described some of the key areas to consider when selecting the right hardware. Bear in mind that this is not a list of dos and do nots but a list of topics to be aware of. Some of these factors will matter more than others depending on your priorities, company policies and available resources. Additionally, to comprehensively assess the suitability of a headset, you will need to consider it in connection to the solution you are building. Headset specifications such as the processor, weight and visual fidelity of the screen and optics systems are important only to the extent that they contribute to higher-level objectives such as the user experience or they align with the objectives of your solution.

## Input functionality

It is important to know what input a headset accepts as it will determine what options are available to you when designing and developing your XR application. Check for the following functionality:

- tracking classification (of headset and controllers);
- microphone;
- eye tracking;
- hand tracking.

The tracking classification of a headset is described by its 'degrees of freedom' (DoF), which determine whether you will be able to change your position and viewpoint in the virtual experience. With 3 DoF headsets, your viewpoint is fixed and you can look around the virtual environment from that perspective. With 6 DoF hardware, you are free to change your position, meaning you can, for example, lean out of the virtual window of a vehicle.

As with headsets, this concept also applies to accessories like controllers. A 3 DoF controller is one that you can rotate from a fixed position. With six degrees of freedom you would be able to move it in three-dimensional space in the virtual world while also being able to rotate it. Headsets with a microphone and eye tracking will allow you to collect voice- and gaze-related data respectively. Headsets with hand tracking offer a simplified user experience as the user doesn't need to know how to hold and operate a set of controllers or learn how to use action buttons on a headset (if applicable).

FIGURE 7.1

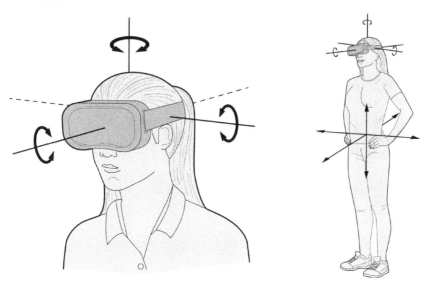

An illustration of the six degrees of freedom concept, three degrees representing how you can rotate your head (left) and the three others (right) how you can physically move.

## User experience

This is a significant area to assess and consists of a lot of different points. Ultimately, this is about examining the process of setting up, using, managing and maintaining the headset, such that it is easy, quick and comfortable to perform each of these procedures.

For a headset to be comfortable, it should be light, the weight should be evenly distributed and it should not produce excessive heat.

Setup and use generally become more complicated and lengthy when items of hardware other than the headset are required. Controllers that are mandatory for the headset to function, tracking technology that requires external elements (outside-in tracking) and external processors (computers or mobile phones) fall into this category. These are additional systems that can fail and need to be maintained separately. They will add to any setup time and can be lost or misplaced. Logistically, this also makes things difficult as it means more components to package and transport successfully.

Other processes that can potentially slow down setup include being required to register and log in to an account prior to using each headset. When you're deploying hundreds of headsets around the world, this can be particularly time consuming.

## *Visual quality*

As consumer interest grows in pushing the resolution of 2D screens from full HD to 4K and 8K, people have come to expect increasingly crisp results from their viewing experiences. The sharpness of many XR screens may not match up to such expectations built from many years of viewing traditional media at a distance. For some projects, such as VR soft skills training, this may not pose an issue, but for others, such as virtual cockpit simulators where the user's focus needs to be quite detailed (to read text labels on buttons, for example), it can be a deal breaker. It is not impossible to achieve, but for these specialist cases you may need to engage with a headset vendor targeting the higher end of the market.

---

DID YOU KNOW?

Thanks to the advancement in the visual quality of high-end VR headsets, astronauts can now use VR for training on operating spacecraft as they can see even the smallest of details on the virtual dashboards.[8]

---

For transparent AR displays, being outdoors often represents a problem in that the digital images appear washed out in direct sunlight, making them difficult and uncomfortable to focus on. This is less of an issue for opaque screens that are usually quite capable of adjusting the brightness and contrast levels to remain clear in outdoor conditions. If your intended application of AR requires your users to be outdoors regularly, it is worth ensuring that the device is capable of operating under direct sunlight.

When you look through a pair of binoculars, your field of view (FOV) is limited to what you can see through the lenses – everything outside that is black. A similar concept applies to VR headsets: the greater a headset's FOV, the more you can see in your peripheral vision and the more it emulates how you see the physical world. For AR headsets with transparent displays, the FOV refers to the largest size of digital image that can be displayed to you without being cropped.

Humans normally have a field of vision of around 180 degrees horizontally and 135 degrees vertically.[9] Most VR headset FOVs tend to be within the range of 90–130 degrees (although some headset manufacturers are pushing this to human limits of approximately 220 degrees).[10] AR headsets meanwhile typically allow for viewing digital objects within a range of 19–50 degrees.

When reviewing manufacturer figures, bear in mind that there is no consistent and globally agreed method of calculating FOV, so close comparisons are difficult. It's also important to look out for horizontal versus vertical versus diagonal clarifications. If there is no clarification, it is likely the figure refers to the diagonal, which would be the highest number of the three. Part of the reason for the difficulty in declaring a single, true FOV is that it is affected by differences in face shapes and how the headset is fitted – too loose or too off centre and the FOV suffers.[11] The FOV is also slightly reduced by the use of a 'glasses spacer'. This physical interface creates more room between the user's face and the headset's lenses to provide more comfort for glasses wearers. The trade-off is often worth it to support the 54 per cent of people who wear glasses on nearly a full-time basis.[12]

While a greater field of view creates a stronger sense of immersion, some studies indicate that this is also linked to a greater sense of nausea and therein lies a conflict: on one hand we want to increase the field of view to maximize immersion, but on the other hand we want to reduce it to minimize nausea. Unless your application requires a very high FOV and your users are comfortable with it, the experience provided by most headset manufacturers should suffice.

On some headsets, visual artifacts may be more noticeable than on others due to their design and the optics the manufacturer has chosen. Some of these artifacts include lens glare, an ability to discern individual pixels on the screen (commonly called the screen door effect because of the likeness) and crepuscular rays (or 'god rays' as they're colloquially called).

It is important to consider all of these limitations in line with your project, its requirements and your end users when assessing hardware. This will help determine what trade-offs are acceptable.

## Ruggedness

This is generally a consideration mostly for AR headsets in industrial settings as these tend to get used outdoors more compared with VR headsets. As VR provides access to a virtual environment, it is most often used indoors as being outdoors offers no specific advantage.

A device's level of ruggedness describes its ability to function in harsh conditions with consideration to the design of its internal components and external housing. Such challenges include extremes of temperature, dust, humidity, wetness, vibration, pressure (including changes caused by altitude), corrosion, abrasion and electromagnetic interference.

There are many standards for assessing levels of ruggedness, including those determined by the United States military, the Institute of Electrical and Electronics Engineers (IEEE), the National Electrical Manufacturers Association and the International Electrotechnical Commission (IEC).

The IEC created the IP or Ingress Protection code (sometimes also referred to as International Protection rating), which is the system most adopted by XR hardware manufacturers where relevant. It is also often applied to tablets and smartphones. IP ratings take the form of 'IPAB', where A and B are two digits indicating protection against solid foreign particles such as dust and protection against foreign liquids such as water, respectively.[13]

## Personal protective equipment (PPE) compatibility

AR headsets that are capable of attaching to and working with existing hard hats, bump caps, face shields and other head-protection equipment offer a distinctive advantage when trying to integrate the technology into your workforce's operations as the headset represents an add-on to existing familiar equipment and as such does not compromise the protection that the existing equipment affords. A headset that is incompatible with mandatory PPE cannot be used on a project that requires it.

## Technical support and warranties

Business-focused XR vendors should be able to provide a suitable level of technical support. Assess the availability, response time and method of such support – phone, e-mail, instant chat. What software development kit (SDK) is available? How detailed is the accompanying documentation? This will help determine how easy it will be to develop and maintain software.

What level of warranty is provided and how long is it valid for? What is the approximate failure rate of the hardware and how quickly can the vendor replace dud units? For orders of hundreds of headsets, it may be expected that some will fail over a period of time – as long as these can be replaced quickly and hassle-free, this is generally not an issue.

A second line of defence for time-critical deployments of headsets is an extra hardware buffer which you can control. For example, if you know 50 headsets are required at a specific site, ensure there are 55 available (a 10 per cent contingency).

## Vendor policies

One of the most significant policies to investigate with a prospective XR vendor relates to privacy and data protection: what data (if any) does the vendor collect? Is it optional or part of the purchase contract?

Other vendor policies that may impact your decision relate to device management and white labelling on both a hardware and software level. Can the exterior of the headsets you purchase be branded? Can the loading screens be modified to display your company's logo? What is the vendor's policy on device management software? Do they support third-party solutions or are you locked into their device management system?

---

IN SUMMARY

- There are a number of aspects to consider when deciding on which headset to select for your project. These relate to the capabilities of the hardware as well as to the policies of the hardware vendor.

- Always test the hardware with your end users as they may be able to identify niche issues, particularly around user experience, that are difficult to determine through a written specifications sheet.

---

# Notes

1  www.youtube.com/watch?v=dRnwT3O7cWQ (archived at https://perma.cc/ TCN2-4HAG)
2  https://www.forbes.com/sites/erikaandersen/2013/10/04/it-seemed-like-a-good-idea-at-the-time-7-of-the-worst-business-decisions-ever-made/#2d5089233e80 (archived at https://perma.cc/87R6-R39G)
3  https://www.wired.com/2014/09/tech-time-warp-of-the-week-watch-steve-ballmer-laugh-at-the-original-iphone/ (archived at https://perma.cc/2JEJ-BSXG)
4  https://www.zdnet.com/article/blockbuster-takes-aim-at-netflix/ (archived at https://perma.cc/EVE6-DPK7)
5  https://www.businessinsider.com/rise-and-fall-of-blockbuster?r=US&IR=T (archived at https://perma.cc/M3PE-UWKH)

**6** https://medium.com/@rumblepress/if-only-blockbuster-had-listened-to-enron-4166752a78de (archived at https://perma.cc/9QQU-FLXU)

**7** https://www.businessinsider.com/blockbuster-ceo-passed-up-chance-to-buy-netflix-for-50-million-2015-7?r=US&IR=T (archived at https://perma.cc/RQX7-2FA6)

**8** https://varjo.com/boeing-starliner/ (archived at https://perma.cc/2MC8-98VM)

**9** https://emedicine.medscape.com/article/2094663-technique (archived at https://perma.cc/XU5M-QQTY)

**10** https://sites.cs.ucsb.edu/~holl/pubs/Rakkolainen-2016-ICAT-EGVE.pdf (archived at https://perma.cc/9324-DFV7)

**11** https://www.valvesoftware.com/en/index/deep-dive/fov (archived at https://perma.cc/7FBE-XW4R)

**12** https://www.cbs.nl/en-gb/news/2013/38/more-than-6-in-10-people-wear-glasses-or-contact-lenses (archived at https://perma.cc/7XX3-X68P)

**13** https://uk.rs-online.com/web/generalDisplay.html?id=ideas-and-advice/ip-ratings (archived at https://perma.cc/7Z25-RMKQ)

# 08

# Design and develop challenges

## Selecting the right type of content for your project

*360 video vs computer-generated graphics*

Both 360 video and computer-generated (CG) graphics are valid choices for use in VR business applications. Each comes with pros and cons.

CG content is what you are likely used to seeing in digital applications already. It is a combination of 3D and 2D objects that were created using computer software. It started life within the digital world and never left. This is in contrast to 360 media, which is captured from the physical world and then displayed digitally. It is similar to taking a regular photo (or video) – the difference with 360 shots, though, is that they capture the entire 360-degree environment around you (Figure 8.1).

FIGURE 8.1

An example of a 360 image taken of a room set up for a presentation. The distortion you see is a result of 'squashing' the spherical 360 image flat so the whole of it is more easily viewable on this 2D page.

FIGURE 8.2

A screenshot of a computer-generated application built for VR designed to immerse users in a city of the future. A joint project between PwC and REWIND.[1]

CG content is produced through 3D modelling software (or bought off the shelf) and tied together using a game engine or other software development packages. To produce 360 media requires a specialist camera. These can range from portable, pocket-sized models costing a few hundred dollars to weighty, bowling ball-sized behemoths that will put you back up to $20,000.

> In AR, most content is computer-generated apart from a few unique cases such as AR portals where users, usually through their mobile device, can access a fully digital environment by walking through a digital doorway in the physical world. This digital environment can be composed of 360 video content.

360 video, like regular video, is actually recorded flat. It is then wrapped around the user to create an immersive environment. There is no depth information recorded so you are limited to looking around from a fixed perspective (3 DoF). In contrast, CG assets are placed in three-dimensional space so the application has enough information about how far away other objects are to allow you to roam those environments realistically (6 DoF).

It is generally easier to create 360 video than CG content given the wide range of consumer-grade, ready-to-shoot cameras available in the market. However, both require a significant amount of experience and skill to develop high-quality content. The importance of this cannot be overstated as quality content is one of the key pillars of any VR project.

There are many companies doing a great job in lowering the barrier to entry for 360 production. Camera manufacturers have created lighter, simpler and more portable options; there is a greater range of tools for editing and optimizing 360 video; and more software platforms are available to help users create and distribute interactive 360 experiences without any technical or programming knowledge. Some vendors I have spoken to are even providing clients with pocket-sized 360 cameras as part of a sales package to encourage them to develop more content themselves and thus feed the usage of the vendor's platform.

The danger of democratizing 360 technology so quickly without allowing users to develop a grounding in best practices is that a significant portion of user-generated content will be of a low standard. This content will then be shown to others, who will be underwhelmed. As a result, the project may fail and perception of the technology will diminish.

To combat this, I asked 360 video director Alex Rühl whether she would be willing to put together a layperson's guide to creating 360 video – when to use it, the steps involved and the pitfalls to be aware of. I have worked with Alex on numerous corporate 360 video projects where she brought a wealth of knowledge in the area of immersive storytelling. You can find her guide in Chapter 10.

## Volumetric video: the best of both worlds

Volumetric video capture is the process of taking three-dimensional videos of an individual, object or scene.

There are a few methods to achieve this. One which produces high-quality results involves a dedicated studio in which many pairs of infrared and video cameras (usually at least 30 and sometimes more than 100) surround an individual, object or scene. These cameras capture information about millions of points in the scene.

To bring this to life, suppose you were taking a video of a fairly simple scene: a person delivering a dynamic talk in which they walk, gesture and speak animatedly about a topic. Stop that video at any point and examine it. You have visual information – you know how the person looks: their height, their body shape, their facial features, the type of clothes they're wearing, and the various colours of their hair, skin and clothing. This is one aspect of the information these volumetric systems capture.

The second is related to distance and position. While the human visual system is far from being accurate, in many situations it does a good enough job. From being in front of an individual with outstretched arms, you can tell that their hands are in front of their arms, which are in front of their torso, which is below their head and above their legs. You could probably also make a reasonable estimate for how far away from you all of these areas are. Taking this to the next level, suppose you could calculate the distance to the tip of the finger of the individual's left hand and, similarly, a point a few millimetres away from that tip as the finger curves around. Apply this exercise to every point on the person from head to toe and repeat this exercise 60 times every second for the duration of the video. Now you have some idea of how a volumetric capture system sees the world.

If you can record colour and distance information about every point on an individual in a scene with enough frequency and at a high enough resolution, you have the basis for a 3D model. This model can then go on to live in any type of 3D application, including XR applications.

Given the vast amount of information being recorded in a volumetric capture – 10GB every second[2] – you might think that these models require processing which can be achieved only through a high-powered computer system. In fact, when converted to the right format, volumetric video is more than capable of running on consumer mobile devices.

I visited Dimension in London, which was the first volumetric capture studio of its kind outside of the US and is a joint venture between Microsoft, Hammerhead VR and Digital Catapult. Hammerhead is an immersive media company based in Newcastle, UK and Digital Catapult is the UK's digital technology innovation centre which aims to grow the UK economy by encouraging business adoption of innovative technologies.

Dimension's permanent studio uses 106 synchronized cameras, 53 of which are RGB cameras that record colour information while the other 53 are infrared cameras that record depth (Figure 8.3).

High-end volumetric capture systems, as you can imagine, require a lot of investment, in terms of both cost and space, so they tend to be located in permanent installations. Microsoft technology powers a number of them across the globe. Portable systems that can be transported and set up at different locations are also becoming more widely available.

Sky's virtual reality division commissioned a project called 'Hold the World' in which Sir David Attenborough, the world-famous naturalist, meets you in virtual reality in a 3D recreation of London's Natural History Museum. You are able to explore parts of the museum, including the

FIGURE 8.3

Left: me at Dimension's volumetric capture studio. On the right, the result: my volumetric 3D model. Content and images captured at volumetric capture studio, Dimension, London.

Conservation Centre, the Cryptogamic Herbarium and the Earth Sciences Library, areas that are usually out of bounds to the general public. There, you are given the opportunity to examine and handle various rare specimens that the museum has collected and maintained, from giant butterflies to dinosaurs, manipulating their size, rotating them and placing them on the table in front of you. Meanwhile, Sir David sits opposite you, explaining the stories of these creatures in intricate detail.

As you've probably gathered, Sir David's realistic appearance in this virtual reality environment was enabled by volumetric capture technology at Microsoft's Mixed Reality Capture Studio in Redmond, Washington.

This project, and in particular the use of virtual reality, made it possible to communicate with and educate people worldwide about the history of our world that previously would have been limited to photos and videos for those who were unable to visit the Natural History Museum. Even those who are lucky enough to visit the museum in person are still unable to get the intimate feeling of sharing a moment with Sir David Attenborough as he talks about the giant butterflies of Papua New Guinea:

'Sharing my passion for the natural world is something I have done for many years through different technologies, from the days of black-and-white TV to colour, HD, 3D, 4K and now virtual reality.'

TINO KAMAL: VOLUMETRICALLY CAPTURED FOR A MUSIC VIDEO

English rapper Tino Kamal was volumetrically captured and his resultant 3D model was used to create a 2D music video for his single, 'VIP'.[3] Effects studio Prodigious then created a computer-generated environment around him complete with lighting, smoke, freeze motion and other effects.

In addition to being an impressive form of artistic expression, there are business benefits to conducting a music video in this way. The equipment and materials needed to produce these effects in real life would have been very costly compared to having them generated on a computer around Tino's 3D model. Capturing Tino volumetrically also created flexibility: the director of the video would have the ability to modify shots, insert different effects and try different angles and video methods, all after the filming, in post-production. This would likely require fewer takes and limit the danger of a reshoot because the performance is captured from all angles. As a result, different shots can be explored while the performer, Tino, only has to get the performance right once.

Volumetric capture has also been used in healthcare training using AR. Global learning company Pearson created a number of immersive applications which it spun off into a separate organization called GIGXR. One of these applications is called HoloPatient, which uses volumetrically-captured professional patient actors. These patients can be placed realistically in any environment – sitting on a chair in your room or at the side of a hospital bed. All patients show various forms of symptoms, some of which are visual signs on their body – bruises or marks – and others of which are action-oriented – some will walk disoriented around the room, some will grimace and others will develop itches on their face which they will scratch. When combined with information about these patients' vital signs, trainee clinicians can pause, play or repeat the simulation at any moment and use the information to form an assessment of the patient's condition.

Volumetric capture can also be used to create a digital avatar that can then be animated in a completely separate process at a later date. In other words, a person is scanned in a certain pose to create a 3D model, which is then 'rigged' (ie a digital skeleton is applied to the model which can then be manipulated). This allows you to create a 3D model of someone, which can then be implemented in a multitude of different applications in the future (assuming you have the individual's permission, of course!).

Points to be aware of when using a volumetric capture studio:

1  The colour and material of your subject's attire can affect the capture. Infrared cameras don't play well with shiny, reflective surfaces or dark colours, especially black. So, glasses, sunglasses, large jewellery, leather, sheer or transparent fabric and objects made of glass, plastic or metal can sometimes cause issues.

2  Anything that is in the same colour range as the backdrop material will be ignored by the camera. So that usually means bright green attire is out of the question.

3  Anything that is too thin or small may be difficult for the camera to capture. This includes stiletto heels, hat brims, bag straps and guitar strings, for example.

4  Even long, loose or stray hairs can cause issues in that they may be too thin to capture or they may temporarily occlude parts of the body.

5  Anything that occludes parts of the body or clothing from the cameras will interfere with the capture process. This could be a long cape that covers the feet, a high collar hiding the neck, or even a dress with many deep folds which could end up creating cavities in the 3D model.

As you can see, there are a few considerations to bear in mind about volumetric capture, many of which will affect and constrain creative decisions. This is why it is advisable to conduct a test prior to the actual shoot under exactly the same intended conditions to identify issues and avoid a wasted day during the shoot, which could be a very expensive mistake.

Costs for volumetric captures range widely depending on the location, the technology employed, how long you need the studio or equipment for, and how many minutes of footage you are capturing. Expect it to be the most costly option of the different content types, but you may be able to reduce the cost per capture by batching up a number of captures in the time you've rented the studio for.

If you are looking to capture multiple individuals in a single scene, be aware that many studios are limited to capturing a maximum of two or three people simultaneously due to size constraints and also possible issues with one person occluding another so parts of them are not visible to a camera, which means there will be a lack of information when it comes to creating the 3D model.

A large part of the cost goes into processing the footage so a computer can convert all the information from all the cameras into a 3D model – it's not unusual for a capable computing system to spend 12 hours or more on one minute of footage.[4]

Volumetric capture technology has already been used in education, fashion, marketing, entertainment and video gaming, and we should expect to see this continue in the future, bringing more powerful content to users.

---

DID YOU KNOW?

The volumetric video market is estimated to grow from $1.4 billion in 2020 to $5.8 billion by 2025.[5]

---

*Cost and risk profiles for 360 video, computer-generated content and volumetric video*

Every project is different and there are other factors besides content type that will affect how cost and risk change throughout a project's life cycle, but considered in isolation, there are a few lessons that can be drawn out.

From a risk perspective across all three content types, the design stage represents the least level of pressure – it is the beginning of the project, deadlines are generally not as pressing and, worst case, the project can be abandoned with little to no sunk cost. For 360 and volumetric video, transitioning to development (production) represents a massive ramp-up in risk as this phase is typically characterized by a short burst of filming, which requires intense coordination of multiple resources (crew, actors, venue, props) against an extremely tight timeline. If anything goes wrong during this stage, if it is not resolved promptly, it will result in a reshoot, which means the entire production will need to be repeated another time. Apart from the logistical nightmare of having to pull everything together again, this duplication of cost can be debilitating for a project, particularly as production is the most expensive part of most projects.

Any mistakes made in production that are not significant enough to warrant a reshoot can still also carry consequences to post-production editing. During one of the first 360 productions I was involved in, everyone was so preoccupied with the multitude of tasks that needed to be performed that nobody realized that the keyboard and mouse on the desk needed to be wireless (which the scenario required to be realistic to the users who were going to be shown the video). We had two options: reshoot the scene and reincur the cost of all the actors or make the change during the post-production editing process. We opted for the latter given the difference in cost was a magnitude of thousands instead of tens of thousands of dollars!

There is little flexibility with 360 and volumetric video – once you have finished filming, the movement and delivery of any actors used in the production can't be changed. In that regard, CG content is more flexible as it can be modified and customized to meet a change in direction, or adapted for a new project.

It is difficult during a 360 project to provide stakeholders with a preview part-way through as everything tends to come together quite quickly only near the end after everything has been filmed. A rough preview of the end product can usually be provided shortly after the shoot, but apart from basic feedback such as the chronology of scenes, branding choices and audio synchronization, nothing else can really be changed at this point, especially the delivery of the script and the direction of the scene itself. This is why it is incredibly important to manage the expectations of any stakeholders early on in the project and to keep them involved throughout, especially during production. Have someone on hand during production who can sign off on scenes and voiceover. Provide them with first-hand demonstrations of 360 video projects shot using a similar camera, in a similar location and displayed on a similar headset. Hearing and reading about the plan for a project is a very different beast to seeing the end result in VR.

360 video and volumetric capture tend to have similar risk profiles. Computer-generated projects, meanwhile, are more stable in comparison as risk is quite linear throughout the project, which is built piece by piece. As a result, it is easier to give stakeholders a preview part-way through the project. But getting results that satisfy some stakeholders' desires for realism while maintaining an ability to run on portable hardware is often a challenge.

As a rough guide, 360 video is generally cheaper than computer-generated work, which is cheaper than volumetric video. Based on my experience of a range of different projects, expect to spend the smallest part of your budget but the most amount of time on designing the experience. This might seem unusual but is key to delivering a successful project.

IN SUMMARY

- To create content for a VR experience, you can use 360 video, computer-generated graphics or volumetric video. AR applications are generally composed of CG assets but volumetric video can be effective too.

- 360 video is the easiest for non-technical users to pick up, with many one-click 360 camera options available to the public. It is also generally the most inexpensive option, but the visual quality may not be as clear and you only have a fixed point of reference (ie you cannot move around the virtual environment).

- Computer-generated graphics contain full three-dimensional information, allowing developers to customize the project and users to move and change perspective within the virtual environment.

- Volumetric video produces a three-dimensional video of individuals and objects which can be inserted into XR experiences. Per minute of action, it can be the most expensive form of XR content but produces very realistic results. As it is 3D, it also allows users to change perspectives.

- From a production standpoint, 360 video and volumetric video are quite similar. The most significant costs and risks reside in the production phase, so planning is essential. The equivalent phase for CG content, development, generally has a fairly linear risk and cost profile throughout a project.

## Resourcing the right team in the right way

### Skills required for an XR project

At the beginning of your XR journey, it can be confusing to decide what skills you require when and where to find them. From software developers to user experience designers to 3D modellers, there is a wide range of skills that can be employed to deliver successful XR applications. These skills fall into three main categories:

- business: strategy, project management, change management, stakeholder management, marketing, 360 video production;
- creative: user experience design, sound design, art design, scriptwriting;

- technology: software development, quality assurance (QA) testing, 360 video post-production, audio engineering, technical support.

> Like many a startup and fledgling corporate initiative, when building your own XR team you may find it more efficient and cost-effective to hire individuals with more than a single skill. This can work at the beginning of your journey, but as you grow and your XR product portfolio becomes more numerous and complex, expect to need people dedicated to specific skills.

To successfully deliver an XR solution requires the joining together of skills from all three areas. Creatives need to feed the project with effective content to ensure it has the expected impact on release. Business professionals need to keep the application and any related communications aligned to the project's original vision and objectives. Technologists need to glue these pieces together to deliver the finished product. Not all of these skills will be required on all projects. The decisions you make regarding what content and technologies you employ, how the solution functions and how you intend to deploy it will dictate what skills you need.

It may be easier to find individuals with the above skills from a non-XR background, but it's important that they have at least some knowledge of XR. Understanding the differences between this medium and others is critical to delivering a quality XR project. Without it, project management professionals will have unrealistic expectations of what can be done and when, developers will produce an application that runs poorly on XR devices, and user experience designers will create an interface that works in 2D but falls flat (no pun intended) in XR.

## External vs internal resources

Your XR strategy will influence the makeup of your team and how much of it is outsourced. Assuming you are starting from scratch, your options are to engage external organizations to deliver the entire project, onboard freelancers to assist, or hire permanent employees to join your organization and deliver the whole project in-house.

If you foresee delivering ad-hoc XR projects that require minimal maintenance, it makes sense to work with an external organization on these projects. Most sales and marketing projects fall into this category and are built by digital, immersive, innovation or creative agencies as one-off experiences. For operational XR projects that require continual maintenance and updates, it would be more cost-effective to bring at least some business and technology skills in-house as they will likely be required on an ongoing basis. Creative and niche technology skills can still be fulfilled through freelancers as required.

This hybrid resourcing model of a permanent in-house XR team and a temporary, ad-hoc freelance team is used by many organizations as it provides the best of both worlds: a team that is readily available to deliver a base XR product and is also able to respond to less frequent but nonetheless critical elements of such projects.

> PwC has XR business specialists, software developers, 3D artists and others in-house; however, for projects that require the creation of a narrative, we would usually bring a dedicated scriptwriter on board.

## How to find XR talent

As with any emerging field, it is difficult to find people with direct and comprehensive XR experience. If you have the time, there are dedicated XR job marketplaces which make the process easier, as well as more general job boards. Posting on social media networks such as Facebook, LinkedIn and Twitter can also yield some strong results through the right groups and by using the right hashtags.

Otherwise, there are a number of recruitment agencies which can search and filter for suitable individuals. Note, the cost of this service is usually a one-off fee of 15–35 per cent based on the annual salary of the candidate.

---

### DID YOU KNOW?

Demand for XR software engineers increased by 1,400 per cent in 2019 year on year based on more than 400,000 interview requests from 10,000 participating companies in Hired's 2020 State of Software Engineers report.[6]

---

Because XR is an emerging technology that is evolving rapidly, individuals who can adapt to new tools and methods quickly should be highly valued. New discoveries, research and the natural evolution of both the hardware and the software may open up opportunities for improvement. If you have individuals who can explore and sift through these opportunities, you will be able to take advantage of these developments without necessarily having to hire extra talent (at least at the beginning of your XR journey).

IN SUMMARY

- All three skill sets – business, creative, technology – are required to varying degrees to implement a successful XR solution.

- Everyone in an XR team should have a good understanding of the specifics of XR and what makes it different from other media.

- For ad-hoc XR projects, it makes sense to engage an external agency. For more operational projects, consider building at least a partly in-house team.

- XR talent can be sourced from general and dedicated XR job boards, through social media or via a recruiter.

- Skills and individuals are not a one-to-one relationship – some individuals can be multiskilled but this is difficult to sustain at the later stages of an XR team.

## Improving accessibility

Users may have accessibility challenges that impair their experience with XR applications. This is a consideration not only for your current population of users but for your future ones as well.

There are different types and severities of disability, many of which are very pertinent to XR given how reliant the technology is on the human senses, particularly sight and sound. Accessibility features for XR applications need to be considered at the design stage for implementation during the development of the experience and its deployment. These features can be:

- provided by the XR operating system or platform provider (software);
- custom built into the XR application you are developing (software);
- provided 'outside' of XR to cater to individuals who have difficulties with the hardware.

Accessibility features available at a platform level should be available to all applications running on the platform by default. Explore these first before developing custom accessibility solutions into your XR application to cater to your users. Finally, in addition to these software accessibility solutions, you may still need to develop 'real-world' protocols to take into account some challenges with the hardware.

As an example of such protocols, some users with reduced hearing may wear hearing aids where the microphone is outside of the ear canal. In this case, headphones that sit in the ear or on top of it are unlikely to work, but over-the-ear headphones that sit around and above the microphone may be a suitable option that is easy to make available.

For software solutions, Microsoft released a suite of tools – SeeingVR – to make VR more accessible to those with low vision. SeeingVR can be used when developing VR experiences in Unity.[7] There are also Web Content Accessibility Guidelines (WCAG) authored by the World Wide Web Consortium (W3C). Although these are aimed at making information on web pages or web apps more accessible, some of the guidance can be applied or adapted to XR applications.[8] A set of XR accessibility user requirements is also being developed by W3C's Accessible Platform Architectures Working Group, containing specific recommendations relating to XR.[9]

Accessibility is a complex area and combining it with XR makes it even more complex. In addition to visual and auditory disabilities, there are users who may have physical, cognitive, neurological or speech disabilities. All of these areas have a number of subcategories, each of which can vary with the severity of the user's disability.

It is useful to understand the disabilities of your end users in terms of how they can provide input to the application and receive output from it and then compare that to the options that can be made available in XR. Common input methods include a keyboard, gestures, speech and gaze. Common output methods include a screen (visual), sound (auditory) and haptics (tactile).

While more work needs to be done to achieve greater accessibility in XR, accessibility in traditional 2D media is more mature, and some lessons learnt there can be applied to XR. At a minimum, alternative options based on more traditional media or techniques should be made available.

## Data protection, privacy and cyber security

The concept of data protection is much more widely discussed these days given the scandals that have occurred and the legislation that has been implemented, such as the General Data Protection Regulation (GDPR).

Cyber security and data protection go hand in hand as a failure to adequately shield XR devices from attack could lead to significant data breaches.

This is not an XR-only issue but one that affects any device that stores, processes or transmits sensitive information, especially when connected to a wider network such as the internet. For organizations, the two key areas of concern are company confidential data or employee personal data breaches, both of which could lead to reputational damage, financial loss and a disruption to business operations.

The European Commission defines personal data as 'any information that relates to an identified or identifiable living individual. Different pieces of information, which collected together can lead to the identification of a particular person, also constitute personal data'.[10]

This raises interesting points that directly relate to XR as, unlike laptops and smartphones, many XR devices contain sensors that are needed for them to function. However, this also means that they are capable of tracking unique sets of data, including:

- eye gaze;
- head movements;
- hand movements;
- interpupillary distance (IPD);
- height.

This means VR applications are capable of understanding how you move around, what you're looking at and for how long.

Academic research has shown that the way someone walks can be used to identify them with 99.6 per cent accuracy.[11] Expect to see similar studies conducted on the nuances of a user's body language, including their gestures and body posture, which can be recorded from an XR headset and pair of controllers. Combined with a user's height and IPD, it wouldn't be unreasonable to discover that individuals can be identified by combining this data. Eye-tracking technology is also advancing to the point where it is becoming a commercially viable means of identifying someone.[12] Consequently, these data sets would be classified under biometric data, a special category of personal data under GDPR, and would need to be treated more carefully.

DID YOU KNOW?

The SteamVR tracking system used by a number of VR headsets can provide updates on the position and orientation of the headset and controllers, up to

> 1,000 times a second. In a five-minute VR session, this results in 5.4 million data points being produced. This magnitude of body language data has never been so easy to produce or access.[13]

In addition to potentially personal data being captured, higher-end AR and VR headsets can record data about the environment around them. These devices have a number of outward-facing cameras that are primarily used to create a 3D map of the surrounding space. For AR users, this enables objects to be integrated realistically into the environment. For VR users, they are used to track the position of the headset and controllers as well as warn of any obstacles in the user's vicinity which could be hazardous. The camera feed and the data captured to create these maps, however, may represent sensitive information that could be damaging in the wrong hands.

There are software safeguards to prevent users accidentally hitting or tripping over physical objects while in VR. These systems present a predefined visual boundary to the user in VR when they get too close. Researchers from the University of New Haven in Connecticut, USA demonstrated a series of 'immersive attacks' on one of these systems designed to disorient, disrupt, endanger and manipulate the position of the VR user. This last attack, which they coined the 'Human Joystick Attack', involved slowly moving the virtual environment while the user was occupied with a VR experience. This would encourage the user to make small, often subconscious adjustments to compensate. As a result, attackers were able to physically move the users by almost 2 metres over the course of a few minutes. Only 62 out of the 64 research participants were aware of this happening to them. While care was taken to ensure the participants were never in any danger (the room was clear of obstacles), it illustrates how an attack on a VR device could potentially lead to a user's physical harm.[14]

The attacks were performed on tethered headsets and access to the PCs they were connected to was assumed. This would be possible only where such PCs were already compromised and highlights the importance of effective cyber security practices on systems powering XR devices in order to protect them and their users.

When considering how to appropriately protect XR devices, it is helpful to break down the components. Each device comprises:

- physical hardware;
- operating system;

- middleware (software that provides functionality to the applications beyond what the operating system can provide);
- installed applications.

These represent possible entry points for attack. For a tethered headset, the 'brain' of the system is the workstation it is connected to – the headset itself is, in simplified terms, a screen and a collection of sensors. The workstation is therefore the device to focus on for a tethered headset, which should be covered by existing cyber security protocols.

Things get more interesting for standalone headsets, which are self-contained and can be thought of as another computer. The closest analogous technology is the smartphone, many of which run on a similar processor and operating system.

XR headsets may use an old version of Android which has been modified for optimal use as a VR or AR device with support for functionality specific to the device. In general, older versions of an operating system can represent a security risk unless they are being updated and maintained, which is something to query with the XR headset vendor.

---

DID YOU KNOW?

Despite Windows 7 and older operating systems no longer being supported, 83 per cent of medical imaging devices still use them, opening up healthcare organizations to attacks which could disrupt operations and expose sensitive medical information.[15]

---

This common operating system language is what makes it possible for device management software vendors that are used to supporting smartphones to add support for XR devices with some extra tinkering. It is also why your business may have existing smartphone cyber security protocols that can be applied to standalone XR devices with some modifications.

The channels of attack on an XR device can be either physical or digital. Hardware can be stolen, so physical safeguards will need to be put in place, especially for standalone headsets, which consist of only a few portable components at most. To prevent unauthorized users accessing sensitive data on the headsets, the devices should be locked with a password, online communications should be encrypted, and incoming and outbound connections should be monitored and filtered appropriately. This applies to the entire software stack, from operating system to middleware to applications.

---

**DID YOU KNOW?**

98 per cent of communication from connected devices is unencrypted across organizations in the United States, leaving this data vulnerable to theft.[16]

---

Finally, not all data breaches are malicious. Some are simply a result of signing up to terms that explicitly allow for the collection of such data by XR hardware and software vendors. Query this directly with the relevant vendors from the start – it's best to know early on if their terms are unsuitable.

---

**IN SUMMARY**

- Ensure updates are applied regularly to any software used on the XR device.
- Review existing cyber security protocols on IT assets as they may be applicable to XR devices (with some modifications).
- Stay up to date on legislation to prepare for changes that may impact not only computing devices but also the unique attributes of XR hardware and experiences.
- Read the fine print – understand the terms and conditions of the XR hardware and software you're using.

---

# Notes

1  https://www.pwc.co.uk/services/consulting/technology/insights/experience-future-through-vr.html (archived at https://perma.cc/9E87-7FV6)
2  https://www.dimensionstudio.co/faqs (archived at https://perma.cc/B854-J2L4)
3  https://www.dimensionstudio.co/work/tino-kamal-vip (archived at https://perma.cc/6MVX-F7UJ)
4  https://www.ibc.org/download?ac=6559 (archived at https://perma.cc/TL6E-JHTD)

5  https://www.marketsandmarkets.com/Market-Reports/volumetric-video-market-259585041.html (archived at https://perma.cc/F53T-LS2J)

6  https://hired.com/state-of-software-engineers (archived at https://perma.cc/Q84M-4X3Z)

7  https://www.microsoft.com/en-us/research/project/seeingvr/ (archived at https://perma.cc/A2V4-GPUQ)

8  https://www.w3.org/WAI/standards-guidelines/wcag/ (archived at https://perma.cc/XF5M-DGDP)

9  https://www.w3.org/TR/xaur/ (archived at https://perma.cc/UD7M-R75Y)

10 https://ec.europa.eu/info/law/law-topic/data-protection/reform/what-personal-data_en (archived at https://perma.cc/PQ6G-VXGH)

11 https://www.wired.com/2011/09/walking-biometric-identification/ (archived at https://perma.cc/K5FM-TLCP)

12 https://www.alston.com/-/media/files/insights/publications/2017/07/alstonbird-eyetracking-16pvlr27.pdf (archived at https://perma.cc/E46V-GYLL)

13 https://partner.steamgames.com/vrlicensing (archived at https://perma.cc/67XP-5ZFQ)

14 https://digitalcommons.newhaven.edu/cgi/viewcontent.cgi?article=1087&context=electricalcomputerengineering-facpubs (archived at https://perma.cc/8PJ2-N5AP)

15 https://unit42.paloaltonetworks.com/iot-threat-report-2020/ (archived at https://perma.cc/8LWH-JBC8)

16 https://unit42.paloaltonetworks.com/iot-threat-report-2020/ (archived at https://perma.cc/8LWH-JBC8)

# 09

# Deploy and debrief challenges

## Device management

For small-scale local deployments (fewer than 20 headsets), you can get away with not having device management software if updates are only occasional. For larger-scale or remote deployments, a proper device management solution is recommended as it can save a lot of time and hassle.

Device management solutions are used by businesses everywhere to manage the applications, policies and security of a work device, which could be a laptop, smartphone, tablet or even a wearable. The software creates a two-way communication channel between the device and the company's IT administrators. This allows the company to enforce policies, such as the implementation of a six-digit PIN on a smartphone which must be changed every six months, to ensure a certain standard of security is met.

Should there be any issues – the device may be lost or stolen, for instance – it can be remotely and securely wiped, ensuring that sensitive data is kept away from prying eyes.

As we start to see more and more organizations adopt XR hardware in large numbers, the importance of device management solutions supporting XR has increased. Some XR vendors such as HTC and Oculus have their own systems to manage the business editions of their headsets. There are also dedicated device management providers that support XR, such as 42Gears, Miradore, MobileIron and VMware. Costs start from about $4 per device per month.

Depending on the exact device management solution, administrators are able to perform the following actions on a headset:

- Send files (applications, data files, videos, pictures).
- Install applications silently (ie without prompting the user or requiring any input from them to proceed with the installation).

- Reset the entire device, securely wiping all information on it.
- Save a WiFi profile, including its name and password (so the headset connects automatically when it's in the presence of this WiFi connection).
- View the file and folder structure of the device.
- Stream the visual output of the device (this is helpful when providing instructions to users while troubleshooting issues remotely).
- Modify settings on the headset.

Additionally, administrators can view a vast amount of information about these headsets, including each one's:

- model name;
- device name – a changeable, user-friendly name (eg 'Alice spare' instead of 'PA7650MGD921275X');
- serial number, the unfriendly series of letters and numbers as above;
- Bluetooth name – used to connect to accessories such as wireless headphones;
- status, whether it is currently online or offline;
- last connected timestamp – the date and time of when it was last seen online;
- battery level;
- temperature;
- WiFi network's name;
- operating system;
- firmware version – a piece of software that allows the headset hardware to communicate with the operating system;
- storage and memory usage.

Before there were widely available and compatible solutions to remotely manage XR devices, information like the firmware version and serial number of each headset had to be recorded in a spreadsheet. Any content changes that needed to be made (installing or uninstalling of new applications and media) had to be done manually, one by one, by connecting each headset to a computer.

This information is useful to identify problematic devices, make sure all software is up to date, connect the right accessories to the right devices, and ensure they are charged before an activity or event. This information is all digital. Headsets are cross referenced through a physical asset label, which matches its friendly name in the dashboard.

Your choice of device management solution, if any, will be dictated by the number of headsets you are deploying, their model, and what level of control and functionality you are looking for. Not all headsets are compatible with all device management solutions, so you may need to use a combination of them to achieve coverage across your devices.

---

PWC: REMOTELY MANAGING A 300-HEADSET DEPLOYMENT

PwC built an immersive, interactive cyber security crisis simulation as a way of communicating to clients the issues around cyber security and helping them to understand the reality of such situations. You are placed in the middle of an emergency board meeting where everyone is taking stock of the situation and trying to find a way out of the crisis. From there, you have the option to take on the role of either the CEO, CFO or CISO (Chief Information Security Officer), each of whom has different decisions to make and a different view of the attack as it unfolds.

The VR experience made its debut appearance at a PwC event in Toronto, Canada. Three hundred PwC partners were invited to experience it, each of whom was given their own headset.

It took three months to design and develop the experience and two weeks to deploy. The deployment included setting up our own local network infrastructure at the venue and onboarding the headsets with device management software, which we used to apply the following tasks to each one:

- Download and install the cyber security crisis software.
- Download the software's media files and place them in the correct folder on the headset.
- Load the venue's WiFi network details.
- Change the Bluetooth name of each headset to match its physical asset number (to make it easier to pair each headset wirelessly with a Bluetooth headset).
- Change the settings to keep the headset from falling asleep when inactive.

In total, we sent about 1,600 gigabytes of data over the air to the headsets through the device management software. On delivery day, all 300 headsets successfully connected to the local network we had set up at the venue. Built into the application was synchronization and data collection functionality. Through a tablet (also connected to the network) which acted as a controller system I could tap a button to wirelessly start the application for all users. It also allowed me to see what decisions everyone was making in the simulation, how long they were taking to make those decisions and how far through the experience they were.

FIGURE 9.1

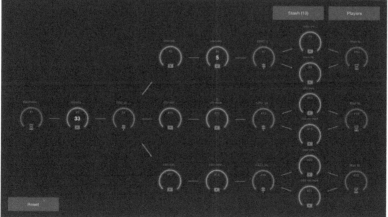

Top: Attendees immersed in the cyber security crisis scenario. Bottom: screenshot of the controller system showing the branching paths of the simulation and the number of users in each scene during a test session.

When the experience ended 15 minutes later, I was able to display the aggregate results of everyone's decisions, which were used to drive a rich and engaging discussion about the challenges of a cyber security attack.

As a result of its success, the VR application is now being used in about 30 different countries around the world and effective device management continues to be an important part of maintaining the hardware it runs on.

## Maintaining headset hygiene

XR headset hygiene is a necessary and critical aspect of their maintenance, especially in settings where sharing is necessary, such as during product demonstrations, at conferences or when loaning out headsets during projects.

There are three main methods for performing these hygiene procedures.

### 1. Disinfectant wipes

This is the simplest way of keeping headsets and any other peripherals clean. Wipes can be purchased from a number of online vendors or at your local pharmacy, and providing the disinfectant strength is high enough to kill pathogens but not high enough to damage the material of the face pad or plastic chassis of the headset, they are a suitable cleaning method.

Although fairly cheap (they can cost less than $0.05 per wipe when ordered in bulk), it is advisable to use one for each piece of equipment to prevent any possible transmission of surviving pathogens or residue, so for frequent-turnover activities, the waste and cost can pile up quite quickly, making them not so eco-friendly and potentially quite costly in the long run.

The material of some headset face pads is porous (such as fabric or foam), making it difficult to effectively clean with a wipe. In these cases, consider either purchasing a covering for the pad made with a non-porous material (silicone or PU leather are commonly used) or using another solution (see below).

A study conducted on infection control of virtual reality headsets showed that the poorest performing headset contained a porous plastic face pad in which 7 per cent of bacteria remained after cleaning with alcohol wipes compared with 1 per cent for the best performing headset which had a non-porous plastic face pad.[1]

## 2. Disposable face masks

These are similar to a surgeon's face masks in that they are held on the face by straps which go around the ears. However, instead of covering the mouth and nose they form a ring around the eyes and over the bridge of the nose – the area at which most headsets come into contact with the face, thus creating a barrier between the headset and the face to prevent any transmission.

They are often used at VR arcades or other entertainment venues so that users can make use of a single one no matter how many times they don a headset or how many different headsets they come into contact with. While more expensive per unit than disposable wipes, less of them will be required if users keep them between headsets, so the relevant cost is not per unit in this case but per headset used. For example, for a face mask costing $0.20 that a user keeps all day and ends up using with 10 devices, that represents an effective cost of $0.02, which makes it cheaper or at least comparable with disposable wipes. If less are used, this also makes them less wasteful than disposable wipes.

However, because they cover only the area around the eyes, they do not provide any protection to other parts, in particular any straps to the side and on top of the head, so these remain a potential hub for pathogen transmission.

## 3. Ultraviolet disinfection

Short wavelength UV light (UVC) disrupts the DNA of microorganisms, rendering them inactive, and is used all over the world to disinfect water, surfaces and equipment. There are more than 2,000 UV water treatment plants in Europe alone.[2]

UVC-emitting machines can come as a handheld model or as a freestanding container. These have a more expensive upfront cost than wipes or masks, ranging from $100 to $1,500, but their effectiveness is scientifically supported, with evidence to suggest that under the right conditions, UVC light can wipe out 99.99 per cent of pathogens.[3]

These devices make a lot of sense for fixed deployments where the headsets are returned to the same location after every session. They are also relatively easy and low hassle for users to operate – for example, the procedure can be as simple as placing the headset inside the UVC container and pressing a button – which makes it ideal for self-management and use by non-specialists.

UVC light on its own is not capable of dealing with makeup, sweat or other debris, however, so the face masks may require supplemental maintenance with a wipe.

## Collecting data on XR solutions

In the hectic rush to build the business case, obtain sponsorship and develop the software for an XR solution, considering what data might be useful to collect and how to collect it can often fall by the wayside despite how important it is.

Both quantitative and qualitative data can be collected in a few ways – through asking users directly for feedback via surveys, by examining their actions within the XR application, or by analysing the user's biometric data (physiological measurements) while they use the XR application (Table 9.1).

TABLE 9.1

| Data collection method | Data type available | Manual or automatic collection |
|---|---|---|
| Surveys presented to the user | Quantitative and qualitative | Manual |
| User metrics directly from the XR application | Quantitative | Automatic |
| Biometrics | Quantitative | Automatic |

Methods for collecting data on the performance of XR solutions, whether such methods produce qualitative or quantitative data, and whether the data can be collected automatically or not.

Table 9.1 is in increasing order of complexity. Surveys can be created relatively easily and given to each user in paper or digital form. Automatically collected data from user sessions in the XR application will need to be built into the application itself. Some biometric measures such as pulse rate require the use of specialist hardware, but voice analysis and eye tracking (or at least head tracking as a proxy) can be conducted on most headsets.

Surveys are a staple data collection method and the main way to collect open-ended, qualitative responses, but automatically collected data requires less follow-up, which will save time if data is being collected regularly. It is also a more direct, immediate and potentially more reliable assessment of user sentiment and behaviours than having to rely on subjective self-analysis or recall.

In any case, the data collection method needs to be assessed and determined at the design stage. The data collected, including any questions asked, will be influenced by the objectives of the project, the end users, the hardware selected and the interactions available within your application.

As an illustration, for a VR experience aimed at training sales executives on how to successfully pitch a product to a potential client, you might collect data on:

- how many times the application was opened;
- the average length of time spent in the application;
- the amount of eye contact each user had with the client;
- the user's confidence, assessed through their tone of voice, spoken words per minute, number of pauses or words indicating uncertainty (umms and uhhs);
- the user's technical score, determined by the use of certain key phrases during the conversation with the client;
- how each user perceived the solution (level of presence, engagement, enjoyment, overall effectiveness and comparison against the usual training method), assessed through a survey.

For an AR solution designed to assist field engineers on a technical task, other data may be useful to collect, including:

- the speed and accuracy with which the task was completed;
- the perceived speed and simplicity in accessing digital diagrams relating to the task;
- the number of times the 'connect to a remote expert' function was activated.

Always design your XR experience with analytics in mind. The data you collect can be compared to that of other solutions to benchmark the effectiveness of XR for your particular application. This will hopefully feed the business case you need to acquire further investment for making improvements and scaling the solution.

## PWC: STEPPING INTO THE SHOES OF COLLEAGUES

PwC ran a VR experience for 2,800 employees over a three-day event. The aim was to help them in their roles as career coaches to navigate an ever-changing world and understand, empathize with and be open-minded towards those they coach and their differing circumstances and motivations.

The experience places them in a common scenario – a project kick-off meeting, in which a leader briefs the team about the client, project and plan of action. Initially, you are in the shoes of an individual on the team who is highly ambitious and willing to sacrifice their personal time to progress their career as quickly as possible. After hearing the project leader speak and the inner thoughts of this individual in response, the scene repeats but this time you are sitting directly across from the first person, embodying another team member. Their inner monologue reveals that they are anxious because it is the end of the working day and they had planned to leave to take care of their child, but felt too guilty about not attending the kick-off meeting to say anything, so now they are trying to make childcare arrangements as discreetly as possible on their mobile phone. As a result, they are not able to focus on the meeting.

After the experience, the audience was split into groups of 4–5 people and encouraged to reflect on what they saw, heard, experienced and learnt. All attendees were given the option to provide feedback through an open-ended survey. Comments received were classified as 'positive' or 'negative' and negative feedback was categorized based on six identified themes: environment, hardware, comfort, facilitation, value, content.

Eighty per cent of responses received were positive in nature. Key findings from reviewing these comments indicated that:

- the vast majority of people found the experience valuable;
- VR is a powerful tool to help build an understanding of different people and situations;
- respondents would like to see VR being used in more training as opposed to e-learning modules and webcasts, especially for soft skills training;
- providing some time at the end of the session for a group debrief created a rich and engaging discussion which would not have been as powerful without the VR experience.

The majority of the comments supported VR's strength as an immersive and empathy-building medium. One comment that summed it up very well was:

'[The most useful thing about the session was the] VR and seeing the same thing from several different perspectives. It felt like we really put ourselves in each other's shoes.'

While this was useful supporting evidence for the investment made in the experience, the most educational comments came from the 20 per cent of respondents that were not so enthusiastic. These are shown in Figure 9.2 in ascending order of number received.

FIGURE 9.2

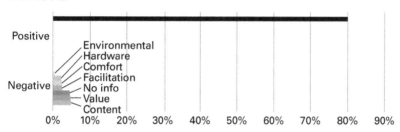

Breakdown of positive and negative feedback from attendees about the VR experience.

ENVIRONMENTAL

These are issues to do with the surrounding environment such as noise or temperature. There were only a handful of these comments, some of which involved users still in VR being distracted by chatter between people who had completed their VR experience. Others noted the creaky floors in the venue, which were a distraction from the immersive nature of the experience. Finally, some complained about the heat in the room, which led to the headset lenses fogging up. Learning points:

- What happens outside the headset is as important as what happens inside of it. To stay immersed in a virtual environment, VR users need to see and hear only what is in that environment for the duration of their experience.

- The electronics within VR headsets generate heat. This should be compensated for by making sure the venue is suitably cooled. When you have a large number of headsets and people (or a relatively small room), this becomes even more important as the heat generated can make the room uncomfortable for both VR users and others.

- Respect the experience of VR users by not talking while they are immersed in VR.

- Be aware of other noises and aim to minimize them for the duration of the VR experience.

- Synchronize the end times of the VR experience for all users as best you can by starting everyone at the same time and giving them suitable induction instructions. If feasible, use synchronization software to kick off their experiences at exactly the same time. For branching narratives, try to design the experience so each path adds up to the same total time.

HARDWARE

These are issues regarding the VR equipment, including its accessories. The vast majority of these comments showed that users had difficulty getting the optical focus right. This was due to the positioning of the headset – too far up or down on the forehead and the content will appear blurry in the same way that it does with your glasses if you try to look through the outer edges of the lens. Others referenced the clunkiness of the headsets and the relatively poor visual quality. In addition to the comments provided, we noted that approximately ten headsets refused to function at one point or another regardless of on-the-fly troubleshooting attempts. This was back in the days of smartphone-based VR – thankfully, things have advanced since then! Learning points:

- Hardware issues are inevitable, but there are some user errors that can be corrected with the right prior instruction. You cannot prevent all issues, but you can prepare to respond swiftly and effectively when they occur.

- Hold a 10 per cent buffer of headsets. If the solution to a hardware issue is not a quick fix or needs any exploration to figure out, immediately give the user a spare headset from the buffer which should be ready to go. Then attempt to solve the issue and either add the headset back to the buffer if fixed or remove it from service.

- Complaints of out-of-focus headsets are frequent, especially with users new to VR. Explain up front that they may need to adjust the headset up and down to bring it into focus. Left and right adjustments are generally not needed.

COMFORT

Any lack of comfort for the user refers to discomfort not related to the environment. Some users mentioned feeling dizzy and one was uncomfortable being disconnected from the physical world. Learning points:

- Acknowledge that a small portion of users may not feel fully comfortable and ensure there are alternatives available for them.
- An alternative option could be a desktop version of the experience.

FACILITATION

This is the way in which the VR experience was introduced and any relevant instructions explained. Some users were confused as to what they should be doing in the VR experience while others felt the instructions given for using the equipment were too long. Learning points:

- There is a fine line between providing sufficient information and too much information. This is exacerbated by the differing levels of experience of the technology in any audience.
- Incorporate initial instructions within your VR experience explicitly stating that users can look all around them, or at the very least mention this before users enter VR.

VALUE

This refers to issues where the use of VR was perceived as not having enough value. Some respondents felt the use of VR was unnecessary to deliver the messages of the session. Learning points:

- Dig deeper into feedback in this category as it may be connected to one of the other areas. 'Value' actually has a hidden component: effort. The more effort a user has to make to overcome obstacles, the less net value there is.
- Environmental, hardware, comfort, facilitation and content issues all represent obstacles for the user to overcome ('effort'). Aim to minimize these and net value will improve.
- Don't expect a 100 per cent positive response rate – some users will simply not connect to the project.

CONTENT

This is what was included within the VR experience (the narrative). Users wanted to see more content, different content or more interactivity in the experience. Learning points:

- Users want to be engaged. High levels of interactivity can enable greater engagement.

- Consider how your experience can be made more interactive by creating decision points or other forms of interaction within it.

- Involve a sample of your intended audience in the design process to gather their thoughts. Incorporate this feedback before development of the experience starts.

This was one of our earliest uses of virtual reality, which I've laid out transparently here as it holds great value in terms of the lessons we learnt from it. I hope you are able to use it to leapfrog some of these issues on your own projects. Applying these lessons, we were able to achieve a 95 per cent positive feedback response on our next VR project.

## Notes

1   http://realitycheckxr.com/Why_Infection_Control_Impacts_Medical_Virtual_Reality.pdf (archived at https://perma.cc/Z9KS-4DDN)

2   www.water-research.net/index.php/water-treatment/water-disinfection/uv-disinfection

3   https://www.ncbi.nlm.nih.gov/pmc/articles/PMC7319933/ (archived at https://perma.cc/RMZ3-ZKFR)

# 10

# A beginner's guide to creating quality 360 video content

*by Alex Rühl*

## Introduction

It's early 2016 and I'm standing in the middle of a field, next to a cluster of action cameras strapped to the end of a pole held together by a DIY 3D printed rig and a strip of gaffer tape. I look at the homespun creation and can't help but think to myself, '*How on earth am I going to pull this off?*'

I don't know whether it was because I love challenging myself, because I've always prided myself on my can-do attitude, or because I felt like I was standing on the precipice of a new horizon in what technology could do, but from that second I knew I had to go all in on a career in VR.

I had been making films since I was 14 years old, had a bachelor's degree in production and had four years' experience in the television industry working on huge shows for national broadcasters like BBC Three, Sky and ITV Studios. But I had no idea what I was getting myself into when I agreed to take on a project to make a 360 film for a well-known brand in the UK.

I rationalized, weighing up the risks and rewards of the project, and eventually landed on the thought, '*It's just a film shoot with a camera that records everything around you. How hard can it be?*'

The night before that shoot I was quietly confident that I would be able to blag it. After all, I had a teaching tool that most of my predecessors didn't when discovering a new technology: Google.

Nothing – and I mean nothing – is more horrifying for a millennial in the information age than turning to Google for advice, instruction and YouTube tutorials and getting literally zero search results back. My search terms yielded nothing with every abrupt tap of the Enter key:

- 'How to set up a 360 camera rig'
- 'What camera settings to use for a 360 video'
- 'How is 360 video different to traditional film?'
- 'How to make a film for a virtual reality headset'

NOTHING.

So I spent a frantic all-nighter wrestling with rented equipment, getting as much hands-on experience as possible to prepare myself for the shoot. The next day I was in the middle of a field with a camera rig and a head full of questions about this new medium I was exploring.

It's been over four years since I first picked up a 360 camera. What I've learned in that time can be distilled into one sentence, one that I think even Google would concede: this is an entirely new medium with new hardware, new workflows and a whole new cinematic language that hasn't been defined yet.

So instead of leaving you stranded in a metaphorical field with an intimidating camera rig and a descending sense of confusion, I'm going to give you an insight into everything I've learned in this quickfire blueprint for creating 360.

## Reasons to use 360 video

So far in this book, you've learned when virtual reality can be a powerful solution for your business, but as Jeremy has outlined, there are multiple forms of content within VR. The key question for a creator is when to use 360 video over computer-generated content – what benefits are there to offering your audience a 360 degree view of a physical environment?

### 1 CAPTURING MOMENTS

Events, industry workshops, demos, conferences or countless other in-person occasions in business are all ideal opportunities to set up a 360 camera. Capturing the moment can allow employees, customers and stakeholders to have an on-demand experience while feeling engaged, as if they're actually part of the action.

This can also double as a stress-free solution for logistical or inclusivity challenges – if you have remote workers who can't travel, or simply want to cut down on their carbon footprint, for example. Or if they struggle with mental health issues that would pose a barrier to them being among crowds, or physical impairments that might stop them from attending in person.

360 video captures are the next best thing to being there in person.

## 2 PHOTOREALISM

Despite massive leaps in computer graphics capabilities, film remains the most realistic way to capture a scene. In my experience with clients, employees engage more when their brain recognizes an environment, or people, in a video rather than an animated scenario. Computer graphics can produce an incredibly powerful experience, but it requires a lot of work and expense to reach that level. If your aim is to evoke empathy and emotion from the viewer, it's often more effective to capture content directly from the world we're used to with 360 technology.

## 3 EASIER FOR FIRST-TIME USERS

Passive 360 is a great entry point to VR for most people because once the headset is on, first-time users can simply enjoy an engaging and often mind-blowing experience. I've found when demonstrating more interactive forms of VR, unless your onboarding process is flawless, or the user is already familiar with video games, the second you hand over a headset and controllers to a user and ask them to interact with something that they've never experienced before, you start to see some problems.

Interactive VR experiences require a lot more expertise, resources and pre/post care, whereas passive 360 video is a simple case of putting on a headset, sitting back and watching a scene play out in front of you.

## 4 EASIER-TO-CREATE CONTENT

Recording videos has become part of our daily lives. Every person who has a smartphone has access to a video camera good enough to produce a Hollywood movie. Although phones can't record in 360 (yet), the familiarity with camera settings, terminology and the culture around capturing videos are all transferable to 360 filmmaking. For the majority of people, it's going to be a smaller step from that to filming on a 360 camera than it would be to upskill in advanced games programming and 3D graphics modelling, which is what is required for CG content for VR. This, combined with the fact you can get a brilliant entry-level 360 camera for less than $500, makes 360 video an attractive option to experiment with.

---

DID YOU KNOW?

Consumer-grade smartphones have become so powerful that they've been used in some professional productions: American filmmaker Steven Soderbergh released several films in cinemas and on Netflix that were shot on an iPhone. Award-winning comedy-drama *Tangerine* and Lady Gaga's latest music video were also filmed on an iPhone.

---

### 5 EASIER TO DISTRIBUTE

In addition to ease of use, 360 content is easier to distribute than other forms of VR. It's the most widely distributed of all content for VR because it requires only a 'three degrees of freedom headset,' the most inexpensive form of VR headset, and it doesn't need a computer or laptop to power it, making it a compact option. The video file sizes can be fairly large in comparison with CG projects, but most online platforms such as YouTube and Facebook can host 360 videos, making it fairly easy to share content quickly. When it comes to putting on VR demos, it doesn't require that much space per person to showcase 360 as users are static, simply sitting and looking around.

Compare that with more complex, interactive VR projects: you'll be limited to a smaller number of users because the equipment is far more expensive, requires more time and people to service and troubleshoot, and you need a lot more space because users will be flailing their hands around as well as potentially walking around the experience.

## Reverse engineering your desired outcomes

So, you've decided you definitely want to create a 360 experience. Now what? The next step is to reverse engineer your desired outcome for the project, starting with what you envisage the project will look like once it's completed.

What do you want the piece to achieve in the business, how do you want users to be impacted by it, and how are you going to facilitate it?

Although my specialism is 360 video made specifically for VR headsets, 360 media can also be displayed in what those in the industry call a 'magic window'. This essentially means you can show 360 content on a tablet or phone or within a browser on a computer. It's called a magic window because it's been likened to opening a window into an alternative reality. You can move your phone or click and drag your mouse to navigate around the video rather than move your head like you would in a headset.

It's important to decide up front which device you're creating for. This is because although the production workflow is the same, the directing style and filming and editing techniques are very different. We'll dig deeper into this in the production process section, but an example is that if you created a 360 experience incorporating fast editing cuts while moving the camera around a lot, that would make a great magic window experience where the user attention is quite short. But translated over to a VR headset it would almost certainly make the viewer feel some element of cyber sickness.

I've been very vocal in my career about my firm belief in the value and return on investment 360 video for VR headsets provides for businesses. This is where a great deal of my expertise lies. So the remainder of my insight will give an overview of these benefits and how to tap into them with your VR content.

A big part of getting the best return on investment for your VR content is deciding whether you will be creating something that will be part of a wider event or a standalone experience.

Why is this important? This may affect the opening of your 360 video, which could include more instructions if it's being used as a standalone experience. Or, if you're using it as part of a wider event and want the 360 video to be a catalyst for discussion, that could shape the narrative and inform the way scenarios play out on screen, leaving them a little more open-ended and thought provoking.

One project Jeremy and I completed together is a great example of this. Project Shift – the very stealthy code name for the project – was a 360 experience created to highlight negative behaviours in senior leadership and to facilitate a dialogue around them, as part of a wider change management programme. To achieve this, we shot scenes that gave examples of good and bad behaviour designed to open up group discussions.

Once you've established whether your piece will be a standalone or integrated experience, you need to decide what you want your user to feel coming out of the experience. Do you want them to feel inspired or entertained? Uncomfortable or pensive? Educated or emotional? This should relate back to the overall objectives of the project, which could include saving time or money with your existing business processes, converting more customers or generating more leads.

To summarize so far:

- you've decided that you definitely want to make a 360 piece and know why you've chosen it over other forms of VR content;
- you know how the piece will be distributed and facilitated;
- you know what you want your user to take away from the experience.

Now it's time to design the actual 360 video from start to finish.

## Designing for 360: the three stages

The process of creating a 360 experience can be broken down into three stages:

- **Pre-production:** this is all the upfront preparation you need to nail down before you pick up a camera rig.
- **Production:** this is the really hands-on part, the time spent actually filming.
- **Post-production:** this is all the work done to the project after filming, including editing, sound and stitching.

When it comes to 360 video, arguably the most important stage is pre-production. Unlike the famous Hollywood saying 'we'll fix it in post', 360 footage is very, very difficult to correct if it is filmed wrongly. Something as simple as not considering a prop choice, or not noticing branding somewhere in the room that shouldn't be there, can cause a real headache when it comes to post-production. So it's important that there is a lot of effort, work and stakeholder approval in pre-production.

# Pre-production

## 1 Key takeaways for users

What do you want your user to feel when they come out of the headset? What are they supposed to have learnt? Are you trying to evoke empathy by putting them in someone else's shoes? Or are they meant to understand how to look out for hazards in an office environment? The more specific you can be outlining your objectives, the better.

So let's say, for example, you want to use this 360 experience to educate employees on the effects of poor leadership. Rather than having someone talk to the camera about best practices as in a traditional training video, you can now put the user in a role-play scenario of poor leadership playing out. This allows users to have a next-level immersive experience that they can recall and draw from in future, as they feel as though they've been through that situation first hand.

## 2 High-level storyboarding

Next you want to break down every scene of the 360 video. This will start to inform everything, from the budget to logistics for filming to timelines for delivery.

Outline every scene with the main action, including what actors will be doing in the scene, how they will interact with each other, where they will be location wise and any key props needed.

What is the key action and takeaway from each scene? For example:

SCENE ONE

Location: Private meeting room

Characters: Freya and Toby

Props: Toby's phone / meeting room decor

Action: Freya is waiting for her annual review. She's nervous because she's missed KPIs. Her manager, Toby, comes storming in on the phone. He's stressed and when he gets off the phone he doesn't let Freya get a word in edgeways and has actually forgotten why she is there. Freya leaves feeling more frustrated, which leads to built-up animosity and impacts her performance.

---

PRO TIP

When you're starting out creating 360 video, resist the urge to move the camera at all during scenes. If done incorrectly, the motion can make your viewers feel nauseous and disoriented and risks deterring them from watching completely.

---

## 3 Perspective

Perspective is the key difference between creating a 360 video and a traditional non-360 video. VR's superpower is the fact that you can put people in someone else's shoes. Not all projects will be shot from the POV (point of view) of a character, but you always need to give your viewer a reason to believe they are actually in the film. This will allow them to really connect with the experience rather than find themselves questioning what they are doing there.

---

FUN FACT

VR industry professionals call traditional videos 'flatties' because they capture only a limited 2D 'flat' portion of the scene.

---

When considering the POV of the piece, think about your key takeaway and which perspective would be most effective to communicate those messages from. In our poor leadership in business example, it makes the most sense to experience the piece from Freya's point of view so you can feel how Toby's behaviour is affecting her.

---

PRO TIP

A mechanic I often use to heighten the feeling that you're in a character's shoes is an internal monologue. This allows you to hear a character's thoughts and deepens empathy towards them. On the projects Jeremy and I have produced together, we've found this technique works very well at establishing the kinds of emotions we want our users to be picking up on.

---

### SWAPPING PERSPECTIVES

A question I often get asked is: can you swap perspectives? The answer is yes, but with one major caveat: you have to make it explicit to the audience when it happens. Personally, I would highly recommend not switching perspectives during the same scene as this risks disorientating viewers.

When Jeremy and I have worked on projects together, we have found it useful to precede some scenes with a brief narrative description, which also explains whose point of view you are seeing the scene from. For example, if you're in Freya's shoes and in the next scene you're in Toby's, I would insert an explanatory screen before each scene to draw attention to the change of perspective. The wording might be something like:

'You are Freya, a junior manager in [a law firm] expecting to have her annual review.'

'You are Toby, partner in [a law firm] on the phone to a board member.'

## 4 Scripting a scene

360 video is a nascent medium. There is no set way to format the script for a project yet. Generally speaking, for business-related 360 video projects the most effective script template follows the style shown in Table 10.1.

TABLE 10.1

| Script | Scene description & set notes |
| --- | --- |
| **Scene 1**<br>*We are in the shoes of Freya – a junior manager – who is having a 1:1 end-of-year review with her manager, Toby – a partner in the same firm.* | **Location:**<br>*We are in Toby's office.*<br><br>*There is an empty coffee cup and stacks of paper on the desk in front of us.* |
| **Freya**<br>*(internal monologue VO)* | ***Over black. Text on screen reads:***<br>***You are in the shoes of Freya – a junior manager working at X CORP.*** |
| I really hope Toby has had a chance to review those numbers. | |
| **Toby**<br>*(surprised)* | ***Toby walks in texting on his phone, laughing to himself.*** |
| *Oh Freya. Sorry, do we have something scheduled?* | |

Project X example shooting script

You'll notice the dialogue and key performance details are on the left and the physical action, description of setting, etc. are on the right. This style allows people very quickly to identify key components for production, such as locations for each scene, which actors are required, whose perspective the scene is shot from, any important props that are required and other key info for the production team.

> PRO TIP
>
> Don't forget to describe how you want your actors to perform. What emotion should they be portraying? Who should they be addressing in the scene? Remember that everyone is in shot in a 360 video so give direction to characters who aren't talking as well.

## 5 Length of scenes

The rule of thumb for scripts is that one page of dialogue will equal about one minute in filming time, so be aware of that when writing your script. 360 scenes are much more like theatre than film so you want them to be a minimum of one minute, but be mindful of scenes that run on for too long. Remember, there is no editing within a scene so the actors will have to memorise the whole script and perform it in one take. This means if your script is six minutes long and there are three actors in a scene, if one actor gets one line wrong at the five-minute mark, you will have to start the whole take over again.

> Of all the projects Jeremy and I have worked on, our record is 18 takes to complete a scene successfully. Although relatively short, this three-minute scene was fairly complex, involving seven characters in a boardroom and two over a telephone, with people moving in and out of the room. Each character's lines were short and had to be delivered off the back of the previous character's dialogue, creating a rapid chain that was prone to failure – 18th time lucky!

## 6 Actors vs contributors

You may have noticed that in all of my examples so far I have referred to using actors and characters, rather than presenters or contributors (someone not media trained such as one of your organization's employees appearing in the film). This is because filming a 360 scene is technically challenging and without excessive prep and rehearsal time, most people won't perform as well as an actor does.

If you are going to use contributors or presenters rather than actors, make sure that they are off-script, which means they know their lines inside out. Be sure to incorporate a lot of rehearsal time for them to get comfortable on camera and also to make sure they know where to stand/move on camera, as these are incredibly important details that can impact post-production.

## 7 Action/props in scenes

Due to technical reasons, which we will explore in the production phase, you need to consider what kind of movement or action and also what decor and props you have in every scene.

For props, remember that the entire location will be in shot because the camera can see everything. It's no good arranging just a corner of the room to look pretty. Everything is in shot so everything has to be considered. Look out for any branding that you need to remove or any unnecessary decor that might affect your story, even small details like a clock showing 5pm when your scene is supposed to be happening first thing in the morning.

## 8 Reconnaissance

Reconnaissance – or the 'recce' as it's known in the industry – involves the key production team scouting the filming locations ahead of time to test ideas, identify and resolve potential issues, and agree on the technical setup of the equipment.

This is where you can plan the specific movements of the actors' action ahead of time (called 'blocking'), test the technical setup of the camera, pre-empt and resolve any problems that may appear in post-production, and test the audio to make sure no appliances in the room will be picked up by microphones. These include fridges, computers, printers, air conditioning and anything else that gives off even the smallest hum.

Why are recces so important in the production process? In the 360 cyber security crisis experience Jeremy described in Chapter 9, one scene required 20-plus actors in a single room to recreate a hectic, high-level press conference. One scene required 20-plus actors in a single room to recreate a hectic, high-level press conference. A recce was crucial for that scene because there were so many elements and so much action that needed to be considered ahead of time.

It was also important to test how far away actors needed to be so as to not cause problems for the camera and we needed to figure out where to hide the crew. In the end, we hid some of them in plain sight, giving them starring roles as camera operators at the back of the press conference room.

We also had to consider the practicalities of the location. What was the lighting like in the room and would that impact filming? How many props would we need and how would we transport them to that particular room? How many crew members would we need to help set out the chairs to make it look realistic? Where could we hide the room's original decor? All of this and many other considerations had to be addressed before we could even pick up a camera.

All the elements listed above are very important to consider ahead of filming a 360 piece. You can save yourself a huge headache and potentially even more budget by being thorough in the pre-production stage.

---

IN SUMMARY

For first time 360 makers during the pre-production stage, here are some summary tips:

- Keep it simple.
- Don't have too many scenes.
- Maintain a single perspective.
- Consider having two actors maximum in a scene at any one time.
- Keep dialogue short.
- Keep action/movement to a minimum.
- Use a location that you're familiar with.
- Do lots of tests in your recce for audio and visual.
- Have plenty of rehearsal time.
- Plan, plan and plan some more.

---

## Production

So, you've done the prep work and your team is ready to film your 360 project. Now you're ready to go into production. This is the point of no return, but it shouldn't feel scary if you've done extensive work in pre-production and you've had the correct approvals from all the stakeholders involved.

## 1 Crew

The minimum number of crew roles with which it is feasible to create a 360 video is four. These roles are:

- **Director:** this is the captain of the ship. They make key decisions for the project, set the creative vision and, on production day, look after what's happening on screen in front of the camera.
- **DOP (Director of Photography):** the DOP operates the camera, making sure it is working properly, recording in the right settings, and oversees the technical aspects of the shoot. On an advanced shoot they will also be the person to set lighting and create a visual aesthetic that evokes a certain mood agreed with the director beforehand.
- **Sound recordist:** this person is responsible for making sure all of the audio is captured clearly and that the microphones pick up no disruptions that would spoil a recording.
- **Production assistant:** this person is the support system for all of the crew members, ensuring they have everything they need, facilitating communication between the crew, and generally looking after actors, contributors and other stakeholders. The essence of their role is to make sure everything runs smoothly.

This is what we would call a skeleton crew, which means it's the bare minimum number of people you need realistically to achieve a good-quality professional 360 video.

Other crew members you might have on a bigger production would include:

- **First assistant director:** the 1st AD is the COO to the director's CEO. They are a senior crew member who makes important decisions to keep the production running on time and on budget. They manage operations, make purchasing decisions, arrange logistics, and all crew members report directly to them apart from the DOP and the director who work together to achieve the desired creative output.
- **Second assistant director:** on larger shoots, the 2nd AD takes on some of the 1st AD duties, such as creating daily call sheets (which have operational

information for crew and actors, such as what time they should be on set, the address of the venue, etc), as well as being the person in charge of liaising with actors.

- **Third assistant director:** on even larger shoots when you're working with a lot of actors and background actors (extras), a 3rd AD will take on the responsibility of liaising with actors as well as supervising the team of production assistants.

- **Script supervisor:** this person sits next to the director on set and their job is to make sure actors hit all of their lines. This is especially essential in 360 projects where scenes are quite long and intricate.

- **Camera assistant:** this person assists the DOP.

- **DIT (digital imaging technician):** this person is responsible for organizing and backing up the large amounts of data produced during a shoot and verifying that the data hasn't been corrupted or lost in the process.

- **VFX (visual effects) supervisor:** a VFX supervisor approves the creative decisions made on set to ensure the footage is suitable for post-production.

- **Production designer:** this person creates a particular aesthetic for your 360 project. For example, if the narrative centred around business negotiations with another culture and took place in a foreign country, this person would make sure everything on set was authentic to that geography and narrative, including location, props, graphic styles, etc.

- **Sound assistant:** this person assists the sound recordist.

- **Gaffer:** sometimes known as the 'chief lighting technician', the gaffer is the head electrician on sets that require complex or large lighting setups.

- **Grip:** a grip is someone who sets up and operates equipment like a track, dolly or crane, which are all ways of moving a big camera setup. They can also organize non-electrical lighting setups such as tripods, stands and ceiling rigs from which lights could be suspended.

- **Make up artist:** this person applies film-appropriate makeup to the talent (actors, presenters and contributors).

- **Hair stylist:** this person styles the talent's hair.

### Directing the action: beware the FOMO

Directing a 360 video is very different from other forms of film directing. One key thing to remember is that when you're creating content for virtual reality headsets, the camera essentially becomes the viewer's head, so any time you want to put something in the scene, really consider what that would be like from the point of view of someone sitting where the camera is.

When you've got multiple things happening in a scene, try not to have them happening at the same time. This will create a FOMO (fear of missing out) effect, which you want to avoid unless that is your intention. Your viewer might get whiplash from spinning their head around too quickly trying to take in everything that's going on around them.

Having showcased 360 to thousands of audience members, I can confidently say that people do not like feeling as though they're missing important action. Instead, pick your POIs (points of interest) carefully. My best advice would be to stand next to the camera and think about how people would naturally react in that particular location and circumstance. Make it feel as natural and intuitive as possible. In traditional filmmaking, in order to get a close-up, you either zoom in or put the camera closer to the actors. With 360, this kind of framing can be achieved with choreography – in other words, by making your actors move closer and further away from the camera you can create different feelings of intimacy and intensity with the viewer.

Think about what the energy of the scene is supposed to feel like and create a pacing with the dialogue that reflects that. If a scene is supposed to be tense or awkward, consider drawing it out with lots of thoughtful pauses or uncomfortable glances. If you want it to feel energetic and exciting, increase the pace and have a bit more movement in the scene.

Another important consideration is how your viewers' gaze will transition between scenes. What I mean by this is you need to make sure that your audience is looking in the right direction so that when you cut to the next scene, the point of interest and where the audience is looking are aligned.

This theory of 360 directing comes from Jessica Brillhart, who was the lead VR filmmaker for Google. She described the process of editing scenes in 360 as jumping between worlds. You want to make sure that when you jump into a new world, your user isn't disorientated and that they are looking in the direction of the next piece of action.

So, for example, if your first scene is in an office and the scene ends with the person leaving the room via the door on the right, when you land in the next scene maybe have the person standing by the coffee machine on the right because chances are the viewer will be looking that way.

FIGURE 10.1

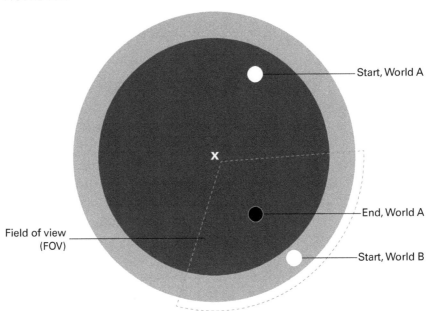

Start, World A

End, World A

Field of view
(FOV)

Start, World B

Pictorial explanation of Jessica Brillhart's theory on editing 360 video showing a user's view at the end of a scene matching up to the right place at the start of the next one.[1]

---

PRO TIP

I recommend filming scenes in single, complete takes wherever possible. Don't assume you can fix a fluffed line in post-production. If you try to cut an awkward pause out of the middle of a scene, the person watching in a headset will see a disorienting jump in the footage as if the scene skipped forward. It's a jarring experience, so avoid it at all costs unless it's an intentional stylistic choice. And even then, really scrutinize your style choices.

---

## 3 Where shall I hide my crew?

This is a really important consideration and it will totally depend on your filming location. If possible, you can make them leave the room or hide. They could even hide in plain sight in the scene and become extras – the people acting in the background that don't say anything or do anything – just make sure they look natural and don't acknowledge the camera while recording.

The key crew members that need to be near the camera, able to watch the scene unfold, are the director and the DOP. If you have a WiFi-enabled camera the DOP could potentially view the scene from an iPad or another device away from the filming area. If you do this, make sure they have a reliable connection and can see the scene play out clearly as they will be looking out for technical aspects that could spoil the 'take'.

> A take begins the second you hit record (usually accompanied by the famous command 'action') and ends when you stop recording ('cut').

On bigger productions, or on productions where you have a budget for advanced post-production, you can have your crew stand in a particular section of the location where they can be removed with visual effects in post-production (Figure 10.2).

If you don't have this luxury I recommend that you have the director sit underneath the tripod or as close to the camera as possible because you will need to digitally remove the tripod that the camera sits on in post-production at the very minimum.

## 4 Camera considerations

The technology of 360 cameras is changing rapidly. Every six months, there seems to be another breakthrough development in the way we capture and process 360 video. Make sure you research the camera you're going to use and make sure it's right for your production at the time of filming.

### STEREO VERSUS MONO

The first decision is whether or not you want to film stereoscopic or monoscopic. I'm not going to go into too much detail about this because (spoiler alert) the answer for any beginner, and anyone who isn't a video professional, is monoscopic – *always monoscopic.*

'But Alex, what even are stereoscopic and monoscopic?' Quite simply, stereoscopic means the film is shot from two different perspectives to imitate the left eye and the right eye, which gives the illusion of depth. It tricks you into thinking something is three-dimensional but really it's your brain doing that work.

Monoscopic is when you deliver the exact same image to both the left and the right eye. Some people watching 360 video that is monoscopic think that it is 3D purely because your brain is so overwhelmed with being in an all-encompassing new reality, it naturally interprets depth.

FIGURE 10.2

Top: Before post-production, me directing a scene alongside some of the crew in one area of the 360 environment. Bottom: After post-production, the crew and I have all been magically removed using a technique called plating – find out more about that in the post-production section.

There is a whole host of technical challenges that come with shooting in stereoscopic, so I would advise that you stay away from that unless you've done some advanced training or have hired a professional crew.

RESOLUTION

The next thing you need to pay attention to is your camera's resolution. Although you are used to 4K being the standard for your smartphone and

TV, in 360 video 4K is the absolute minimum you would want to shoot at. The reason is that a traditional 4K image is thousands of pixels squished down into a 16:9 rectangle that creates a crystal-clear image. In 360, those same thousands of pixels are stretched over a full spherical frame. The image directly in front of you is only a quarter of those pixels and therefore looks distorted and grainy, similar to the quality of a VHS tape.

A lot of consumer 360 cameras now shoot at a minimum of 5.2K resolution and go right up to 8K. Although the image will still not be as crystal-clear as you're used to, this offers much more clarity in your 360 images.

On a professional shoot, the minimum resolution that you would want to use is 8K and could go up to 12–16K, which is getting closer to having 4K in every direction you're looking in a headset.

This could get very technical very quickly: not all pixels are created equally and 8K on one camera may produce different results to that on another depending on the camera's other specifications. But I'm going to leave that information for now because there is another factor that will affect what resolution you can actually shoot at.

### NUMBER OF CAMERA LENSES

The minimum number of camera lenses on a 360 camera is two: one capturing the front and one for the back. The more lenses you have, the more resolution you can likely capture. But on the downside, more lenses also means more stitch lines.

A 360 image is created during post-production processing, stitching together the images from the different camera lenses like you would with a patchwork quilt. There will be seams along the lines where there is no camera lens. You need to be very aware of these stitch lines. If you have an actor too close to the camera on one of them, they risk appearing chopped by the stitch and will quickly resemble a cyclops.

You may also see 'ghosting', when someone moves between one lens and another. This is because of parallax. The easiest way to explain parallax is by taking your index finger – yes, do this now – and stretching out your arm so it's as far away from you as possible. Close your left eye and use your right eye to stare at your finger. Now open your left eye, close your right eye and repeat. Your finger looks like it's vaguely in the same position, right?

Now bring your finger closer – an inch away from your face – and do the same thing. Your finger has completely shifted now, hasn't it? This is because of parallax and the way that your left eye and your right eye see things from different perspectives.

This is why you have to be really careful when plotting out action in a 360 scene. For beginners, ideally you don't want actors crossing any stitch lines. But if it's absolutely essential, make sure they do it from a good distance away as this will decrease the amount of parallax and therefore reduce ghosting and other visual abnormalities.

For locations that are quite small, you might want to consider using a camera with fewer lenses purely to reduce these potential problems. However, remember that reducing lenses reduces quality, so it's always a balancing act when it comes to choosing the right camera for production.

### 5 Lighting

Most 360 cameras do not work well in low-lighting situations. Make sure that you are in a very well-lit location. Outdoor or natural light is the best, but if you are indoors make sure you don't mix too much outdoor and indoor lighting because this will mess with your colour balance. Indoor lighting is more orange and outdoor lighting is more blue, and they will obscure your colouring if they are both present.

If you're shooting in a room with windows, make sure the majority of your action is happening on the side of the camera without the windows. This is because of something called dynamic range. When a camera is faced with two different lighting conditions it has to 'expose' for just one of them.

If I was shooting indoors but I wanted the attention to be on what's happening outside the window, I would adjust the exposure for the window, making the inside room much darker but the outside look crisp and natural. Conversely, if I wanted to focus on the action inside the room (which is usually the case), then exposing indoors would make the room brighter but the window would be blown out, meaning you would see no detail because it would be too bright.

### 6 Plating

If you've got a post-production budget for a visual effects artist to work on your project, you can do something called plating. This is particularly helpful in difficult lighting conditions. Plating is when you film a scene multiple times in different states and combine the results. For example, you might film the main action at one exposure, then, after the take, record the environment again at a darker exposure so in post-production a VFX artist can 'composite' (or overlap) parts from the different videos to make a perfect image with balanced lighting.

Another great benefit of plating is hiding crew. As I mentioned earlier, if you have the crew sitting behind the camera in a specific spot, you can then remove them in post-production. Similar to the lighting scenario, you can record (or plate) the same location without anyone in it. So essentially you have the scene with the action going on and a scene with no one in sight, and the VFX artist then mixes both of those images together to magically erase the crew from the scene.

This same principle can be applied for removing things like props and unwanted action on locations where you can't control the whole environment, like a public park or space.

The most basic example of plating is to remove the camera's tripod which appears underneath you. If the scene is in an office, you can even replace the tripod with a chair, for example.

## 7 Sound

Sound is one of the most important aspects of 360 video production. It's a well-known fact in filmmaking that audiences will forgive bad-quality video as long as the sound is great. But the reverse is not true.

Recording good sound is crucial to having a believable, immersive experience with 360 video. This is especially pertinent if you're creating a piece that has a lot of dialogue.

Make sure your microphone is as close to the person speaking as possible without being in sight. We tend to use lapel radio microphones, which means you can hide the microphone on the actor's body while maintaining a high-quality recording. The recording is then transmitted through radio waves to the receiver, which is being monitored by the sound recordist.

On a professional shoot, you could even record in a format that will allow the user to have the same spatial audio experience as they would do in the real world. Essentially, as well as recording in every direction – much like the camera does – you are recording data about which direction those sounds are coming from. For example, if an actor is sitting on your left, the audio comes from the left side. If that same actor gets up and moves to the right side, the audio will follow them. If the actor is in front of you and you were to move your head so that you are facing the opposite direction, the sound they are making will now come from behind you. This kind of positional audio really enhances a 360 experience and allows your brain to fully believe that what you're viewing is real.

For a director, spatial audio is a very powerful tool because it now allows you to draw the audience's attention to something purely using sound. Imagine if a bang went off behind you right now. Your instinct would be to turn around quickly to see what was there. Delivering sound cues is a powerful way to direct the audience's attention.

But before you consider using this style of audio, make sure that the headset you are delivering to and the software you're using to run your 360 video can handle this format. As this is such a new medium, there is no standardized format yet, which makes it difficult to make audio compatible with all headsets and video player applications.

## IN SUMMARY

For newcomers to 360 video, use the guidance below during production:

- Make sure you have a minimum of three crew members – four if you're recording sound – looking after the key areas of production. By having a specific focus you're less likely to miss any important aspects that will potentially spoil the recorded takes.

- Keep the camera still. Remember, the camera is now a person's head – treat it accordingly.

- Don't have too much action going on. Try to keep the focus on one point of interest.

- Position actors in places that feel natural. Don't have them move around a lot.

- Hide your crew as much as possible.

- Pick a camera with a smaller number of lenses to minimize stitch lines, but with a minimum of 5.2K resolution.

- Don't have your actors positioned near the stitch lines in between camera lenses. If they move, make sure they are a minimum of 1–2 metres away from the camera.

- Film in monoscopic unless you're working with an experienced professional.

- Shoot in well-lit locations and try to keep your lighting as even as possible.

- If you're shooting in a place that has windows, make sure your action is happening away from the windows.

- If you're on a more advanced shoot, consider plating and recording spatial audio.

## Post-production

Congratulations! You finished filming and it went extremely well because you had prepared and followed the advice outlined so far. Now it's time to bring the project to life by pulling all the pieces together and putting the final touches on your 360 video in post-production.

### 1 Data management

First things first: get organized. You want to offload all of your files into structured folders that will allow you to find them and identify them quickly and easily. The number of scenes you shoot, actors you work with and lenses on your camera will all affect how many files you have to look after, so it's really important that you name them and organize them in a way that everyone working on post-production will be able to understand.

360 video file sizes tend to be a lot bigger than normal video files because of the amount of data you're capturing, so make sure you allow enough time to properly offload and back up all of your files.

In a professional production we like to say that if you don't have your files backed up in three places, you don't have a backup at all. I won't scare you with the details of the horror stories I've heard from people on incredibly big, large-budget productions that have been completely lost because someone decided not to back up their files securely. Do yourself a favour and get a couple of external hard drives – you'll thank me later.

### 2 Stitching

As we've talked about in previous sections, because of the way that 360 cameras capture a scene you will need to stitch that footage together like a patchwork quilt.

Most cameras have pretty good automatic stitching software that comes with the hardware.

This might be as simple as opening your files in one of these apps and letting it do its magic automatically.

If you require advanced stitching because you have a lot of movement in your scene, you might have to use specialist software which allows you to manually adjust your stitch lines with pixel-by-pixel accuracy.

---

PRO TIP

Many 360 video industry professionals use specialist software to perform manual stitching, such as Mistika VR and PTGui.

---

After the stitching process is complete you will be left with a single fully panoramic 360 video. This is now ready for further post-production edits.

### 3 Paintwork, compositing and rotoscoping

Once you have a single stitched 360 video file, a VFX artist can do some paintwork on the background of the environment, removing any bits of the scene that need to be erased, such as nails on the wall where clocks have been removed or unwanted props. At the very least, this is where you will remove the camera tripod and replace it with a graphic (often your company's logo) or another object, such as a chair, or even simply paint in the floor.

Compositing is the process mentioned earlier where your VFX artist will take the different plates and combine them to make one polished video.

If you have a really complex scene where people are moving through areas in the scene that need to be painted or composited, you will need a VFX artist to complete some rotoscoping work. This is where they edit each frame individually, cutting around the moving object so that the edited effect remains consistent throughout the scene.

### 4 Editing

Once you've got your final 360 videos of each completed scene polished, you can edit them together as you would with a traditional video or 'flattie'. This is where you place scenes back to back, trim them down to the length you want and add any graphics, title cards or credits.

## 5 Sound mixing

Once you have a 'picture lock' as it's called in filmmaking (that is, you are happy and have signed off all visuals), you can mix your sound. This is basically a fancy term for sound editing.

First, you will need to synchronize the sound from the actors' microphones to the inbuilt microphone from the camera. Then, you need to mute the camera sound and adjust all of the levels – or the volume – of the different microphones to make sure they all match and that none of them are too overbearing.

On a professional audio mix this is where you would do things like remove unnecessary noise such as wind, static or clothes ruffling. You could also add in music, soundtracks or sound effects to enhance the cinematic feel of the project.

If you recorded spatial audio, you then need to go through the process of having the individual sounds placed in time and space using the data captured on location.

Once you've gone through this whole post-production process you'll be left with a 360 video file which you can now load on a VR headset to watch back.

ET VOILÀ! You, my friend, have just become a 360 filmmaker.

---

IN SUMMARY

- Make sure your files are organized and backed up in at least two places.
- Use the camera's automatic stitching software to give you your base 360 video files.
- Edit the scenes together, making sure you don't cut anything out during one scene.
- Replace the camera's audio with the sound from the actors' microphones and make sure the volume is even and clear for the user to hear.

---

## Other subjects of 360 video you might come across

### VR 180

In 2017 there was a surge in popularity of 180 content, where only 180 degrees are captured by the camera. YouTube and Facebook released support for the format and manufacturers started to produce cameras capable of shooting 3D 180 footage.

180 is like the lovechild of traditional video and 360. Its production workflow is a lot more similar to traditional filmmaking and because you're capturing only the front half of the scene, you avoid a lot of the headache that you have to consider in 360 that we've outlined here, including hiding the crew, considering lighting and having to do a lot of paintwork and compositing.

180 is innately stereoscopic because the idea is that you have just two cameras side by side capturing the action in front of you, replicating what your left and right eyes would see. What that means is that you still have to make considerations based on a stereoscopic workflow, which as I suggested earlier is very technical and should be left to a professional.

Having said that, consumer 180 cameras make it very easy to create a 'point and shoot' setup where the camera will do all the work for you. It's essentially recording a traditional video in 3D that can be viewed in a headset. In fact, one of the biggest upsides for 180 is the increase in pixel density, which makes the image look a lot crisper and higher quality than a 360 image when viewing in a headset. That's because you're filming the same resolution in both formats, but with 360, that is then stretched around a full spherical frame rather than just half of one. The main downside is that only half the environment is captured, so it is less immersive for the user, who will see just a black screen if they turn around.

Support for this format has dwindled over the past couple of years and I'm seeing fewer and fewer clients and professionals requesting it.

### Interactive 360

The biggest argument people have against using 360 video in a VR headset is that it's not as interactive as other forms of VR. However, you can incorporate interactive elements into 360 projects.

The cyber security crisis simulation Jeremy and I produced together was a special type of interactive 360 production called a 'branching narrative' in which the user makes decisions which affect how the experience progresses.

The way we produced this was exactly the same as if we were creating a regular 360 experience, only we had to create different scenes for every different 'branch point'. So every time the user made a decision, we would have a different 360 scene for each possible choice made.

You can even make an interactive 360 experience seem non-interactive to users. This is done by putting invisible hotspots in the scene so the user doesn't see anything other than the 360 video, but behind the scenes the content is changing in response to what part of the frame they are looking at. This works really well in scenarios such as hazard awareness where you want the user's natural engagement to trigger certain consequences. For example, in an office scenario, if they don't spot the smoke coming from the bin behind them quickly enough, the next scene could be the bin on fire and causing panic. If they do see the smoke early enough, the next scene could be that character raising the fire alarm or getting the correct office fire hydrant.

Obviously, the more scenes you have to film, the bigger the cost and the longer the project timeline. With branching narratives in particular, each decision point you introduce creates extra complexity, so keep that in mind and make sure you plan accordingly.

The interactive elements themselves can be programmed from scratch in game engines such as Unity and Unreal. Alternatively, you can use off-the-shelf solutions such as WondaVR or Liquid Cinema and many others that allow you to add interactivity using a simple web user interface that doesn't require programming skills.

## The future of 360

As this technology evolves rapidly we will see the film and game technologies in VR continue to converge. Currently, 360 video and computer-generated content are two ends of the same spectrum. As the technologies develop, become cheaper and more accessible, we will see more features available for 360 filmmaking to make projects more interactive and give the user even more agency.

As I write this, we are seeing the advent of 'roomscale 360', which takes an existing 360 video and through the use of some intermediate software makes it seem to the user as though they can walk around the scene.

Some 360 cameras can capture the depth data from a scene and give you what is called a depth map or mesh, which would allow you to make a 3D model of the environment and manipulate it in game engine software.

It's simply a matter of time before we will be capturing 360 videos with technology as powerful and advanced as volumetric video, which enables you to capture an object or a person from various angles with dozens of cameras to create a fully 3D model which can be manipulated in game engine software. Essentially this is a fusion of filmmaking and game development techniques.

Volumetric video captures from the outside in and 360 video captures from the inside out, so if you could achieve the same results and get the same data as a volumetric capture but with a simpler single-camera setup like 360, it would be an extremely powerful production tool for all kinds of VR creators.

## Closing remarks

I hope this guide has given you the confidence and the know-how to go out and start creating powerful, immersive 360 projects that can enhance and transform your business. Taking your first steps into VR production is an opportunity to test yourself, figure out the fundamentals and allow you to work more effectively with a creative partner or professional expert to deliver high-quality 360 content.

It's an exciting time to be pioneering best practices in VR for business. There are endless opportunities to deploy VR in offices, workplaces and businesses, and I feel a sense of genuine excitement at seeing many more brilliant use cases blossom from the people who have followed the expertise of this book.

## Note

1   https://medium.com/the-language-of-vr/in-the-blink-of-a-mind-attention-1fdff60fa045 (archived at https://perma.cc/GCR8-QQEX)

# 11

# Common misconceptions and criticisms of XR

As you continue your journey of introducing XR technologies into business, it is likely you will come across a number of misconceptions surrounding the technology. This chapter will address the more common misunderstandings and enable you to challenge them by drawing on the information, discussions and case studies of the previous chapters.

## 'XR is only for entertainment'

This is the most damaging perception of XR and the cause of missed opportunities for organizations all over the world. The reason for it is simple: we mostly only hear about XR applications from consumer-facing organizations with large marketing budgets to promote and sell their products. When a game like Pokémon GO (AR) or Beat Saber (VR) becomes popular, it makes the news, appears in TV shows and movies, and gets discussed publicly.

On the other side, commercial use of XR is generally not as well publicized – the technology is used internally to achieve a business objective and at best it may appear in a few niche business publications. Improving the efficiency of warehouse operations may be exciting to the business implementing it, but it is unlikely to make 'The Tonight Show With Jimmy Fallon' (unlike Brie Larson, who made an appearance playing VR title Beat Saber).

These two forces act together to bring the consumer uses of XR to the forefront while keeping the business applications in the background.

In earlier chapters, I discussed in detail the numerous ways XR is being applied in businesses across all industries, so I won't repeat that here. XR is clearly not all about gaming and entertainment, but it does owe a lot to gaming. Gamers constantly strive for increasingly engaging and immersive forms of entertainment and are continually driving XR to the peak of such media. Engagement and immersion are essential components of many business areas, including learning and development, operations, sales and marketing, and more.

Gaming and business are two worlds that are becoming increasingly intertwined. We will discuss their intersection further in Chapter 12.

## 'VR makes people sick'

The truth is far more nuanced than this and compared to the human history of discomfort from technological innovation, it is neither surprising nor unique.

### MOTION SICKNESS THROUGH THE AGES

Humans suffering forms of motion sickness is nothing new: more than 2,000 years ago, the Greek physician Hippocrates first described such symptoms when he wrote that 'sailing on the sea proves that motion disorders the body'. The word 'nausea' itself is derived from 'naus', the Greek word for ship, a testament to the potent effect of seafaring on human physiology.[1]

---

DID YOU KNOW?

During the 18th century, the famous British naval commander, Lord Nelson, suffered from seasickness for the entirety of his 30-year naval career.[2]

---

Fast forward to the mid-1900s and history repeats itself: Ernie Pyle, an American journalist and winner of the Pulitzer Prize, covered stories of American soldiers during World War II. He witnessed first hand the beach landings at D-Day and noted that it resulted in 'the greatest mass vomiting ever known in the history of mankind'.[3]

Even nowadays, from sea to sky and land to space, millions of people around the world suffer from sea sickness when on a cruise, air sickness when flying between countries, car sickness when travelling in a vehicle. Astronauts even contend with space sickness during spaceflight.

There are some theories to suggest that motion sickness is not a bug but a feature of human evolution, one that evolved to let our ancestor, the chimpanzee, know that a swaying tree or branch was not the safest place to be. This is not our primary concern nowadays so feeling ill while riding in a car, bus, train, boat, plane, while watching films or playing video games, or while using a VR device, is rather inconvenient in the modern-day world.

---

DID YOU KNOW?

There is a website dedicated to rating regular movies based on how motion-sick they are likely to make you feel. Even watching traditional 2D media has the potential to make people feel ill.[4]

---

WHAT CAUSES CYBER SICKNESS?

Significant studies on discomfort within immersive environments were conducted as far back as the 1970s thanks in large part to NASA and the US military. These are still referenced today as they provide a wealth of insight into the symptoms, theories, factors and solutions connected to user discomfort in immersive environments.

There are multiple hypotheses for the cause of motion sickness (or cyber sickness as it is called when specifically referring to similar symptoms caused by digital technology). The most widely publicized theory is that there is a mismatch between your visual and vestibular systems. In basic terms, there is a disagreement between what you're seeing and what you're feeling. In VR, this sensory conflict typically manifests itself when you are physically stationary but the virtual environment around you appears to be moving in direct conflict to your stillness.

> Many have fallen victim to the infamous VR rollercoaster experience and I ask you to resist the urge to try it (at least if it's your first experience of VR as there may not be a second!).

The factors influencing whether someone experiences cyber sickness and how severely they're affected by it are numerous and complex. They can be related to the:

- **Individual:** age, sex, ethnicity, sleep patterns, previous exposure to similar technology, negative experiences from those exposures, susceptibility to migraines, the time since they last ate – even one's personality has an effect!

- **Hardware:** type of display (headset, projection system or large screen); how comfortable the system is; calibration – if the headset is not sitting properly on your face or the IPD (distance between the pupils of your eyes) is not set correctly it can exacerbate feelings of discomfort; how powerful the hardware is – underpowered VR equipment may cause a small but perceptible delay between when you move your head and when your view of the digital environment follows, which can induce nausea.

- **Software:** duration of the experience; direction of the content – wild, erratic camera movements or simply a camera view that strays from your own field of view can instigate cyber sickness. The user's ability to control their navigation in the virtual world is key.

- **Environment:** uncomfortable conditions such as a hot, humid or noisy atmosphere can also exacerbate a reaction.

---

DID YOU KNOW?

Even the day of a user's menstrual cycle will affect their susceptibility to cyber sickness.

---

### AR USERS ARE SAFE FROM CYBER SICKNESS

Augmented reality does not induce the same ill effects as there is no visual–vestibular mismatch: users walking while using AR are still walking with almost full sight of the physical environment so the two systems are in agreement. Digital objects that are moving in AR are unlikely to cause a sensation of movement for the user – unless an application smothers your view with overly dynamic AR advertisements, pop-ups and other unsolicited information.

> An equally overwhelming but more static world to the one described above on the evolution of advertising was made famous through a concept film by Keiichi Matsuda called 'Hyper-Reality', which he created 'to explore this exciting but dangerous trajectory'. It shouldn't make you sick – at least not physically; emotionally, many are appalled by this vision of the future![5]

### WHAT PERCENTAGE OF PEOPLE ARE AFFECTED BY CYBER SICKNESS?

This is a difficult question to answer as it depends on the many factors described above. There are also varying intensities of cyber sickness, so setting the bar higher or lower will change the prevalence.

One option is to examine how sensitive people are to motion sickness (which is strongly linked to cyber sickness). According to the US National Library of Medicine, about one in three people are highly susceptible to motion sickness, but almost everyone will suffer from motion sickness if provoked with an experience that is intense enough.

The Cyber-Human Lab at the University of Cambridge regularly conducts experiments involving VR and other technologies. From one of their studies involving more than 700 participants, they had no cases of serious sickness.[6] The Royal Shakespeare Company conducted a market research study which involved users sitting through a three-hour theatre performance in VR – no issues were reported.[7] There are many similar conclusions from academia and industry that would indicate that when VR is implemented correctly and optimally, cyber sickness is a much smaller issue than its reputation would imply.

### WHAT CAN YOU DO ABOUT IT?

While some people may feel sick or know someone who was sick while in virtual reality, it is important to recognize that this is not purely connected to VR technology, and making a case to dismiss VR as a result would make as much sense as calling for cars and trains to be boycotted because a portion of passengers feel unwell while using them.

All of the information in this section may seem overwhelming, but the good news is that a significant portion of these factors is within your control to manage. Individuals and their attributes are obviously not influenceable, but your choice of hardware is. So is software that you design and develop. Even the environment in which you deploy the experience is within your control. The vast majority of people are comfortable in well-developed VR applications and well-planned VR environments. As you continue to discover and implement best practices through experience, research and collaboration, this will only improve.

---

IN SUMMARY

- Feeling uncomfortable after using technology is nothing new and not specific to VR.

- Some users will experience discomfort from using VR, especially those who are susceptible to motion sickness.

- The severity of the discomfort will depend on a number of factors relating to the hardware and software used as well as the individuals themselves.

- One of the most prominent theories for cyber sickness in VR is a conflict between what you see and what you feel.

- AR technology does not induce cyber sickness as users are still in the physical environment so there is no such conflict.

- The exact prevalence of cyber sickness is difficult to measure, but a number of studies have found no symptoms among users which indicates that its reputation may be more widespread than its effect.

## 'VR is an isolating technology'

Virtual reality is an easy target for this argument. To a lot of people, it appears that users put on a headset and are instantly disconnected from the world around them while they stand slack jawed, brandishing oddly shaped controllers and reaching out to grab non-existent objects. Augmented reality, meanwhile, does not suffer as badly from this accusation as the user remains firmly in the physical world and is still capable of engaging with those around them.

This stereotypical image fails to consider the multitude of applications where virtual reality accomplishes the exact opposite of isolating people – it brings them together. When we discussed collaboration in Chapter 4, we showed that virtual reality enables employees in different parts of the world to share the same digital environment and work together.

So why do some people still consider VR to be isolating? Partly due to a lack of understanding of the technology and partly due to the infancy of VR etiquette. VR and non-VR users regularly find themselves in the same room and this can be awkward for both parties: VR users may feel uncomfortable and vulnerable with others watching them; the onlookers may feel the need to keep quiet so as not to disturb those in VR while simultaneously feeling pressure to remain in conversation with one another to avoid an awkward silence.

History is littered with examples of technology that could be considered antisocial. Books, newspapers, computers and mobile phones all potentially involve solitary activity, but all have positively contributed to greater connectedness in the world.

As society becomes more familiar with VR, as the user experience of the technology develops, and as we develop an understanding of the unwritten social rules surrounding such situations, we should expect to see these situations become more commonplace and more comfortable.

## 'VR will replace real-life experiences'

There is a lot of concern in society that virtual reality will replace real-life experiences. There are worries about vacations becoming VRcations and the impact this will have on various industries, including tourism, hospitality and aviation.

First, as impressive as the technology is, virtual reality is not capable of fully emulating the real world completely. While it can communicate with our sense of sight and sound, it cannot communicate a sense of touch, taste or smell in a simple, accurate and portable way. Yes, there are devices out there that do a very good job of engaging with our other senses via vibrational feedback, but most of them are not yet mature enough to be used in earnest.

Second, virtual reality is not about replacing experiences in totality – it is a supplement to these experiences and in some ways may even encourage people to enjoy them in the real world. Before Thomas Cook ceased trading, its use of virtual reality helped boost helicopter tours of New York by 28 per cent and sales of Royal Caribbean cruises by 45 per cent.[8] These VR experiences gave prospective holidaymakers a taste of what it could feel like being in a real helicopter or on a real cruise. And once you've been teased with that almost-but-not-quite experience, it becomes a tantalizing prospect to complete the experience in reality.

Then there are those who simply cannot travel. Uluru is a large rock formation in central Australia made of sandstone and measuring an impressive 9.4 km in circumference. From most major Australian cities, it requires a 2–3 hour flight to the local Yulara airport. The nearest town, Alice Springs, is 335 km to the north-east – a 4.5-hour drive over 450 km of road. If this sounds arduous, consider having to get to Australia first!

Despite the logistical challenges, this UNESCO World Heritage site received 300,000 visitors in 2015. But what about those who don't have the money to make the journey, those who suffer from illnesses and are bedridden, or those who simply can't afford to take enough time off to complete the visit? Through virtual reality they have a means of experiencing the beauty of this natural landmark and can share in the fulfilment of being part of its wonder. For those people, virtual reality is a technology that promotes greater accessibility to experiences that would otherwise be inaccessible due to health, money or time constraints.

## 'XR is just headsets'

XR headsets are most commonly pictured whenever VR, or to a lesser extent AR, is mentioned. However, both technologies take a variety of forms, some of which are already integrated into our lives that we don't notice.

As you'll see in Chapter 14, VR can be experienced through a headset, a projector system and even a large enough screen – any system that provides an immersive enough experience. AR can be accessed through a headset, projector system or mobile device – any system capable of presenting digital information against the physical world.

Then there are other unique methods that don't fall neatly into any category. Head-up displays used in vehicles and in fighter jets are a form of AR. Even in the sports world, digital game data is superimposed on the physical pitch or court to give viewers information and insight into the performance of players and teams. The only difference between your mobile screen and the TV screen in this case is that you don't control the TV screen. This type of AR is so widespread and familiar that not much thought is given to it anymore.

LaLiga, the top professional football league in Spain, partnered with Vizrt to superimpose digital fans into games (Figure 11.1). The games were played in empty stadiums due to the Covid-19 pandemic and this was a way to create a sense of normality. EA Sports supplied sounds that it had recorded for its FIFA video game franchise to complete the augmented experience.

## '360 video is not VR'

The two arguments I regularly hear about this relate to 360 video lacking interactivity and depth. While interaction and depth can certainly create more powerful experiences, neither is a prerequisite for a VR experience, which is largely a factor of immersion.

Additionally, while the majority of 360 content out there is passive, as you will have seen in previous chapters, interaction within 360 video is indeed possible, just not to the same extent as it is with computer-generated

FIGURE 11.1

A LaLiga football match before and after fans were superimposed into the stadium to create a more familiar atmosphere for remote viewers during the Covid-19 pandemic. Photo credit: LaLiga[9]

content. At its most basic level, even the ability to look around an environment is a form of interaction as it is a decision by the user to select their own frame within the experience as opposed to traditional 2D video where that frame is dictated to you.

The lack of depth data in a 360 video results in a 3 DoF experience where the user can look around but not change their position. 3 DoF is a recognizable and accepted attribute of many VR headsets and experiences, so it makes little sense to use depth as an argument to disqualify 360 video from VR.

360 video, like computer-generated graphics, is simply a form of content that can be used in VR (or even non-immersive media) – sometimes the two are even combined within a single experience. While there are some limitations on what you can do with 360 video, it is nonetheless a valid form of immersive content within VR.

## 'Can't they just watch a regular video?'

If someone asks this question, it is likely they haven't experienced VR. The best response is to introduce them to the technology through a first-hand demonstration of relevant and powerful content. This is usually far more effective than citing supporting data as the experience should show them the impactful nature of VR. However, they may need convincing to get to that stage, in which case it is worth mentioning the advantages of VR over traditional media:

- a more focused, distraction-free environment;
- a first-person perspective;
- a more engaging and emotionally impactful experience.

A study of 150 participants was conducted by Nielsen and YuMe to gauge their emotional engagement while watching video content across three systems: a VR headset, a tablet and a regular, flat-screen TV.[10] Nielsen's neuroscience team used eye tracking and biometric monitoring technology to analyse the eye movements, skin conductance and heart rate of each participant as well as a post-experience survey to capture their attitude. When viewed in VR, the content elicited the following benefits over its equivalent on the TV:

- 27 per cent higher emotional engagement;
- 34 per cent longer emotional engagement.

Even when the 360 video content was viewed on a tablet (with the ability for the user to navigate around it), viewing it in VR was still 17 per cent more emotionally engaging for 16 per cent longer.

## 'XR is not scalable'

If you're relying on your users' own mobile devices, then deploying your XR solution in large numbers is not a major issue. If you need to procure new XR devices for a large population of users, it is challenging but certainly not impossible.

### WALMART: DEPLOYING VR TRAINING TO 1.5 MILLION EMPLOYEES

Walmart is an American retailer and the world's largest private employer. Founded in 1962 in Rogers, Arkansas, Walmart has over 11,000 stores and 2.2 million employees globally.

The United States is home to almost 70 per cent of its staff (1.5 million), who are distributed over 5,000 stores in 50 states. It is a tremendous challenge to deliver effective training at this scale, yet starting in 2017, Walmart kicked off a colossal virtual reality training programme in collaboration with STRIVR to equip its US staff to better handle everything from operating new in-store technology and managing difficult customers to dealing with active shooters.[11,12]

Headsets were initially delivered to every Walmart training academy in the US, giving managers and department managers access to bespoke VR training experiences. Following the success of this programme, more than 17,000 headsets were deployed to individual Walmart stores, giving store associates access to the same training. Every Walmart supercentre (hypermarkets ranging in size from 6,400 to 24,200 square metres) received four VR units and every neighbourhood market (smaller stores 2,600 to 6,000 square metres in size) and discount store received two.

Two hundred live stores and 10 distribution centres are physically adjacent to a Walmart training facility. These facilities are located in such a way that 80 per cent of associates are within driving distance of one, meaning they can travel there in the morning, undergo a day of training and then travel back home in the evening. Creating a network of centres like this is a great way to make VR training more available to larger groups without having to invest in a headset for every single individual or location.

In total, more than 45 VR training modules were created and deployed using both 360 video and computer-generated graphics to cover the following topics and more:

- **Workplace induction:** check-in procedures, introduction guides to existing equipment, what devices colleagues carry, different employee grades and identification badges, workplace facilities such as lockers.

- **New technology:** introducing new physical equipment that will be rolled out in stores and getting employees used to the processes involved so they are ready to hit the ground running when it arrives.

  VR was used by Walmart to introduce employees to 'pickup towers', 16 ft high in-store structures that can hold and distribute hundreds of online orders to customers conveniently. Four five-minute modules provide training on how to set up, maintain and use the towers. As a result, pickup tower training time was reduced from 8 hours to about 15 minutes.

- **Operational tasks:** including how to load and unload trailers delivering goods.

- **HR assessments:** to see if someone has developed their skills enough to perform a role successfully. This helps reduce turnover by ensuring employees are placed only in roles that they are ready for.
- **Situational training:** public speaking during large staff meetings, active shooter response and customer holiday rush scenarios (Black Friday).

  'How on earth do you prepare somebody for the holiday peak season – the rush of a busy store and all of the action going on around you? With [immersive training], we can really prepare these leaders.' – Tom Ward, Vice President of Digital Operations, Walmart[13]

- **Store compliance:** identify and resolve issues such as low stock or incorrectly stocked sections, sections missing produce bags, etc.
- **Customer service:** teach instinctive actions such as responding quickly and pre-emptively to customers who are likely to require attention.

Data is collected on employee performance during these VR experiences, which can be used to tailor their future training.

As a result of implementing VR at this scale in combination with its latest training programmes, Walmart found that:

- training time is reduced;
- associate engagement is higher;
- associates reported 30 per cent higher employee satisfaction;
- associates scored higher on tests 70 per cent of the time;
- knowledge retention is 10–15 per cent higher;
- customers think there are more associates in the store because they are effective at their job and more confident in approaching and helping customers;
- clean, fast and friendly (CFF) scores – a Walmart measure used to gauge customer happiness – are going up;
- utilization of front-end systems is increasing following training in those systems;
- turnover continues to decrease (at the lowest it's been in 10 years).

  'We've seen that VR training boosts confidence and retention while improving test scores 10 to 15 percent' – Andy Trainor, Senior Director of Walmart US Academies

As the world's largest employer, Walmart had a massive challenge on its hands introducing VR training to its workforce. With a clever deployment model, dedicated resources and the right external support, it managed to overcome this challenge. While smaller organizations may have fewer resources to work with when trying to scale XR, they also have a smaller target to hit, with fewer complexities and fewer employees.

## 'XR is expensive'

XR projects can cost anything from $500 to $500,000 and beyond depending on the objective and the scope of the project. For a large number of users and bespoke software, XR solution costs can certainly rack up quite quickly, but this is not wildly different from other technology implementation programmes. The key difference is that the benefits of XR are less understood so there is less willingness to even consider the cost, especially when it is large. Cost is a gate that will open when the benefits of the proposed solution are positive and well articulated. In other words, when the return on investment is favorable, conversations about cost become easier to navigate.

Many organizations take an 'all or nothing' attitude towards investment in technology solutions and projects when there is a middle ground alternative such as creating a basic prototype that is piloted to an initial group of users. There are always ways to build an XR pilot programme to meet most budgets. Consider the following factors:

- Application scope – what are the minimum features required to prove the value of the initiative?

- Content type – can the project objective be achieved using a more inexpensive form of content?

- Application assets – what is already available? Can any assets be reused from previous projects or bought instead of created from scratch?

- User deployment model – does everyone need to have their own hardware or can it be shared?

- Hardware deployment model – have you considered leasing versus buying equipment? For your VR application, have you looked at the different device options? Do you need a 6 DoF headset or will 3 DoF suffice? For an AR application, do you need a headset or can the objectives be achieved on a smartphone? If a headset is required, does it need to be able to map the physical environment or will a basic digital overlay be enough?

- User deployment population – does the application need to be rolled out to everyone or can you start with a more limited group of users?
- Team resourcing – what elements can be confidently outsourced without compromising on quality?
- Level of software customization – does it need to be custom-built or is there off-the-shelf software that can be licensed to achieve what you need? Is there an option in the middle to license a platform which makes it easier for you to create the bespoke solution you need? Are any vendors offering a solution that is close enough to what you need which they are open to customizing?

> Don't discount the possibility of using an off-the-shelf solution for training or collaboration purposes. There are many on the market which can be licensed on a monthly basis. For example, under a headset-sharing model, including all hardware and software costs, running a three-month pilot programme for hundreds of people could cost less than $10,000.

The key to tackling an argument about XR programme cost is to start small with a pilot programme, use it to build a business case, and focus on the resultant return on investment. This will have the strongest credibility because it is based on a specific company problem or opportunity rather than having to make the connection to reports whose findings relate to a different context. Don't be afraid to make compromises as noted above as long as the expected return on investment is not jeopardized.

> With an initial fund of only $7,000, 3D solution provider Hobs 3D set out to produce a prototype VR experience to protect the well-being of workers in the construction industry. The prototype was enough to show stakeholders the value of such a solution and its success led to Hobs 3D receiving an additional $115,000 of funding to develop the concept further.[14]

## 'XR only appeals to younger generations'

The stereotypical view is that older generations spend less time engaging with new technologies and are less interested in using them, but the data says otherwise. A cross-generational survey indicated that the majority of Baby Boomers (64 per cent) and Generation X (70 per cent) were excited to experience VR.[15] This was backed up by later research from the University of Cambridge Cyber-Human Lab, which found that none of its VR or AR experiments showed any influence of age on performance.[16]

Walmart found that generational differences were not significant in the adoption of new technology such as virtual reality. When it introduced VR technology into its training programmes there was no negative feedback as a result of disparate generational views. Members of all generations enjoyed using it for its ability to create a fun, useful and efficient training environment.

In fact, there are indications that it is even more positively received by and inspiring to older generations compared with younger ones, who already view it as the status quo and something they are used to seeing in their everyday lives. This makes sense when you consider the fast pace of technological change that is taking place in the world now and the daily interactions with new technologies that each generation has. In my interactions with a Scandinavian high school that was looking to introduce a VR training programme, they revealed that their preliminary explorations showed that students displayed an indifference towards the technology unless it was of the quality they were used to seeing at home while playing video games. Considering that most popular video game titles can cost anywhere from $20 million to $150 million to produce, expectations may need to be managed.

On the other side of the world, a survey of over 3,000 people in China across multiple generations was conducted to gauge interest in popular emerging technologies by generation. The result was that 33 per cent of millennial respondents indicated an interest in AR compared with 32 per cent of non-millennials. On the VR front, the results were 48 per cent and 46 per cent respectively. In summary, there was a difference of 2 per cent or less between millennial and non-millennial populations interested in VR or AR technology.[17]

## 'AR will make VR irrelevant'

Analyst data from multiple sources and public opinion generally concur that the AR market will be significantly larger than the VR market as both technologies mature. This is understandable as AR interfaces with the physical environment where there is a greater number of applications and possibilities. It is also becoming increasingly available as consumer smartphones advance and is more comfortable as a concept as you are not disconnected from reality.

PwC's *Seeing is Believing* report estimates the global economic potential for VR and AR separately through to 2030. The expectation is that AR will contribute more than double that of VR by 2030.

However, it is important to recognize that these technologies are not at war. While they may be closely related and even share a limited number of applications, they are not substitutes for one another. VR immerses users in alternative environments, AR informs users within their physical environment.

---

## VODAFONE: WORKING AT HEIGHT IN VR

If your goal is to recreate the experience of climbing a telecommunications tower without needing to travel to one, then it makes most sense to look at VR for its ability to provide that level of emotional immersion. With VR, you have a safe environment for users to explore tasks and their associated risks while also helping them to understand how they might react so that they can manage those emotions during a real-world scenario.

Vodafone did just this, working with Make Real to build a VR experience to help communicate the risks facing telecommunications engineers working at height as part of a wider initiative to reduce health and safety incidents.[18,19]

Aimed at team managers of maintenance crews, the experience covered the typical risks found during these jobs and raised the importance of personal protective equipment. At the beginning of the experience, the user is asked to identify and collect required gear before heading to the rooftop. Once there, they conduct a risk assessment of the area, identifying potential hazards and taking any necessary precautions. Following the risk assessment, the user proceeds to climb the tower while applying the appropriate safety procedures. At the top, the user can hear the wind whipping hard against them while they try to adjust a microwave antenna. Once successful, the user is debriefed on how they performed. They are rated on their preparations, risk assessment, procedure and time taken, and asked to reflect on the task.

The application was built for tethered VR headsets. A number of these were deployed to the main Vodafone headquarters, giving 80 per cent of its employees access to the experience. To scale it further, a portable version was created for a standalone headset, allowing employees to borrow it for use at work or home. The computer-generated content was also adapted to a 360 video experience, which was deployed to Vodafone's learning management

---

system – this could be accessed by all employees on either their work laptop or mobile.

As an effective way for users to step into the shoes of a telecommunications field engineer, it helped managers to develop greater empathy for their maintenance crews. This encouraged everyone to align to Vodafone's 'Work Safe, Home Safe' global directive to reduce fatalities on the job.

The VR experience was also a great way for Vodafone to engage with the public. The application was released externally, installed over 4,000 times, and received largely positive feedback, with many reviews highlighting Vodafone's focus on employee safety and wellbeing.

## 'This is going to be the year of VR'

Each year since 2014 when Facebook bought VR startup Oculus, the world has impatiently predicted the mainstream adoption of virtual reality, forgetting that this is not a new mobile phone release or software update but a completely new medium for humanity to explore and experiment with.

The first handheld mobile phone was showcased in April 1973 by Martin Cooper, a researcher and executive at Motorola, and it was not until 1997 – 24 years later – that the mobile phone achieved what could be considered mainstream adoption (more on that definition soon). And that is after significant investment at a global level, which we are seeing only now in this latest phase of VR that has yet to reach the 10-year milestone.

Does a 'year of VR' even make sense? This indicates that in a single year we should expect to see some earth-shattering rapid adoption of the technology. Was there a 'year of the mobile phone'? You might be tempted to point to 2007 when Apple released its first iPhone – the global mobile phone penetration in that year had tipped past halfway to 51 per cent, which makes for a tantalizingly good story when combined with the furore over the iPhone's release.[20,21] Such was the anticipation from the public that thousands of people queued up to purchase it, some days before it was released, and marketing efforts had been so intense that 6 out of 10 Americans surveyed were aware of its imminent release.[22] Despite all the excitement, this time period coincided with the beginning of the decline in the rate of market penetration of mobile phones, which grew at a yearly rate of 54.7 per cent before reaching an inflection point in 2008, after which it followed a slow decline – growth from 2009 to 2017 was a mere 6.6 per cent.

To summarize the point, mainstream adoption of a significant technology that continues to impact our lives every day – the mobile phone – took a long period of time during which there was both positive and negative progress. No single year was responsible for mobile phone adoption and there is no reason to think that virtual reality technology will suddenly experience what could acceptably be called 'the year of VR'. Instead, we should expect that, as it was with the mobile phone, the integration of the technology into our everyday lives will be a slow but steady burn.

Let's also examine how we've used technology in the past. All technologies are composed of input and output systems: in computing, a keyboard and mouse is the most common input and a 2D screen is the most common (visual) output. On mobile phones, it's a series of finger taps that produces output on a touch-sensitive screen. Smart home assistants take voice input and output audible responses via an in-built speaker.

In VR, there is a multitude of potential inputs based on your natural, physical actions: the movement of your head and hands and your gaze are most common. This form of input is natural from a human perspective but is not part of the history of our digital interactions – we were brought up on keyboards, mice, touch screens, and are currently adding voice to our input repertoire. On the output side, things differ even more wildly. We are no stranger to screens, but to date these screens have stayed at a comfortable distance from our face (with the exception of those who were glued to the TV while playing Super Mario back in the day, of course). This allowed us to deal with the digital while simultaneously remaining cognizant of the world around us. Virtual reality breaks our cultural comfort by shutting out the physical environment. The input it expects from us is still relatively alien in comparison with our past digital interactions.

In contrast, mobile phones benefited from a shared user experience with their predecessor, the landline telephone – people were already used to holding a device to their ear after pressing a series of buttons or rotating a dial. Strapping a screen to your face that blocks out the physical world for the duration of your experience is not something that we were able to grow accustomed to with predecessor technologies.

Virtual reality can be thought of as the 'final medium' as along the spectrum of this technology lies the closest we will come to creating a full sensory emulation of the physical world. But achieving this will be an incredibly complex objective that has scientific, technological and societal hurdles which will not be surmounted overnight. So while it may not be 'the year of VR', the technology is accelerating towards mainstream adoption with each passing day.

## 'VR is dead'

### THE ESSENCE OF VR HAS EXISTED SINCE THE DAWN OF TIME

This misconception stems partly from the belief that VR is a new technology. As a concept, virtual reality has been around for as long as stories have been told. The Lascaux Cave near the village of Montignac in south-western France is a UNESCO World Heritage Site, home to over 600 paintings that cover the cave's walls and ceiling. These paintings depict a variety of animals, humans and geometric signs. In an attempt to interpret the paintings, one theory put forward by some anthropologists and art historians is that they could be a record of past hunting success. Another theory suggests that they represent a ritual to encourage the success of future hunting activities. Whatever the true reason, these paintings are a medium of primitive communication estimated to date back as far as 15000 BC.

Although recent findings suggest that written text goes back further than 5000 BC, the Sumerian civilization is often credited with developing writing around 3400 BC. The 'Epic of Gilgamesh' is probably history's oldest known fictional story, starting out as a series of Sumerian poems that dates back to 2100 BC.

These ancient examples show storytelling through two different forms – pictorial and textual. But we also communicate stories through what is perhaps the oldest medium that until relatively recently has been difficult to historically record: speaking. Every day, we speak to colleagues, friends and family. In a professional context, we tell and listen to stories every day, from coaching conversations to pitch presentations.

The objectives of storytelling and VR are similar: to immerse you in the narrative of the storyteller. The reasons for this are many, but can include entertaining, socializing, informing, educating, persuading, training and so on. It is the job of the storyteller to evoke an emotion in the receiver: fear of missing out on a good deal, empathy towards a refugee living in difficult conditions, excitement about a new product being released, fright while watching a horror film.

VR, in its present-day technological form, is simply the latest evolution in the medium of storytelling. As a concept, it is grounded in the very essence and history of humanity and is consequently not going anywhere any time soon.

## ADOPTION TIME OF VR VS OTHER TECHNOLOGIES

'VR is dead' is a favourite line for news articles, tweets and blog posts everywhere due to the supposedly 'long' time it has taken to reach a relatively small level of adoption. This perception pervades because most people don't attempt to benchmark VR against the adoption times of past technologies. It is the result of examining VR in isolation and against a backdrop of expectation that technologies are widely adopted in a matter of a few years.

Figure 11.2 shows adoption rates of old and new technologies. It includes domestic appliances such as microwaves as well as media sources such as radio. It covers technologies as pervasive and complex as the internet as well as hardware devices such as tablets. Analysing this diverse range of technologies provides useful insight to better understand the question of how long technology adoption takes.

This data is taken from publicly available sources and is based on US household adoption. Most records, particularly older ones, are usually gathered once a technology has reached a significant point such as the 10 per cent penetration mark. Hence, granular data below this point is sometimes not available. However, by considering the year that the technology was first sold to the public, we can calculate how long it took from that moment to reach mainstream adoption.

Mainstream adoption is a largely subjective concept, but by defining it clearly and applying this definition consistently across all technologies, we can develop an analysis that is useful for making comparisons. In 1962, sociologist Everett Rogers released a book titled *Diffusion of Innovations* in which he theorized how new ideas and technology are spread.[24] To do this, he pulled together research from more than 500 studies across a range of fields. The result is what is known today as the technology adoption lifecycle, a bell-shaped curve which categorizes consumers into five groups based on their buying habits. These are listed below with interpretations inspired by organizational theorist Geoffrey Moore.

- **Innovators:** the first 2.5 per cent of adopters. They represent the technologists and enthusiasts for whom having the latest innovation is core to their life interests.

FIGURE 11.2

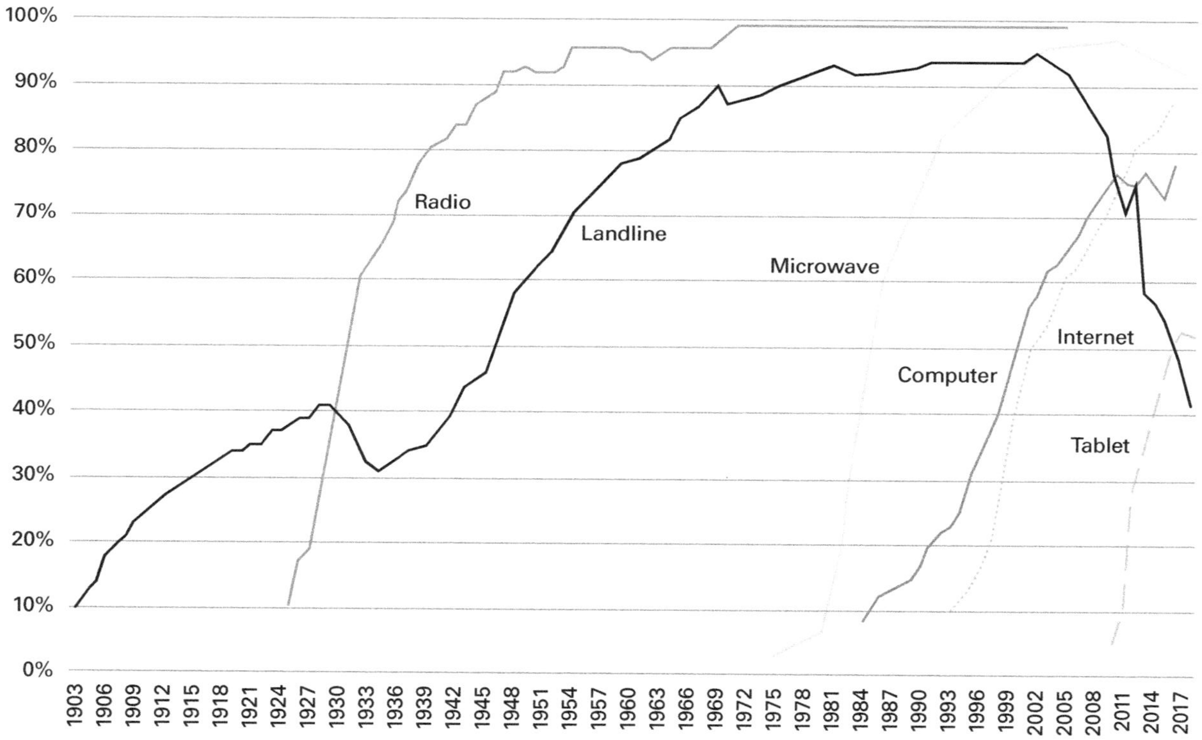

Adoption rates by US households of various technologies from the early 1900s to the modern day.[23]

- **Early adopters:** the next 13.5 per cent. These are visionaries who are not necessarily technologists but who are willing to take a high risk on an early product to reap its benefit.

These two groups, the first 16 per cent of adopters, represent the early market.

- **Early majority:** the following 34 per cent. Pragmatists who represent the start of the mainstream market. They are comfortable with new products but want to see evidence of their usefulness before adopting.
- **Late majority:** the penultimate 34 per cent. Conservatives who are steeped in tradition rather than progress. They will only engage with deeply established products.
- **Laggards:** the final 16 per cent. Skeptics who actively avoid technology and innovation.

These three groups, taking us from 17 per cent to 100 per cent adoption, represent the mainstream market.[25]

In his book *Crossing the Chasm*, Moore outlines the challenge of establishing a foothold in the mainstream market, which he defines as the early majority onwards.[26] This indicates that once you have almost 1 in 5 people that have adopted a technology, it can be considered mainstream. This would seem to be a reasonable assumption, if slightly conservative, but that's okay as it will only strengthen our findings. On that basis, let's examine a variety of technologies through the ages and see how long each one took to reach mainstream adoption status (or 17 per cent by our agreed definition).

### LANDLINE: 29 YEARS

Following Alexander Graham Bell's telephone patent being granted in 1876, the first home telephone was installed in April 1877. It took until 1906 for landlines to reach 17 per cent adoption.[27]

### MICROWAVE: 26 YEARS

Raytheon, a developer and manufacturer of radar systems, accidentally discovered a new use for its microwave-producing radars after the end of World War II: heating up food.[28] The first consumer-targeted microwave oven, the Tappan RL-1, went on sale in 1955 and reached 17 per cent adoption in 1981.

## TABLET: 23 YEARS

The first tablet device was actually released in October 1989. It was called the GRiDPad and cost $2,370 ($5,000 in 2020 money). It didn't catch on fast, with tablets taking 23 years to hit 17 per cent adoption.

## COMPUTER: 19 YEARS

The Kenbak-1, arguably the world's first personal computer, was sold in 1971 for $750 ($4,800 in 2020 terms). The manufacturer, Kenbak Corporation, shut down after producing only 50 of the machines; 19 years later, in 1990, 17 per cent of US households had a personal computer.

## INTERNET: 8 YEARS

The internet originated as a United States Department of Defense project in 1969. However, it was only made commercially available to the public in 1989 when The World became the first internet service provider (ISP), offering dial-up access to the internet. Growing at a blistering pace, eight years later 17 per cent of US households had internet access.

## RADIO: 6 YEARS

In November 1920, the first commercial radio station, KDKA, was broadcast from Pittsburgh, USA. The local Joseph Horne department store offered ready-to-go radio receivers. Prior to this, getting a system in place to receive radio transmissions was very much a DIY job for the geek of the day. It could be built from scratch or through a kit which came with all the parts and instructions. They weren't incredibly expensive as far as new technologies go, with some kits being sold for $17 in the early 1920s (about $250 in 2020 terms). Radio took only six years to reach 17 per cent of US households.

---

FUN FACT

The term 'broadcast' actually originates from the agriculture industry and refers to a method of sowing seeds by scattering them over a wide area of soil.

---

Despite a fairly low bar of 17 per cent adoption to qualify as mainstream, it still took some technologies like the telephone up to 29 years to reach this level. And long adoption times like this are not only limited to old technologies – a relatively modern one like the tablet still took 23 years to reach the mainstream market.

The first VR headset was offered to consumers as a commercial product in 1993. By 2020, VR penetration was somewhere between 6 per cent and 16 per cent based on different estimates, and despite a lull of almost two decades in lost time, its progress is still within the range of mainstream adoption times of the technologies that came before it.

## Notes

1. https://theconversation.com/motion-sickness-it-all-started-550-million-years-ago-121789 (archived at https://perma.cc/9LMQ-DBXJ)

2. https://www.reuters.com/article/us-britain-nelson/letter-shows-depth-of-admiral-nelsons-seasickness-idUSBRE8BA0PP20121212 (archived at https://perma.cc/WZ26-P7XH)

3. https://www.semanticscholar.org/paper/Configural-Scoring-of-Simulator-Sickness%2C-and-Space-Kennedy-Drexler/e2987901888a9631ea5f13cf02daa3c0e16c11eb?p2df (archived at https://perma.cc/F6CU-HF6N)

4. http://moviehurl.com/ (archived at https://perma.cc/8MKX-2F22)

5. https://www.youtube.com/watch?v=YJg02ivYzSs (archived at https://perma.cc/7VME-59C3)

6. https://www.youtube.com/watch?v=XIzIN8kmd1M&feature=youtu.be (archived at https://perma.cc/S6PS-TLKR)

7. https://gorillaitr.com/project/shakespeare-theatre-vr-market-research-case-study/ (archived at https://perma.cc/J7LF-NLGG)

8. https://www.thisismoney.co.uk/money/holidays/article-4618554/Will-virtual-reality-help-shape-future-holiday.html (archived at https://perma.cc/48KQ-SFCA)

9. https://uk.reuters.com/article/uk-health-coronavirus-soccer-spain/la-liga-to-use-virtual-stands-and-audio-for-broadcasts-idUKKBN23E0VG (archived at https://perma.cc/9STZ-M4BH)

10. https://www.businesswire.com/news/home/20161109005274/en/Groundbreaking-Virtual-Reality-Research-Showcases-Strong-Emotional (archived at https://perma.cc/9FT4-UAUR)

11. https://corporate.walmart.com/newsroom/innovation/20180920/how-vr-is-transforming-the-way-we-train-associates (archived at https://perma.cc/9PY7-C438)

12. https://www.strivr.com/resources/customers/walmart/ (archived at https://perma.cc/UX8G-8E4Z)

13  https://www.hrtechnologynews.com/news/learning-and-development/
    the-shifting-reality-of-employee-training/101054 (archived at https://perma.cc/
    XJL4-6YHQ)
14  https://hobs3d.com/news/thames-tideway-tunnel-boring-machine-vr/ (archived
    at https://perma.cc/ZET4-LTE9)
15  https://touchstoneresearch.com/vr-and-consumer-sentiment/ (archived at
    https://perma.cc/QG2R-FPYP)
16  https://www.youtube.com/watch?v=XIzIN8kmd1M&feature=youtu.be
    (archived at https://perma.cc/S6PS-TLKR)
17  https://www.statista.com/statistics/805322/china-interest-in-popular-emerging-
    technologies-by-generation/ (archived at https://perma.cc/EW2Y-KY5D)
18  https://www.vodafone.com/perspectives/blog/virtual-work-vr-telecoms-mast
    (archived at https://perma.cc/KN6V-7P7N)
19  https://makereal.co.uk/work/vodafone-working-at-height/ (archived at
    https://perma.cc/KEZ5-ZDBL)
20  https://www.cartesian.com/the-rise-of-mobile-phones-20-years-of-global-
    adoption/ (archived at https://perma.cc/9ND5-DJVY)
21  https://stats.areppim.com/stats/stats_mobilxpenetr.htm (archived at
    https://perma.cc/SLD7-LP49)
22  https://www.theguardian.com/news/2007/jun/29/usnews.apple (archived at
    https://perma.cc/K2AH-A66P)
23  https://ourworldindata.org/grapher/technology-adoption-by-households-in-the-
    united-states (archived at https://perma.cc/Z9F5-HKU8) – adapted from data
    by Comin and Hobijn (2004) and others, licensed under the Creative
    Commons BY licence
24  https://books.google.co.uk/books?id=9U1K5LjUOwEC (archived at
    https://perma.cc/9ZJX-5M5B)
25  https://www.business-to-you.com/crossing-the-chasm-technology-adoption-
    life-cycle/ (archived at https://perma.cc/5EX2-W4W7)
26  https://www.goodreads.com/book/show/61329.Crossing_the_Chasm (archived
    at https://perma.cc/Q5HQ-PGM3)
27  http://www.telegraph-history.org/charles-williams-jr/part2.html (archived at
    https://perma.cc/35YR-AWEB)
28  https://spectrum.ieee.org/tech-history/space-age/a-brief-history-of-the-
    microwave-oven (archived at https://perma.cc/33SG-XR7B)

# 12

# Why now?

Before XR as a digital technology was widely available to consumers, it underwent decades of research and numerous attempts to bring it into mainstream use.

In the early 1960s, when the first digital form of XR was born, a user could view a primitive geometric digital object like a cube in their physical environment through a headset, the perspective of which would change in line with the user's movements. This was incredible from an academic standpoint as this form of natural interface between the physical and the digital hadn't been accomplished before. From a practical point of view, though, the many applications we explored in previous chapters had yet to be discovered.

The VR of the early 1990s was rough: imagine a 3–4 kg headset weighing down on your head with an octopus of thick cables arcing between the headset, the controller and a giant computing system. The computer churns away, processing the virtual world and your movements in it, but is not powerful enough to deliver updates to your screen at a fast enough rate. The result is that what you are seeing lags behind your actions – not immensely, but enough to make many feel sick. 3D graphics at the time were in their infancy, so the visual quality of the virtual environment comprised blocky graphics, simple textures and basic animations. Despite these shortcomings, the cost of VR equipment could breach $100,000 in some cases.[1] In summary, it was a long run for a short slide. Effort exceeded value. This was largely why virtual reality fell out of favour as the 1990s wore on.

While it is easy to point to the inadequacies of past technologies when compared to their modern-day equivalents, the technical achievements of these VR systems were incredible for their time and without them the industry wouldn't be where it is today. Together with the research conducted, lessons learnt and knowledge gained from building and deploying these systems, a number of trends contributed to the resurrection of VR technology.

## Decreasing costs, increasing power

From whatever angle you look at it, technology costs have dropped tremendously over the last several decades.

- **Storage:** In 1964, it cost $3.5 billion to purchase a terabyte of space. By 2020, this had fallen to a mere $15.

- **Computing:** In 1961, it cost $1.1 trillion for computing power capable of processing 1 billion calculations per second. By 2020, this could be done for a few cents.

- **Connectivity:** In 1998, it cost $1,200 per megabit per second of data transfer speed. By 2020, the same internet connection cost had dropped to about 20 cents.[2]

While technology costs have been dropping, availability of computing power has been increasing drastically. In 1965, Gordon Moore (who would later cofound Intel) predicted that the number of transistors on a silicon chip would double every year (revised in 1975 to a doubling every two years). Moore's Law has since held true, with more and more computing power being crammed onto smaller chips. This has allowed us to move on from the low-level graphics of previous eras of VR to create richer experiences. The increase in processing power has also enabled these experiences to run more smoothly, reducing the number of users who feel unwell while using VR.

Virtual reality experiences require immense amounts of computing power. In an average 3D application, a computer needs to calculate and send instructions for what to display on your screen 30 times a second. Assuming the screen's resolution is 'full HD', that is 1920 pixels wide × 1080 pixels high × 30 frames per second = 62 million pixels that need to be processed every second. Considering a VR headset that operates at a resolution of 2880 × 1600 and a refresh rate of 90 frames per second, that leads to 415 million pixels that need to be calculated each second – a nearly seven times increase over a regular 3D application.

From the astronomical costs of VR systems in the early 1990s, much progress has been made. The Oculus Rift CV1, introduced in March 2016, retailed at $599 and didn't have 3D tracked 'touch' controllers (they were released about eight months afterwards for another $200). Additionally, you needed a powerful PC to run the headset that would set you back at least another $900. Altogether, this system of components cost in excess of $1,500, which was what you needed to get started with high-grade VR. Three years later, in 2019, consumers had the option to purchase the Oculus Quest – a standalone device that didn't require an external computer – for $400 (and that included the touch controllers!). Its successor, the Quest 2, which released in October 2020, cost even less, retailing at $299.

## Investment in XR

With decreasing costs of increasingly powerful computer hardware, it became more viable for smaller enterprises to create an affordable and effective VR headset. On 1 August 2012, a young man called Palmer Luckey launched a Kickstarter crowdfunding campaign to raise money for a prototype VR headset – he called it the 'Oculus Rift'.[3] Luckey set a goal of $250,000, which was reached through public contributions within 24 hours. By the time the campaign ended a month later on 1 September, $2.4 million had poured in from more than 9,500 people all over the world – almost 10 times his initial target.

The success of this campaign attracted the interest of Facebook, which acquired Luckey's company, Oculus VR, for $3 billion in March 2014. This sparked a slew of corporate activity and investment that poured into the XR space in a way that it hadn't seen before.

Investment came from many places – venture capital (VC) funds, corporations, private individuals (angels), government grants and crowdfunding platforms. Between 2012 and 2019, approximately $17 billion of VC money was invested in XR by funds all over the world. Some of these investors are part of the Virtual Reality Venture Capital Alliance (VRVCA), a consortium of 49 global investors with over $18 billion of deployable capital and a mission to invest in the 'world's most innovative and impactful VR technology and content companies'.[4,5,6,7]

In addition to the above specialist investors, corporate venture capital funds from established companies such as Google, HP, Intel and Qualcomm have invested in XR startups, while companies including Apple, Facebook,

Microsoft and many others have spent hundreds of millions of dollars acquiring them. XR startups across the globe were valued at $45 billion in total near the end of 2019.[8]

Governments have started to recognize the value of XR. In November 2017, the UK Department for Business, Energy and Industrial Strategy published a white paper setting out 'a long-term plan to boost productivity and earning power of people throughout the UK'. In this paper, a $41 million fund was announced to support the immersive technologies sector. This fund acknowledged the approximately 1,000 specialist XR companies in the UK generating $830 million in sales.[9] The '2019 Immersive Economy in the UK' report detailed that UK Research and Innovation, which directs funding to promote innovation and positive economic, social and cultural impact in the UK, had supported over 500 immersive technology projects worth more than $275 million since 2018.[10]

In 2016, HTC partnered with the Shenzhen Municipal Government to create a $1.5 billion VR investment fund, covering a number of areas, including design, defence, engineering, healthcare and manufacturing, to promote the development of the VR industry in Shenzhen, China.[11] At the 2018 World Conference on VR Industry in Nanchang, the government of China's Jiangxi Province announced a number of incentives to encourage XR startups, including plans to raise $460 million of investment for companies focusing on XR.[12,13] The South Korean Ministry of Science, ICT and Future Planning also announced funds totalling $62 million to advance the development of XR and immersive content.[14,15]

None of the above figures includes the tremendous amount of time and resources being invested internally every day by large organizations like Facebook, HTC and Microsoft, as well as the thousands of startups that are researching, developing and improving XR technologies for businesses and consumers around the world.

## Backing of multinational corporations

Aside from the companies that are using XR across every single industry (of which there are too many to list in this book), there are companies all over the world, small and large, that are involved in the development and advancement of XR technologies. To give you an idea, I've included some of the more well-known companies and their XR-related activities below:

Acer, Asus, Dell, Epson, Facebook, Google, HP, Huawei, Lenovo, Microsoft, HTC, Samsung, Snap Inc, Sony, Valve, and Xiaomi have all shipped XR devices.

Alibaba, Amazon, Apple, Canon, Facebook, Google, Huawei, IBM, Intel, LG, Microsoft, Nokia, Qualcomm, Samsung, and Sony have collectively registered thousands of XR patents.

Bosch created a ready-to-use solution enabling manufacturers to create lighter AR-enabled smart glasses.

Intel and Microsoft invested in the creation of volumetric capture studios, enabling 3D video recordings of individuals to be used in XR applications.

Apple and Google are at the forefront of mainstream mobile AR technology with their continual development of ARKit and ARCore.

IBM developed object-recognition technology for AR applications and has released design guidelines for XR experiences.

Amazon, Unity and Unreal created tools to allow software developers to build powerful XR applications.

ARM and Qualcomm developed processors and chips optimized for XR applications.

Adobe and Autodesk have multiple software packages that can be used to develop XR content.

Sennheiser developed audio-specific augmented-reality hardware and software.

AMD and Nvidia are developing central and graphics processing units optimized for XR applications.

Garmin, GoPro, Kodak, LG, Nikon, Ricoh and Samsung released 360 video cameras.

Facebook, HP, Lenovo and Microsoft built ecosystems to help businesses use XR technologies.

This is only a selection of big names that are working to grow the XR landscape. There are countless other businesses involved in building applications and infrastructure to support the industry.

## Global economic impact

In its *Seeing is Believing* report, PwC predicts that immersive technologies will contribute a $1.5 trillion boost to global GDP by 2030.[16]

*Seeing Is Believing* was a six-month collaboration between PwC's Economics department and its VR/AR department. Altogether, more than

50 people were involved in the report, in a range of capacities including research, content writing, marketing, economic analysis, immersive consultancy and webAR development. The report provides a credible scenario for what impact XR could have if uptake of the technology is reasonable and the quality of products and services available develops as expected.

$1.5 trillion is a hefty number, but the working behind this figure has a strong economic and business foundation. By considering a variety of XR applications, the economics team was able to assess the resultant effect on productivity and use it to model the macroeconomic, global impact of XR. The analysis comprised three phases and involved a bottom-up approach, which is summarized below.

## Phase 1: Researching and identifying XR applications

PwC's VR/AR team provided input here on the list of potential XR applications that could realistically be implemented by 2030. This was complemented and cross referenced with interviews from third-party stakeholders in the XR industry to form a comprehensive list, which was cut back to remove applications not likely to have a significant impact on the global economy. The analysis also included economic impacts resulting from applications that were not transformative at the time the report was written but were expected to have significant productivity effects, such as impacts on flexible working and organizational meetings.

## Phase 2: Estimating the uplift in productivity

For each shortlisted application, PwC looked at existing research on adoption and productivity impact together with forecasts from ABI Research. Combined with PwC's own economic analysis, productivity estimates were created for each application and categorized into 12 areas. These were later consolidated down to five main categories to make it easier to communicate the information. Eight countries were selected – China, Finland, France, Germany, Japan, UAE, UK, USA – based on the strength of their immersive markets and the existence of reliable data that could be used as an input for the economic analysis. All the factors were then applied across these countries through to 2030 based on an assumed S-shaped adoption curve, the Global Innovation Index[17] and the projected uptake of VR and AR.

> Adoption of a technology is S-shaped when it is adopted slowly but steadily at first followed by exponential growth and then a return to a plateau as it reaches

the majority of the population. Radio, television, mobile phones, computers and more have all followed this adoption curve (as you may have noticed from the 'VR is dead' section in Chapter 11).

### Phase 3: Running the findings through an economic model

The final stage involved inputting the productivity figures into a dynamic computable general equilibrium (CGE) model to estimate the aggregate effects of VR and AR adoption on global GDP up to 2030 and the total number of jobs enhanced as a result. The CGE model is built on the Global Trade Analysis Project database,[18] which provides details on the size of 57 different economic sectors in 140 different countries, and captures economic interactions in the global economy, including trade and spending between firms on one another's goods and inputs; spending by consumers on goods; investment decisions and dynamics in the market such as demand for factors like capital and labour, trade, employment and wage effects. Ultimately, this model simulates how households, businesses and governments interact.

> CGE models are widely used in policy-making around the world and so represent a credible approach to modelling impacts on a global economic level.

### The result

The analysis and results span multiple dimensions:

- time: each year from 2019 to 2030;
- technology: VR and AR are considered separately;
- geography: eight key territories are examined;
- application: five consolidated categories are included;
- jobs: how many are enhanced by immersive technology?

Technology-wise, AR accounts for more than double the economic contribution of VR ($105 billion versus $43 billion in 2021 respectively) and this will continue to 2030 ($1.1 trillion versus $451 billion).

From a country perspective, the USA shows strong results, expected to account for just over a third of the global economic impact of XR in 2030 ($537 billion). Together with China and Japan, these three economies represent over half of the economic impact expected by 2030. In Europe, Germany is expected to lead the pack with a $27.1 billion contribution to global GDP in 2030 through XR-related 'product and service development' enhancements alone. This is partly thanks to a strong manufacturing sector in the German economy.

The five key applications of XR examined in this analysis are listed below in order of decreasing expected boosts to global GDP by 2030.

### PRODUCT AND SERVICE DEVELOPMENT

VR and AR have the potential not only to enhance and augment existing product design and development but also to enable entirely new techniques, accelerating the creation of more accurate and realistic concepts, shortening the product development pipeline, and saving significant time and money.

### HEALTHCARE

The impact of VR and AR on the healthcare sector could be huge over the next 10 years, for front-line patient care and also for training. VR is already being used to give medical students greater access to operating theatres, where there are restrictions on the number of observers. The technology is also being used to enable consultants based in different locations to collaborate remotely and discuss upcoming surgical procedures.

### DEVELOPMENT AND TRAINING

The use of VR and AR in training boosts engagement and knowledge retention and enables organizations to enforce consistent, measurable standards at scale. The technology also provides a way to train employees where it is not always practical, or safe, to do so in the real world – for example, to simulate emergency situations or asset maintenance in dangerous environments.

### PROCESS IMPROVEMENTS

VR and AR are opening up exciting new ways to improve the efficiency, productivity and accuracy of employees and processes. Engineers and technicians can be fed information such as repair diagrams using an AR interface, enabling them to quickly identify problems and conduct repairs and maintenance. In the logistics sector, smart glasses can display picking information for workers, highlight relevant locations, and display product details as well as packing instructions.

### RETAIL AND CONSUMER

VR and AR offer new ways to engage, entertain and interact with consumers, creating new possibilities in film, gaming and retail.

TABLE 12.1

| Area | Consolidated category | Predicted boost to global GDP by 2030 |
| --- | --- | --- |
| • Organizational meetings<br>• Design, visualization and build<br>• Flexible working | Product and service development | $359.4 billion |
| • Healthcare | Healthcare | $350.9 billion |
| • Organizational training<br>• Education | Development and training | $294.2 billion |
| • Asset repair and maintenance<br>• Logistics and location mapping | Process improvements | $275 billion |
| • Retail processes<br>• Consumer experiences<br>• Video gaming | Retail and consumer | $204 billion |

Consolidated application areas of XR and their expected boost to global GDP by 2030

## Jobs enhanced by XR

PwC predicts that 2.6 million jobs are being enhanced through XR technologies as of 2021. And this is only the start as the figure is expected to rise to 23.4 million by 2030. These are connected to the application areas above and apply globally across sectors.

These figures are part of a wider analysis of the impact of immersive technologies on business and the economy, which features in PwC's *Seeing Is Believing* report. The web page hosting the report includes a data explorer which allows you to examine each year individually, select different countries, and see the result in terms of monetary and percentage boosts to GDP, across both VR and AR, as well as the number and percentage of jobs enhanced.

IN SUMMARY

● XR technologies are already adding value to the global economy by creating efficiencies and increasing productivity.

● They will continue to do so at an increasing rate through to 2030 (where the forecasts for this analysis end, but the effects are expected to continue).

● Millions of jobs worldwide will be enhanced by these technologies across numerous sectors.

## Academic research in XR is surging

Universities are an incredibly important stakeholder in the XR landscape. Alongside leading research divisions within large corporations, they are responsible for improving our understanding of these technologies and their advancement from a technical, functional and commercial perspective. The work they conduct uses scientific rigour and methodology to inform what problems the technologies can be deployed to effectively solve.

Examining papers published in academic journals, research in both AR and VR has been climbing steadily. In 2000, about 600 papers were published relating to VR and 50 for AR; in 2016, yearly VR publications had doubled to about 1,200. AR, meanwhile, saw an almost 15 times increase in that same period, albeit from a very small start. Over the next three years, a surge in research interest led to another doubling in the rate of published papers for both VR and AR.

There is a clear acceleration in the rate of XR publications starting in 2016, as seen in Figure 12.1. This was two years after Facebook bought Oculus for $3 billion, which likely had a knock-on effect in both industry and academia.

Although academic research in XR is not focused solely on business requirements, through the increased focus and sheer number of studies conducted on the technology, some will naturally be applicable. Others, conducted in partnership with organizations, will directly improve the mounting evidence to support the effectiveness of using XR to solve a multitude of business problems.

FIGURE 12.1

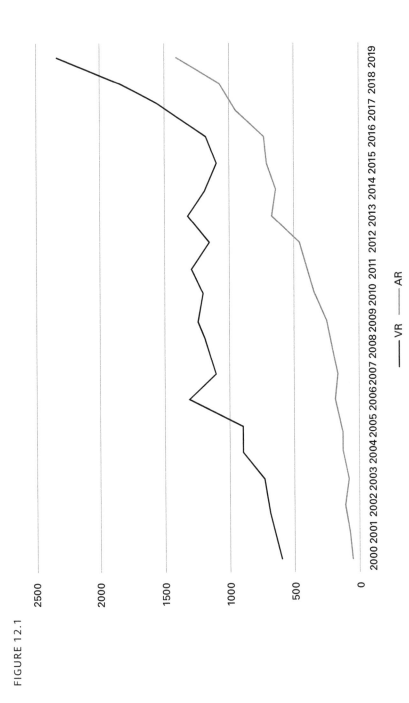

Academic journal publications on VR and AR from 2000 to 2019 based on search results for these topic areas in Microsoft Academic.[19]

## UNIVERSITY OF LEEDS: STUDYING THE VALUE OF VR IN DENTAL EDUCATION

The University of Leeds (UoL) is a research-focused public university with origins that date back to the founding of the Leeds School of Medicine in 1831. It is a top 10 university for research power in the UK and is home to more than 38,000 students.[20]

In 2012, the UoL School of Dentistry invested almost $2 million in a suite of VR dental simulator systems to create the largest of its kind in the UK and one of the largest in the world, enabling a full classroom of students to practise simultaneously. These systems are all-in-one devices featuring positionally tracked physical implements ('dental VR controllers' effectively), a display which presents a 3D image to the user who wears a pair of polarized glasses, and a touch-screen panel to navigate through the training modules and virtual patient notes. The system also contains built-in haptics technology that gives the user force feedback, creating a realistic feel as they perform various dental procedures.

Researchers at UoL have been using these VR systems to examine their value in dentistry education from different perspectives. One of their studies of nearly 300 participants showed that the VR simulator is capable of distinguishing between different levels of dental ability – this provided confidence in the simulator's ability to assess trainee dentists. Another study concluded that a student's early performance using the VR simulator can be used to successfully predict their real-world dental ability even more accurately than traditional training methods conducted later in their studies. Following many years of analysis and published research, a summary of their findings is that VR can be used to train dental students:

- faster;
- safer;
- more effectively;
- more cost efficiently.

Traditionally, students without the VR simulator would be taught using a physical set of real and plastic teeth that would be set into a 'phantom head' – an open-mouthed, toothless manikin. This relies on a continuous supply of disposable items, including the teeth and drill pieces. By using VR instead of relying on these physical items, wastage is reduced, water consumption is lowered and cost decreases. Additionally, more granular, objective data can be collected directly from the VR system compared with the external observations of an instructor. For example, a student's hand–eye coordination can be assessed through the system and the resultant data can be used to categorize them by skill level, identifying those who may need extra support.

About 5 per cent of the population suffer from an underlying neurological condition which makes it challenging to acquire the fine motor skills needed for a career in dentistry. Using a VR dental simulator can help reveal this information more quickly.

In a direct comparison of dental novices using either the VR simulator or traditional, instructor-supported training, UoL's studies found that although students learnt in both cases, needing only a single instructor to manage an entire classroom practising on simulators means progress can be made more quickly with VR.

The VR simulator is an effective training system available on demand to students, which gives them the ability to load up and practise on a theoretically unlimited number of dental cases to hone their skills. This provides them with more opportunities at the earlier stages of their studies to practise in a way that is representative of a real patient but without the risk of harming one.

This is an example of how, through rigorous academic research, UoL has shown the increased effectiveness, efficiency and safety that come from using virtual reality for dentistry training. This and other academic studies around the world continue to give us a better understanding of the benefits of XR across different applications and industries.

## Acceptance of video gaming trends and technologies in organizations and society

### When games became serious

Video games, with which VR and AR are stereotypically associated, are viewed as a form of entertainment, but organizations have been using video games and their related mechanics to achieve goals unrelated to entertainment for a long time. In fact, there is an entire field related to using games for purposes other than entertainment – it is aptly named 'serious games'. Clark Abt, an American researcher, is author of a book of the very same name (released in 1970), in which he introduced the term.[21] Abt summarizes the idea of serious games well and the paradoxical perception some people have with the term: 'Games may be played seriously or casually. We are concerned with serious games in the sense that these games have an explicit and carefully thought-out educational purpose and are not intended to be played primarily for amusement. This does not mean that serious games are not, or should not be, entertaining.'

Serious games were being used long before the term was even coined. Militaries use game-like simulations as a way to replicate the complexities of the physical world. These have been employed to deliver cost-effective training since the end of World War II when, in 1948, the US military created 'Air Defense Simulation' in collaboration with the Operations Research Office at Johns Hopkins University, leading to what could be argued was the first computer game.

The US military has created a number of simulations since the early days of computer technology, some of which have intersected with the consumer world. 'America's Army', first released in 2002, is a series of video games developed by the US Army as a marketing avenue for the public. The idea was conceived by Colonel Casey Wardynski, a director at the United States Military Academy, who 'envisioned using computer game technology to provide the public a virtual soldier experience that was engaging, informative and entertaining'.[22]

---

DID YOU KNOW?

Some simulations which started their life as training tools have become video games in their own right. Consumers all over the world purchase and play these simulations, which cover everything from driving trains and flying planes to running hospitals and zoos.

---

## The gamification of corporate and academic work

In a similar fashion to the military, corporations have been using video gaming technology and techniques to encourage various behaviours and achieve business outcomes – this tends to get called 'gamification'. A number of organizations and products use gamification to enhance learning by creating engaging and interactive narratives that can turn even the driest compliance e-learning into a more enjoyable experience. Corporate software used by businesses to manage customer relationships and internal communications, such as Salesforce, Yammer and Jive, either contain inbuilt gamified elements or have such modules available for purchase. These usually introduce game mechanics, such as profile badges, points or other types of rewards. Rewards are provided in return for desired actions, such as posting information and sharing knowledge, stoking and stroking the competitive spirit and ego of the platform's users. Such recognition is nothing new – organizations all over the world, both civilian and military, use medals, awards and titles in a similar fashion. UK insurance company Vitality encourages its customers to rack up points from walking and exercising to earn rewards from coffee to cinema tickets.

Even in the consumer world, serious games have made an appearance in the intriguing area of citizen science. An application called Foldit encourages people to contribute to scientific research by playing a game in which they attempt to 'fold' proteins in different ways and submit their highest-scoring solutions for further analysis.[23]

### The video gaming industry and the upcoming generation of leaders

The video gaming industry is a force to be reckoned with – it is bigger than both music and film combined. To put this in perspective, consider that the highest-grossing film in the decade leading up to 2020 was *Avengers: Endgame*, released in April 2019.[24] It made $305 million globally in its first two days.[25] By comparison, the video game *Grand Theft Auto V*, released almost six years prior in September 2013, made more than twice that – $800 million – in half the time: one day.[26]

Video games have become embedded in the fabric of the modern world. Nearly one in every three people on the planet plays video games on either a PC, console or mobile device.[27] Millennials are the most significant generation here in terms of their expenditure, spending an average of $112 every month on games, almost double that of Gen X, who spend only $59 per month.[28]

From 2020 to 2030, many millennials will be moving into senior leadership positions in organizations and will bring with them a culture of greater acceptance of video games and understanding of their potential within business.

'It's a digital age. Virtual reality is not uncommon. Rapid change is the norm right now. So, yes, VR and augmented reality technologies are of huge importance in the way we innovate moving on, because that's what this generation is used to.' Alethea Duhon, Technical Director at the Air Force Agency for Modeling Simulation[29]

---

### RED CROSS: VR 'GAMES' FOR DISASTER RESPONSE TRAINING

There are many organizations using game engines to build games for corporate purposes. The International Committee of the Red Cross (ICRC) is one such example.

> Most of the XR experiences mentioned in this book were built on 'game engines' – computer programs traditionally used to create video games for PCs, consoles and mobile phones, and now also used to build applications for business.

The ICRC works on the ground in over 90 countries to help people affected by armed conflict and to promote compliance with international humanitarian law. Headquartered in Geneva, Switzerland, the ICRC employs more than 18,000 staff worldwide. It has a dedicated VR team that uses virtual reality to immerse staff and partners in disaster scenarios for training purposes.[30]

One such scenario immerses users in a forensic examination during a disaster and was used in Thailand's Chonburi province. Before setting out, each user needs to (virtually) dress in appropriate PPE and pack relevant materials as they would in the physical world: a full-body coverall with gloves, boots, goggles, helmet and face mask, varying sizes of evidence bags, and a camera. Once ready, they set off to explore the virtual city, wading through wastewater and removing debris to uncover disaster victims, complete forensic examinations on them and finally place them in a body bag for transportation. Along the way, the trainees need to take relevant photographs, including any unique features of each body, such as faces, tattoos and scars, while checking for items to help uncover the identity of the victims. Dangling electrical cables and wild animals are constant hazards they need to deal with during the experience.

> 'In the past, training was based on repeating [the same exercise] again and again, and it was a waste of time and money. Thanks to virtual reality, we can simulate different scenarios from crime scenes to the chaos of a natural disaster'. – Police Major General Nithi Bundhuwong, Commander of the Institute of Police Forensic Science Training and Research, Royal Thai Police

FIGURE 12.2

The view of a user (pictured top right) as they explore the scene of a disaster in VR.

It was with the advent of the digital age, the prevalence of smartphones and the improved connectedness of devices that gaming technologies and techniques gained a foothold in the corporate world. Learning technology market research firm Metaari predicts that the serious games industry is in a boom phase and will see revenues quadruple to more than $24 billion by 2024.[31] Video gaming technology with VR and AR at the forefront of innovation will inevitably be a part of this growth.

## Maturity of XR

Research and advisory firm Gartner provides organizations with information and insights across different industries and functions. The company analyses emerging technologies with the aim of helping these organizations understand their progression and effect. One of its methodologies, the Gartner Hype Cycle, is a graphical representation of the evolution of a wide range of technologies from smart dust and quantum computing to augmented reality and virtual reality. The Hype Cycle plots expectations of the technology (represented on the vertical axis) against time (on the horizontal axis) (Figure 12.3). There are five phases each technology goes through as it progresses along the Hype Cycle (Table 12.2):

TABLE 12.2

| Phase | Expectations | Technology viability in business | General business interest |
|-------|--------------|----------------------------------|---------------------------|
| 1. Innovation trigger | Low growing to high | Proof of concept | Observation without investment |
| 2. Peak of inflated expectations | High to peak | Low | Some business interest |
| 3. Trough of disillusionment | High falling to lowest point | Low | Waning |
| 4. Slope of enlightenment | Recovering from lowest point | Growing | Growing |
| 5. Plateau of productivity | Stable | Stable | Stable |

A summary of the five phases of the Gartner Hype Cycle.

1 **Innovation trigger:** a potential breakthrough with a new and upcoming technology that sets off a chain reaction of growing excitement, which ignites a growth in the expectations of what the technology can do.

2 **Peak of inflated expectations:** where enough publicity has been generated around a technology that expectations of what it can do are at their highest.

3 **Trough of disillusionment:** the inevitable realization that the technology cannot live up to the high expectations that have been set, which causes confidence in it to plummet.

4 **Slope of enlightenment:** the technology matures as its applications become clearer and easier to implement.

5 **Plateau of productivity:** the beginning of mainstream adoption of the technology.

Gartner released its first Hype Cycle in 1995 and has been updating it annually ever since. 'Virtual reality' appeared in this very first edition, tumbling down into the trough of disillusionment. For the next two years, VR continued to fall further and by 1998 Gartner had removed it from the Hype Cycle, a sign of the troubles the technology was facing at the time. In 2013, the year after Palmer Luckey proposed the Oculus Rift to the world, Gartner brought VR back to the fold, placing it just beyond the lowest point of the trough of disillusionment. It spent two more years fighting its way out

FIGURE 12.3

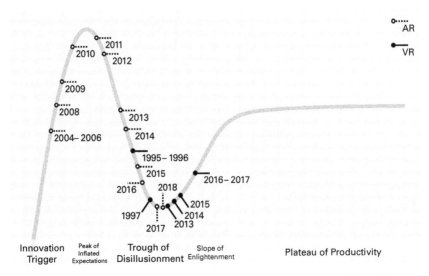

The location of VR and AR technology from 1995 onwards on a representation of a typical Gartner Hype Cycle diagram.[32]

before finally breaking free into the glorious slope of enlightenment in 2016. By 2018, Gartner had again removed VR – not because the technology had failed but because it had succeeded. At this stage, VR headsets were being sold to consumers online and in stores by the millions – by Gartner's reckoning this was evidence enough that the technology should be unceremoniously stripped of its 'emerging' title and booted off the Hype Cycle to make way for some unsuspecting emerging technology such as 'flying autonomous vehicles' to start at the beginning of the innovation trigger phase and run the gauntlet again.

If the Hype Cycle were around before 1995, VR would likely feature in the 1960s at the innovation trigger stage as a result of the many head-mounted displays that were developed during the decade. The excitement around VR in the early 1990s would land it a place on the peak of inflated expectations.

---

DID YOU KNOW?

The term 'virtual reality' wasn't actually popularized until the late 1980s by computer scientist Jaron Lanier, who was heavily involved in researching the technology.

Augmented reality made its debut on the Hype Cycle in 2004, although, like VR, its history dates back to the 1960s when AR was a research topic within academia. It started to gain traction in industry in 1990 when the term was coined by Boeing engineer Thomas Caudell and his co-worker David Mizell. They proposed that AR headsets be used to assist workers with aircraft wiring instructions. In the late 1990s and early 2000s it had made its way into entertainment, where broadcasters used it to superimpose informational graphics onto video feeds of live sports matches. Between 2009 and 2010, AR stepped into the peak of inflated expectations at a time when print media was starting to explore AR, giving *Esquire* magazine readers the experience of bringing Robert Downey Jr to life on their mobile phones.

For the next eight years, AR slid down to the bottom of the trough of disillusionment amidst a lot of activity and progress: in the business world, Google and Microsoft released the first iteration of their AR headsets (both of which received a second-generation upgrade in 2019); in the consumer world, Niantic and Nintendo launched Pokémon GO, which helped to spread the word about AR technology even further. From 2019 onwards, Gartner removed AR from its Hype Cycle in a similar fashion to VR, stating that 'augmented reality is rapidly approaching a much more mature state, which moves it off the emerging technology class of innovation profiles'.[33] This decision was likely spurred by the rapid innovation in the industry that has led to billions of AR-capable devices, many of which are in our pockets and travel with us every day, everywhere.

## Omnipresence of the smartphone

If you own a smartphone, then it is likely that you already have a very AR-capable mobile device. By the end of 2020, there is estimated to be approximately 7 billion mobile users and 14 billion mobile devices worldwide.[34] In other words, about 90 per cent of the world's population are mobile device users, and on average those users have not one but two devices each.

Let's scrutinize this a bit further, though: from an AR perspective, not all mobile devices will be capable of running all manner of augmented reality applications. However, at the most basic end of the spectrum, all that is needed is a camera, and those have become ubiquitous on mobile devices. In fact, I struggled to find a widely available mobile device without a camera when researching online. The best I could come up with was an Amazon page for 'phones without camera' that comprised three models, two of which were no longer available.

What if we considered only 'high-end' mobile devices? From an AR perspective, a high-end mobile device could be defined as being capable of understanding the geometry of physical surfaces – in other words, it is able to build a 3D map of the world simply from the information it is getting from the camera.

Android and iOS represent the operating systems on more than 98 per cent of the mobile devices out there.[35] As mentioned earlier, the software that enables high-end AR on these devices is ARCore and ARKit respectively. ARCore generally requires at least an Android 7.0 operating system, a device that originally shipped with the Google Play Store, and internet access. If we also apply the internet access criterion to Apple's ARKit-supported mobile devices (which require an A9 processor or later), then there are still approximately 2 billion mobile devices out there that are capable of running high-end AR applications.

For those of you who live in the UK, you can download the Royal Mail application for a practical example of how the company is using AR to help its customers. The app's AR functionality is summarized below.

---

### ROYAL MAIL: AR PARCEL SIZER FOR CUSTOMER POSTAGE

Royal Mail is a British postal service and courier company that has been delivering mail throughout the UK for more than 500 years.

In October 2018, as part of a campaign to make more services available online, Royal Mail released a mobile app (for both Android and iOS) to help its customers track their parcels, arrange for the redelivery of missed packages and locate the nearest customer service point. According to surveys, a key pain point for some customers was a lack of confidence in assessing the size and cost of their postage and, as a result, the worry that their parcel would be delayed.

A year after its release, Royal Mail updated its mobile app to include an AR function which helps customers correctly size and price items they intend to post.[36] While customers navigate the buying journey to send an item, they are asked to enter its dimensions. Here, they have the option to enter values manually or use the AR parcel sizer feature (Figure 12.4). Upon selecting the latter, a digital box appears in the user's physical environment. The user can select from Royal Mail's three categories of parcels – large letter, small parcel and medium parcel – and this modifies the box's dimensions accordingly.

FIGURE 12.4

A screenshot taken from Royal Mail's iPhone app showing the AR parcel sizer functionality in action.

The digital box can be placed on any surface and locked to the environment with a press of a button. Once locked, it can be compared with a physical parcel next to it, allowing customers to visually determine what category their parcel falls into. This saves them time and increases their confidence in paying the appropriate postage.

The Royal Mail mobile application has been downloaded more than 2 million times and, together with its AR functionality, provides reassurance to customers all over the UK when buying postage online.

## Smartphones and VR

The proliferation of smartphones in the world is mainly a bolster to AR technology. Using smartphones to act as a power source and display for VR devices is fraught with issues, from overheating to the poor user experience of having to fiddle your phone into the headset slot – not to mention that it rapidly depletes the battery, meaning you might be without a phone for part or all of the day unless you can quickly and conveniently recharge it nearby. These issues contributed to the decline of smartphone-based VR and the subsequent evolution of the standalone VR headset.

There are some niche cases where it still makes sense to use smartphones for VR experiences. One of these is for consumer research purposes where immersion is important but required only for a brief period of time. The other is education. Both applications benefit from the main hardware (smartphone) already being with the end user, meaning a much lower deployment cost that is required only to distribute a simple VR headset body for the phone.

## Notes

1  http://www.retro-vr.co.uk/test/inside.html?LMCL=l_IerV (archived at https://perma.cc/Q7KS-ZS5J)

2  https://www.pwc.com/gr/en/publications/assets/tech-breakthroughs-megatrend-how-to-prepare-for-its-impact.pdf (archived at https://perma.cc/V8A2-9X2Q)

3  https://www.kickstarter.com/projects/1523379957/oculus-rift-step-into-the-game (archived at https://perma.cc/P7J7-FBVR)

4  https://www.cbinsights.com/research/ar-vr-startup-funding/ (archived at https://perma.cc/J62L-LPTK)

5   https://www.digi-capital.com/news/2018/01/record-over-3b-ar-vr-investment-in-2017-1-5b-in-q4/ (archived at https://perma.cc/FG5K-5J35)

6   https://www.digi-capital.com/news/2019/01/ar-vr-investment-stabilized-in-q4-2018/ (archived at https://perma.cc/N2KP-KH2P)

7   https://www.digi-capital.com/news/2020/03/4-billion-ar-vr-investment-2019/ (archived at https://perma.cc/FZR3-7G5N)

8   https://www.digi-capital.com/news/2019/10/virtual-reality-and-augmented-reality-startup-valuations-hit-45-billion-on-paper/ (archived at https://perma.cc/J5T5-WXDL)

9   https://assets.publishing.service.gov.uk/government/uploads/system/uploads/attachment_data/file/730048/industrial-strategy-white-paper-web-ready-a4-version.pdf (archived at https://perma.cc/8FWH-CWRZ)

10   https://www.immerseuk.org/resources/immersive-economy-report-2019/#:~:text=The%202019%20Immersive%20Economy%20in,Economy%20in%20the%20UK%20Report (archived at https://perma.cc/W3XY-LZKC).

11   https://assets.publishing.service.gov.uk/government/uploads/system/uploads/attachment_data/file/730048/industrial-strategy-white-paper-web-ready-a4-version.pdf (archived at https://perma.cc/8FWH-CWRZ)

12   https://www.roadtovr.com/china-jiangxi-nanchang-promises-invest-480-million-ar-vr/ (archived at https://perma.cc/X3QW-7SQG)

13   https://www.roadtovr.com/china-jiangxi-nanchang-promises-invest-480-million-ar-vr/ (archived at https://perma.cc/X3QW-7SQG)

14   https://koreajoongangdaily.joins.com/news/article/article.aspx?aid=3022874 (archived at https://perma.cc/AK4J-CR2E)

15   http://www.theinvestor.co.kr/view.php?ud=20190502000549 (archived at https://perma.cc/QQ6M-VFMS)

16   https://www.pwc.com/SeeingIsBelieving (archived at https://perma.cc/9U2P-AY9L)

17   https://www.globalinnovationindex.org/Home (archived at https://perma.cc/9KWD-6D32)

18   https://www.gtap.agecon.purdue.edu/ (archived at https://perma.cc/6JPD-9EVN)

19   https://academic.microsoft.com/home (archived at https://perma.cc/V9S4-PHCA)

20   https://www.leeds.ac.uk/info/5000/about/140/facts_and_figures (archived at https://perma.cc/49RU-5APA)

21   https://books.google.co.uk/books?id=5z-QAAAAIAAJ&dq=editions:0AFLRE73VcDZA6oN1U8ReScOkguIz9pUDsbKxgCziOjtvaDnjnBkI33J3D6DaQ7RjV7sRua0us3qJ (archived at https://perma.cc/JPX6-GVY4)

22   https://www.army.mil/article/11935/improving_americas_army (archived at https://perma.cc/LH5J-Z8KK)

**23**  https://fold.it/ (archived at https://perma.cc/FU85-BMFD)

**24**  https://www.cnbc.com/2019/07/21/avengers-endgame-is-the-highest-grossing-film-of-all-time.html (archived at https://perma.cc/4MDV-6APH)

**25**  https://www.cnbc.com/2019/04/26/avengers-endgame-smashes-thursday-night-record-with-60-million-haul.html (archived at https://perma.cc/7KYX-SKRH)

**26**  https://variety.com/2013/digital/news/grand-theft-auto-v-earns-800-million-in-a-day-more-than-worldwide-haul-of-man-of-steel-1200616706/ (archived at https://perma.cc/L69F-GYE3)

**27**  https://newzoo.com/insights/articles/the-global-games-market-will-generate-152-1-billion-in-2019-as-the-u-s-overtakes-china-as-the-biggest-market/ (archived at https://perma.cc/9GSV-6DTL)

**28**  https://www.nielsen.com/wp-content/uploads/sites/3/2019/06/millennials-on-millennials-gaming-media-consumption-report.pdf (archived at https://perma.cc/2DNG-RG7Q)

**29**  https://fedtechmagazine.com/article/2020/04/air-force-turns-vr-ar-training-and-maintenance?utm_source=Spatial+Insights+Weekly&utm_campaign=721abdc477-EMAIL_CAMPAIGN_2020_04_21_11_41&utm_medium=email&utm_term=0_3bd0cb579a-721abdc477-364219542 (archived at https://perma.cc/K6QD-SYZ7)

**30**  https://www.straitstimes.com/asia/red-cross-turns-to-vr-for-disaster-response-training (archived at https://perma.cc/3CRU-ABVZ)

**31**  https://www.slideshare.net/SeriousGamesAssoc/the-20192024-global-gamebased-learning-market (archived at https://perma.cc/E9MM-39SV)

**32**  https://commons.wikimedia.org/wiki/File:Gartner_Hype_Cycle.svg (archived at https://perma.cc/66AC-NJET) – built on a graph by Jeremy Kemp, licensed under the Creative Commons BY-SA licence

**33**  https://skarredghost.com/2019/09/04/augmented-reality-mature-gartner/ (archived at https://perma.cc/UF3K-66MF)

**34**  https://www.radicati.com/wp/wp-content/uploads/2019/01/Mobile_Statistics_Report,_2019-2023_Executive_Summary.pdf (archived at https://perma.cc/CU7V-TEM5)

**35**  https://www.statista.com/statistics/272698/global-market-share-held-by-mobile-operating-systems-since-2009/ (archived at https://perma.cc/2ELP-6GNZ)

**36**  https://blog.postofficeshop.co.uk/parcel-sizing-royal-mail-app/ (archived at https://perma.cc/TJG7-MX3A)

# 13

# Conclusion

I hope you've enjoyed reading about the wonders of virtual reality and augmented reality technology in business and have a better idea of how they can be used and to what benefit. I believe they will form a significant part of our everyday personal and professional lives in the future.

On this reading journey, you will have explored a vast range of topics and information. If I were to summarize it as concisely as I can, this is what I'd say.

## XR's impact is global across all industries

XR holds value for businesses today, as showcased by the numerous case studies we've seen. Originally an item of academic interest and military potential, it has evolved a variety of applications in business.

VR, which immerses users in a different environment, has been used to:

- transform training for millions of employees on a combination of soft skills and practical skills;
- create effective ways of collaborating and working remotely;
- design and visualize assets and environments that don't yet exist or which are inaccessible for financial, time, health or safety reasons.

Meanwhile, AR, which conveniently displays information relevant to a user's surrounding environment, has been used to:

- help businesses optimize operational tasks;
- provide effective remote assistance;
- enhance product sales through the ability to try on personal items and try out physical goods in a customer's environment.

Most of the case studies in this book are from large companies, not because they are the only ones capable of implementing XR but because they are widely recognized and publicize more details on their XR solutions. In many ways, smaller companies have an easier time implementing XR as they have a smaller number of employees, which leads to less costly and complex projects.

## Challenges exist but the rewards are great

XR suffers from a large amount of misinformation and preconceived notions which hold it back from being acknowledged and implemented in business. To set the record straight:

- XR is not just for gaming and entertainment. While it can be an incredibly fun and engaging experience (which itself is a rare business benefit), organizations are using XR to derive tangible business outcomes.

- XR projects don't have to be expensive and complex. Smaller pilot programmes offer multiple benefits: they are simpler, cheaper and less resource intensive, and also give organizations the targeted data they need to build a business case to take the solution to the next level.

- From a macro perspective, societal unfamiliarity with XR and how we interface with the technology makes it more difficult to introduce into the workplace; however, the value is there for those who are willing to invest the time in understanding the technology, its strengths and its limitations. Practically, this means XR project stakeholders need to experience the technology and its many forms first hand and keep up to date on advancements through their own research. When the time comes to deploy, some work will need to be done from a communications and facilitation standpoint to help introduce the technology to employees.

- XR is neither a passing fad nor even a new technology. It's been around in digital form since the 1960s and in more abstract forms for long before that. Having already proven its value in business, it will be around for many more years to come.

For those willing to invest the time and money in better understanding XR and its applications in business, there is a multitude of benefits to be gained in the form of cost and time savings, improved health and safety outcomes, greater sustainability, closer alignment with project stakeholders, and other job-specific efficiencies.

## Expect to see XR more often

All stakeholders connected to the XR industry have now come together in a significant way to advance the technology.

- Major XR industry players are researching and developing new hardware and software designs to improve the experience of using the technology.

- Many large corporations are devoting a significant amount of resources to implement XR as part of their business strategy.

- Smartphone manufacturers are delivering XR-enabled phones to a large part of the world's population, giving users access to XR technology by default.

- Investors of all kinds, from individual angel investors to private and corporate venture capital arms, are funding startups, which are bringing innovative XR applications to the market.

- Governments are creating networks, funds and subsidies to assist with the growth of XR in different countries.

- Academic institutions are producing research papers on XR at a faster rate than ever before, helping us to understand even more clearly how the technology can help specific sectors and applications.

While the concept of the 'year of VR' makes as much sense as the 'year of the laptop', there can be no argument that both VR and AR technology have tremendous value to offer. Meanwhile, the hardware and software required is becoming smaller, simpler and cheaper with every passing day, which will attract an even greater number of applications and users.

# 14

# The machinery behind XR

Having read the conclusion, you may feel that the journey is over, but it needn't end here. For those of you who are looking to dig deeper into the technical detail, I leave you with this final section, which provides an overview of the different manifestations of XR interspersed with some historical tidbits.

XR hardware can be categorized into four main areas:

- head-mounted displays (HMDs);
- handheld devices;
- projection systems;
- large screens.

## Head-mounted displays (HMDs)

This is the most common of devices and the image that generally springs to mind whenever anyone thinks of virtual reality or augmented reality. Also colloquially known as headsets, goggles or glasses, this category encompasses any form of technology worn on the head that displays digital objects or environments for the user to see.

## Virtual reality

All VR headsets are composed of a tracking system, display, processing system and power source. As users move and look around a virtual environment, the tracking system keeps tabs on these movements and sends them to the processing system, which works out where they should be and what they should be seeing and updates the display accordingly. On modern VR headsets, these updates to the display occur up to 120 times every second, creating the illusion that you are actually navigating the virtual world.

When the processing system is external to the headset – for example, a desktop computer – a cable is used to link the two together and the VR headset is referred to as a tethered headset. Being tied down in this way is inconvenient at best (consider users wrapping themselves up in cables as they turn around in virtual environments) and hazardous at worst (tripping over an unseen cable isn't pleasant!). This system defined VR headsets until companies like Google and Samsung considered alternative processing sources, creating headsets that were powered by mobile phones. What followed was the birth of the Google Cardboard (Figure 14.1) and the Samsung Gear VR in 2014, with Google claiming to have shipped more than 15 million units of the former by November 2019.[1]

FIGURE 14.1

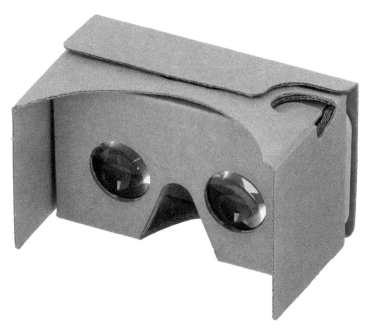

The Google Cardboard is controversial. Per its name, it is made almost entirely out of cardboard. It is inexpensive, able to be branded, accepts a variety of smartphones and is easily transported as it can be flat-packed. It spread far and wide and was an entry point into VR for many. But it had significant limitations: it suffered from low-quality content, was not durable, had only a single mechanical button for input, needed to be held up by the user, and produced sub-standard visual results compared with many other headsets. As you saw in an earlier chapter, however, these limitations do not preclude it from being used by organizations if the application is fitting.

These efforts evolved ecosystems around them, with Google creating Daydream, which ran on select, high-end phones, to support consumer interest further in VR. In October 2019, Google discontinued the Daydream project, stating, 'We noticed some clear limitations constraining smartphone VR from being a viable long-term solution. Most notably, asking people to put their phone in a headset and lose access to the apps they use throughout the day causes immense friction.'[2]

By this time, a new breed of headset had entered the market that promised to give users a more streamlined experience: a portable device that didn't require a mobile phone, computer or any other external system. Thus, 'standalone' headsets were born (Figure 14.2).

Standalone headsets could initially track orientation but not position. In other words, you could look around but not move around the virtual space. These are referred to as 3 DoF (degrees of freedom) headsets as you can look:

- up and down;
- left and right;
- clockwise and anti-clockwise.

FIGURE 14.2

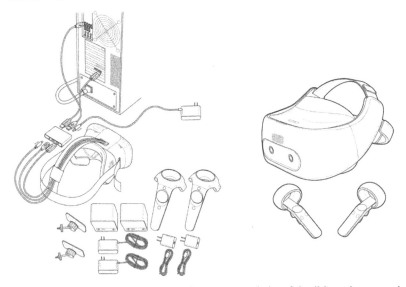

The journey from tethered to standalone headsets was an evolution of simplicity and user experience. On the left, components of a tethered headset released by HTC in April 2016. On the right, one of its standalone headsets released in April 2019.

FIGURE 14.3

Testing out a glasses-style VR headset tethered to a mobile phone which powers it. Thanks to Thomas Gere for taking this photo.

Soon enough, advances in technology meant it became possible for even standalone headsets to track a user's change in position. This enabled not only portability but full 6 DoF functionality. Users could now physically look and move around a virtual environment without having to get caught up in cables.

## VR form factors

Thanks to advances in VR optics, some VR headsets look like a supersized pair of goggles rather than a hefty, front-heavy headset. They are worn like a pair of glasses, with arms on either side that rest over the ears. Generally, they are powered by an external processor such as a smartphone, creating a tethered but portable experience (Figure 14.3).

Most recognizable, though, is the larger box-type VR headset that can be either tethered or standalone (Figure 14.4). These feature in most of the VR case studies and discussions in this book.

FIGURE 14.4

An example of the common box-type form factor for standalone VR headsets. Thanks to Nev Bharucha for letting us take his photo.

## Augmented reality

On the AR front, you can trace augmented reality technology back to 1968 when Ivan Sutherland, an American computer scientist working at the University of Utah, with the help of his student Bob Sproull, created the 'Sword of Damocles'. This headset could overlay outlines of basic 3D objects like a cube on the physical world. A user could move around the room and see the virtual object from different angles – the first 6 DoF headset.[3]

---

DID YOU KNOW?

The Sword of Damocles was named after the ancient tale of the same name, made famous by the Roman philosopher Cicero. As the story goes, Damocles, a courtier of King Dionysius II of Syracuse, was offered the opportunity to experience the life of a king, which he readily accepted. While Damocles made himself comfortable on the king's throne, Dionysius arranged for a sword to hang above his head, held up by only a single strand of horsetail hair. Damocles, upon noticing this, quickly relinquished his title, having understood the lesson that with great power also comes great peril.

> The ancient sword and Sutherland's pioneering AR hardware share one thing in common – both were hung from the ceiling above the user's head, though the latter was thankfully secured with a safer material than horsehair.

Like virtual reality, there are augmented reality headsets that are powered externally by mobile phones, which work by projecting content from your phone onto a transparent visor. These are generally more inexpensive compared with other options. Some of these are even made of cardboard – an AR equivalent to the Google Cardboard. At the higher end of the AR headset market are standalone models that require no phone or other device as they have all the processing power and computer vision hardware self-contained.

## Optical see-through vs video see-through AR

Optical see-through (OST) AR is the more common and easily understood form of AR where you can see straight through a headset's visor, which is usually made of glass or hard plastic. The headset contains a number of cameras and sensors that understand and process the world around you, effectively building a 3D model of the environment you are looking at in real time. Once the system understands its surroundings, it is then possible to introduce digital elements into that environment in a realistic, spatially connected way: virtual machines can be placed on factory floors, a virtual home printer can be positioned on your table, and physical buttons on a device can be highlighted, for instance.

Some VR headsets are also capable of AR functionality through an onboard camera (or via an attached smartphone camera). The VR headset's screen displays the camera's video feed, showing the physical world in front of you, and any 'augmented' features or digital information can be overlaid on that view (Figure 14.5). This concept is referred to as video see-through (VST) or pass-through AR as the view of the augmented physical world is 'passed through' to the user via video from the camera.

Video see-through is a more accessible and affordable AR technique as it requires only a camera and some processing power. It is also possible to modify the brightness, contrast and other visual parameters of both the physical and digital elements so the whole video is optimized before it is delivered to the user. Unfortunately, the quality of most cameras is not good enough to match the human eye, there can be a perceptible delay to the

FIGURE 14.5

The view of a physical parking lot seen through an XR headset using the video see-through technique. The result is an AR experience in which the vehicle, a digital 3D model, appears to be realistically parked in one of the bays. Image taken from the Varjo XR-1 Developer Edition headset. 3D vehicle data courtesy of Volvo.

screen being updated after you move your head, and the field of view usually isn't equivalent to the human field of vision, so the end result doesn't quite match reality. This incongruence gets smaller with headsets at the higher end of the market.

## Assisted reality

Assisted reality is augmented reality at its most basic level: a small screen in your field of view that gives you hands-free access to digital information. The screen can be either opaque or transparent and is usually monocular (ie information is presented only to one eye through a small single display on one side of the head). Assisted reality differs from more advanced forms of augmented reality in that assisted reality devices do not have any onboard computer vision capabilities. As a result, the digital elements displayed are not anchored to the physical world – they are merely presented in the user's field of view for easy and convenient access. While assisted reality devices may not garner the same level of attention as more fully-fledged AR hardware, they are often far cheaper while still offering valuable hands-free access to users.

## AR form factors

AR headsets come in many shapes and sizes. The form factor most of us are familiar with is smart glasses – these look like regular, if slightly bulkier, glasses. You can usually find at least the battery and projection system squeezed into the arms of the glasses on either side. This form factor is the bridge between the consumer and corporate worlds due to the comfortably familiar design. In order of increasing size, next up are smart glasses that are clearly built for industry. They are significantly bulkier than regular glasses and sometimes even have an attachment on one side: an arm that holds a display in your field of view. This display is either a transparent rectangular pane or prism on which the digital elements are projected, or an opaque screen. The third type of form factor is a chunkier headset, usually used in industry and secured to the user's head by tightening straps or twisting a locking wheel.

# Tracking technology

## Tracking in VR

Tracking three degrees of freedom (rotation) on VR headsets is relatively simple and can be done with a set of sensors that you would find on most smartphones. Tracking six degrees of freedom is a more complicated and challenging problem that originally required external hardware to monitor a headset's position from the outside ('outside-in tracking'). Thanks to advances in SLAM (simultaneous localization and mapping) technology, modern 6 DoF VR headsets have cameras that note recognizable points in your physical environment (such as the corners of your dining table) and combined with the 3 DoF sensor data, form an understanding of where you are in that environment and how you're moving within it. When tracking technology like this is embedded within the headset, it is referred to as 'inside-out tracking'.

---

DID YOU KNOW?

The tracking technology used by many VR headsets can determine a headset's position to an accuracy of less than one millimetre.

---

*Tracking in AR*

If you're looking to anchor digital objects in the physical world convincingly, you can do this in three main ways:

- **Marker:** marker-based tracking involves using a static pattern or image which acts as a visual cue for a device to place the digital object.
- **Markerless:** this tracking uses an AR device's sensors to map the physical environment, allowing a user to anchor a digital object to a certain point within an environment without the need for a visual marker.
- **Location:** this uses an AR device's GPS system primarily to identify its location. Based on that, it can place digital information in the right place in the user's view. This is mainly used for macro-level AR experiences, where, for example, a user can point their phone during a crowded music festival for a visual indicator of where the toilets are; at a historical building, structure or landmark in the distance to get more information on it; or even at the night sky to identify planets and stars.

## Application technology

XR experiences can be launched on devices through a dedicated app or via a web browser. These are referred to as native and web apps respectively. AR/VR/XR web apps are sometimes specifically called webAR/webVR/webXR apps. Both methods come with pros and cons. Native apps generally support a greater level of functionality and run more smoothly when there is a lot of information to process, including high-quality graphics. WebXR apps are easier to distribute and offer a more seamless user experience as nothing needs to be downloaded from a store and installed on a user's device. Coupled with the wide availability of smartphones, webAR in particular is a popular method of distributing AR experiences as it requires little more than a web link for the end user to access.

## Input technology

There are many ways of controlling an XR headset and its applications:

- hand controllers;
- headset buttons;

- gaze;
- voice;
- hand tracking.

Different headsets and software will support different methods.

Hand controllers are the most popular and familiar method for VR headsets. Almost every VR headset will ship with at least one (in the case of 3 DoF headsets) or two (for 6 DoF headsets). They usually come with a combination of buttons, thumbsticks, triggers and trackpads. Some of them can detect the position and pressure of your individual fingers, allowing you to express an extensive set of gestures in the virtual world through the controller. This can be helpful when using tools or operating machines during training scenarios, or for enhancing non-verbal communication and building rapport during virtual meetings.

Note that controllers themselves can be either 3 DoF (rotatable only) or 6 DoF (rotatable and moveable in 3D space) and generally match the degrees of freedom of their headset, so 3 DoF headsets have 3 DoF controllers and 6 DoF headsets have 6 DoF controllers.

While most headsets will have buttons on them that allow you to turn the headset on and off and control the volume, some (usually 3 DoF headsets) have action buttons and swipeable trackpads that enable you to navigate through menus and select options. This is quite a simple input method that most users shouldn't have trouble with, but it limits the level of interactivity and therefore the type of experiences that you can have. To make things even simpler, you can dispense with buttons and have an option select itself after looking at it for a second or two (gaze control).

Voice is already an accepted method of interfacing with digital devices outside of XR through smart speakers such as Amazon Alexa and Google Home, and can also be used in some instances to control XR headset and application functionality.

---

DID YOU KNOW?

More than 200 million smart speakers were predicted to have been sold worldwide by the start of 2020 and almost a quarter of individuals in the United States own one.[4,5]

Hand tracking is used on high-end AR headsets and is fast becoming a popular input method for VR as well. It was originally made possible by using an attached system of cameras and infrared LEDs which could track the 3D position of your hands and fingers, recreating them digitally in real time and making them available in VR applications. That functionality is now built into some VR headsets.

---

DID YOU KNOW?

Our very thoughts could be an input method. Our brains produce small amounts of electrical activity when we think. This can be measured and converted to digital signals which can be used in XR and other applications. The technology to do this is available right now but still needs time to mature to produce reliable results.

---

IN SUMMARY

- XR head-mounted displays come in many forms, from ones that look like bulky glasses to larger units that are secured over the head.

- XR headsets need, among other things, a screen and a processor. These can be contained within the headset itself, in which case it is referred to as a standalone headset. Otherwise, if the processor is an external system such as a computer, it is a tethered headset.

- 3 DoF VR headsets allow you to look around a virtual environment from a fixed position. 6 DoF VR headsets support that plus the ability to move within the environment.

- The position of a 6 DoF XR headset needs to be tracked in 3D space. If the tracking system is contained within the headset, it uses 'inside-out' tracking. If it is external, the tracking is 'outside-in'.

- Augmented reality can be achieved in two ways: by overlaying digital elements onto a transparent visor (optical see-through) or onto a video feed of the physical world (video see-through).

- AR objects can be placed on a visual marker in a physical environment, anywhere else within an environment after scanning it (markerless), or at a rough location determined by your device's GPS and other sensors (location-based).

- Assisted reality is a term sometimes used to denote a basic AR experience used for industrial purposes in which information is presented hands-free within the user's field of view. This information does not connect to the user's physical environment.

- XR experiences can be launched natively (via their own app) or via a web browser.

- XR headsets can be controlled via one or more of the following methods: hand controllers, headset buttons, gaze, voice, and hand tracking. The availability of these options will depend on the device itself and the software you're using.

## Handheld devices

### Virtual reality

While smartphones have been used with other accessories to create VR experiences, on their own they are generally too small to effectively immerse users in virtual worlds, so these devices are primarily used for AR scenarios.

Some minimalist solutions exist to convert a smartphone into a basic VR viewing device through a pocket-sized set of foldable lenses that clip onto the phone. When an application is displayed in the right format, where the images are side by side on the phone, each eye receives one of the images through each lens, creating a stereoscopic effect in the same way that more substantial VR headsets achieve this. While far more limited, when high-end headsets are unavailable or unattainable, the pocket lens solution can be useful to provide stakeholders with a quick preview of products and environments in a more immersive manner.

### Augmented reality

Using augmented reality on smartphones made sense once cameras were integrated. By using the live feed from the phone's camera, you can overlay digital imagery and objects to create a basic augmented reality experience.

With the advent of Google's ARCore and Apple's ARKit – software development kits that enable augmented reality applications to be built – more advanced forms of augmented reality were made possible on smartphones. Using the same SLAM technology VR headsets use for inside-out tracking, an advanced AR-enabled smartphone can 'see' your environment in three dimensions through its regular camera, recognize surfaces, and therefore place digital objects in context with the physical environment (for example, placing digital furniture in an office to assess how it looks before buying it) or provide information about the environment itself (for example, being able to measure the width of a recessed section of wall).

## Projection systems

### The CAVE

Before headsets became the stereotypical representation of VR, projection systems were used in scientific and industrial applications to immerse users in a three-dimensional digital environment. These systems comprise a series of projectors that cast images onto the interior walls, floor and ceiling of a room. In conjunction with a set of positionally tracked 3D glasses, user movements in the room cause the perspective of the digital environment to change accordingly. A 6 DoF controller provides interaction capabilities. Such a system is referred to as a CAVE, a recursive acronym which stands for CAVE Automatic Virtual Environment. The name is also a nod to Plato's 'Allegory of the Cave' thought experiment, which discusses themes such as human perception, illusion and reality. The first CAVE was deployed in 1992 at the University of Illinois at Chicago, which is where the term was coined. Nowadays, the word CAVE is used colloquially as a generic term to refer to an interior, projection-based, immersive environment (Figure 14.6). Note all CAVE systems will necessarily use projectors to display the virtual content – some may use screens instead.

> 'In engineering, CAVEs are used to better analyse and understand ways to plan things such as factory floors, complex 3D constructions, flow visualization and simulation analysis. In sciences like biology, chemistry, astrophysics or mathematics, they allow users to experience three-dimensional structures, concepts and data and exploration of worlds that are too small, too large, too hostile or just plain impossible in ways that support faster and more complete understanding.' – Professor Carolina Cruz-Neira, National Academy of Engineering and inventor of the CAVE

CAVE systems have the advantage of being able to support multiple users without isolating them from the physical environment as is the case with VR

FIGURE 14.6

Visualizing a virtual retail avenue through a CAVE system at University College London. Thanks to David Swapp and Anthony Steed, Department of Computer Science, University College London, for the picture.

headsets. Users are able to see their own physical body as well as those of others while immersed in a digital environment.

With the right expertise and software, projectors can even be used in differently sized and even oddly shaped rooms. The interior of dome structures has become a favourite type of room in which to use projection systems due to the smooth 360 digital environment they create.

CAVE systems comprise a number of high-quality projectors, a powerful computer system and accompanying software. They require a dedicated room which once fixed cannot be easily moved. Despite this complexity, most of the equipment can be hidden out of sight – even the projectors can be rear projection units that cast an image from behind the (translucent) walls.

Many CAVE systems are a costly initiative compared with head-mounted displays, but they can provide a significant positive return on investment if used in the right way, as you'll see from the 'MAN CAVE' case study.

## THE MAN CAVE: A PROJECTION SYSTEM FOR VEHICLE DESIGN

FIGURE 14.7

An engineer at MAN Truck & Bus explores a vehicle design in 3D using the company's CAVE projection system.

MAN Truck & Bus, a German-headquartered transport engineering company, uses a CAVE system to create realistic virtual mockups of vehicles so that potential issues can be identified and eliminated before anything physical is built.[6] Housed in a 46m$^2$ design facility in Munich, their CAVE features infrared cameras and stereo projectors, which project images onto four large surfaces.

The processing requirements for this setup are quite intense – five powerful computers with high-end graphics cards compute slightly higher than full HD output for each of the projectors.

It cost MAN more than $500,000 to build this system, which was a joint undertaking by its Development, Logistics and Production functions. According to MAN, the company quickly broke even on the investment due to the number of vehicle design issues that were identified and resolved through the system prior to finding out in the production process or during a physical inspection, at which point a lot of the costs would be irrecoverable.

'The advantage of virtual reality is that it saves us time, material and a lot of money.' – Martin Raichl, advance development and prototyping engineer, MAN Truck & Bus

The CAVE system helps MAN identify as many as half of all potential issues up to a year before any building takes place. Engineers are able to physically explore the virtual bus or truck model as their 3D glasses are tracked, enabling the system to identify their position and how they are moving. They also have a controller which they can use to interact with the vehicle, helping them to figure out whether all the necessary components are accessible, and if not, how the product or manufacturing process should be adapted to enable and optimize the build and repair of the vehicle.

MAN uses a modular kit system, meaning it aims to use the same components regularly across a range of different commercial vehicles. This saves on cost and reduces complexity as fewer new parts need to be produced, stocked and ordered. However, while a component from a specific coach model may technically fit a new service bus model, it may not be physically possible to install due to other design elements of the bus getting in the way. In these cases, using VR through the CAVE system helps MAN to identify such conflicts in advance.

The success of its CAVE system in Munich has led to further investment in virtual labs at MAN sites in Steyr, Austria, Starachowice, Poland, Ankara, Turkey, as well as another city in Germany, Nuremberg. The CAVE systems in these labs have been linked up, enabling colleagues from different countries to simultaneously collaborate on the same virtual vehicle without having to leave their individual work sites.

## Projection mapping

A niche technology, projection mapping is the act of projecting digital imagery onto the surface of objects, sometimes to create an artistic visual effect, but it can also be used to present information in the right place. This technique used to be called spatial augmented reality as it is a form of AR that enhances a physical environment with digital information.

As with other projection techniques, projection mapping negates the need for individuals to wear a headset or take out their mobile phone as the technology is contained within the environment. However, that is also its downside as the effect is available only in the room in which it has been installed, and portability can be an issue. As a result, projection mapping is often seen in product advertising, art installations, events and museums where the solution, once implemented, is not expected to be moved.

Projection mapping can be static or interactive. Users can tap on parts of a projection to see more information about an exhibit, or they can pick up a shoe in a retail store to activate a new projection offering customization options, for example.

---

### LAING O'ROURKE: INCREASING CONSTRUCTION PRODUCTIVITY WITH PROJECTED AR

Laing O'Rourke, headquartered in Dartford, is the largest privately owned construction company in the UK, employing approximately 13,000 people.

In collaboration with the High Value Manufacturing Catapult, a UK government-backed technology innovation centre, Laing O'Rourke deployed a portable projection mapping system to increase the speed and quality of the 'set out' process during construction.

'Setting out' traditionally involves measuring and marking up items such as light switches, sprinklers and electrical sockets in a room with reference to a fixed point like the edge of a doorframe. This is a time-consuming, labour-intensive task requiring a lot of attention to detail, which needs to be maintained across multiple rooms.

A prototype was produced by attaching a projector to a hand truck, which could then be wheeled to any location in the building. Based on the ability of the projector to cast an appropriately sized image given the space restrictions of various rooms, approximately 90 per cent of the building could be covered using this prototype. Building information modelling data, which is regularly used in the design and planning of such projects, was used in this case as part of the build phase as well: it fed into an off-the-shelf projection mapping software package, which instructed the projector on what to display on each wall or ceiling.

Workers who were assisted by the projection system were able to complete the set-out process of an entire floor in 34.5 hours instead of 80, representing a 57 per cent time saving. This time saving could be applied to the entire project as the new, shorter set-out process was no longer a part of the critical path of the project.

## Large screens

When it comes to experiencing digital worlds, they have always been displayed on screens. In the consumer world, this includes movies and video games that we watch and play on a television. In the business world, we might examine 3D models and digital twins (digital recreations of real equipment and environments) on our laptops. Using this medium of viewing has obvious disadvantages in that the immersion is not as strong compared with being absorbed in an environment at the right scale within a VR headset. There is also limited ability to look around the world naturally – instead, a keyboard and mouse are used to navigate the environment.

Large screens have been used for some time in academia and industry to achieve immersion. Many provide a good enough level of presence to qualify as a virtual reality experience, albeit a more limited one. This is part of the reason why many people are drawn to IMAX theatres, whose screens are many times larger than regular theatre screens.

### DID YOU KNOW?

The IMAX cinema in Sydney holds the title for the largest screen in the world at a whopping 117 feet wide by 96 feet tall (36 metres × 29 metres). That's enough real estate to pack in 21 double decker buses, 3 across and 7 high.[7]

As well as providing a powerful visual experience with sharp and vivid images, IMAX theatres offer a high-quality audio system that contributes equally to the immersive experience. But given the size and complexity of such a setup, this immersion comes at a cost, both financially and in terms of its portability, which is understandably limited compared with a VR headset.

## GLAXOSMITHKLINE: LARGE SCREENS TO UNDERSTAND SHOPPER BEHAVIOURS

GlaxoSmithKline (GSK) is a global pharmaceutical and consumer healthcare company headquartered in London. It sells a range of medications, oral healthcare products and other items in pharmacies around the world.

To market its products more effectively, GSK aims to understand how shoppers react when faced with different store layouts and shelf arrangements. This insight allows GSK to advise pharmacies on optimal merchandising practices.

Testing this in a live store would be incredibly time-consuming and disruptive to customers, so to gather this data in a more efficient and cost-effective way, GSK created the Shopper Science Lab, a 930 $m^2$ facility that houses a physical and virtual retail environment and also makes use of facial scanning biometric equipment to analyse the emotional reactions of shoppers.

One of the methods GSK employs to immerse users in a virtual retail environment is a seamless touch screen. It is called the 'Virtual Insight and Engagement Wall' and is 5.32 m wide and 2.55 m tall (Figure 14.8).

Using this technology, different store layouts can be loaded and tested on the fly, and shoppers can explore the virtual environment through a handheld controller or via the touch screen. Their path choices, what they look at and how long they spend in each area are examples of data points that can be tracked to provide insight into their shopping behaviour and help pharmacies optimize product placements to improve sales.

FIGURE 14.8

A large screen used at the GSK Shopper Science Lab to immerse users virtually in a pharmacy. Photo credit: GSK Shopper Science Lab.

## IN SUMMARY

There are four different types of XR device: headsets, handheld devices, projection systems and screens – each has advantages and disadvantages (see Table 14.1).

- XR headsets can be portable and provide deep immersion, but that comes at the cost of isolating the user from the physical world, making it uncomfortable for some.

- Many handheld devices are capable of running advanced AR applications; however, they occupy the user's hand, making it inefficient for some applications and unviable for lengthy use.

- VR projection systems create a good level of immersion and can support multiple users without isolating them from the real world, but they can be complex, costly and immovable.

- AR projection systems require no preparation or hardware setup from the user, making them very convenient to access but only when in the same location as the user. As a result, their applications are more limited than handheld devices or headsets and they cannot be easily moved to other locations.

- Screens are a technology we are used to and so are very comfortable with. However, they do not provide a strong sense of immersion without being physically large – and at that point they suffer from limited portability and high costs.

TABLE 14.1

|  | Headset | Handheld | Projection system | Screen |
|---|---|---|---|---|
| Immersion | High | Low | Medium | Medium |
| Hands-free | Yes | No | Yes | Yes |
| Cost | Low | Low | High | High |
| Scalability | Medium | High | Low | Low |
| Portability | Medium | High | Low | Low |
| Multiple users | No | Yes | Yes | Yes |

The advantages and disadvantages of different XR devices

# Notes

1   https://www.theverge.com/2019/11/6/20952495/google-cardboard-open-source-phone-based-vr-daydream (archived at https://perma.cc/2VDF-XLSX)

2   https://www.theverge.com/2019/10/16/20915791/google-daydream-samsung-oculus-gear-vr-mobile-vr-platforms-dead (archived at https://perma.cc/Y8WN-YQDH)

3   https://arxiv.org/ftp/arxiv/papers/1305/1305.2500.pdf (archived at https://perma.cc/3YN7-84B4)

4   https://www.statista.com/statistics/1130208/smart-speaker-ownership-worldwide-by-country/ (archived at https://perma.cc/TLC5-EMVU)

5   https://www.canalys.com/newsroom/canalys-global-smart-speaker-installed-base-to-top-200-million-by-end-of-2019 (archived at https://perma.cc/29X6-FRCW)

6   https://www.truck.man.eu/de/en/man-world/man-in-germany/press-and-media/Precision-in-the-virtual-world_-MAN-using-the-CAVE-337280.html (archived at https://perma.cc/ET53-PU94)

7   https://theculturetrip.com/europe/united-kingdom/england/london/articles/scaling-up-to-truly-giant-cinema/ (archived at https://perma.cc/9DFQ-PZSH)

# GLOSSARY

If you come across an XR term in this book or elsewhere that leaves you utterly bewildered, feel free to refer to the below list of terminology. Note that some of the terms may have slightly different meanings outside of the industry but are defined here in relation to XR technologies.

## All the Rs

**VR – virtual reality** Immerses users in a fully digital environment through a headset or surrounding display. This environment can be computer-generated or recorded from the physical world.

**AR – augmented reality** Presents digital information, objects or media in the physical world through a mobile device or headset. These elements can appear as flat graphics or can behave as a seemingly real 3D object.

**MR – mixed reality** Represents the spectrum of technologies from the part-digital world of augmented reality to the fully immersive experience of virtual reality. However, the term is regularly used in conversation to define a specific subset of AR in which virtual objects are capable of being anchored within the user's physical environment.

**XR – extended reality** Represents the spectrum of technologies from the part-digital world of augmented reality to the fully immersive experience of virtual reality.

**immersive technology** See **XR – extended reality**. The term has no acronym as 'IT' was already taken in a significant way.

**spatial computing** See **XR – extended reality**. The acronym 'SC' hasn't really taken off so is not generally recognized.

**assisted reality** A domain of AR where digital information is displayed in a user's view, allowing them to examine it hands-free, but which is not anchored to the physical environment.

## Other terms

**3 DoF (degrees of freedom)** Tracking technology where the device's rotation is tracked but not its position. See 'Hardware considerations and selection' in Chapter 7 for an illustration.

**6 DoF (degrees of freedom)**   Tracking technology where the device's rotation and position are tracked. See 'Hardware considerations and selection' in Chapter 7 for an illustration.

**360 video (or photo)**   A video (or photo) of the full 360 degree surroundings of a physical environment.

**AI – artificial intelligence**   A branch of computer science focused on building digital systems capable of simulating human intelligence.

**AIO – all-in-one**   See 'standalone'.

**AR pass-through**   See 'VST – video see-through'.

**AR portal**   Usually accessed via a mobile device, this is an AR experience in which a user is able to walk through a digital door placed in the physical environment that leads to a fully digital environment.

**ARCore**   A set of software development tools released by Google for building AR experiences on Android.

**ARKit**   A set of software development tools released by Apple for building AR experiences on iOS.

**avatar**   A digital personification.

**BIM – building information modelling**   Use of an all-encompassing shared data environment to help architecture, engineering and construction stakeholders to plan, design, construct and manage buildings and infrastructure.

**biometrics**   Metrics relating to human features, often used in the context of authentication, but also valid in other areas such as research.

**Cardboard**   A type of VR headset made out of cardboard and lenses into which a mobile phone can be inserted for a rudimentary VR experience. Sometimes called Google Cardboard as it was initially designed by Google.

**CAVE – cave automatic virtual environment**   A VR environment achieved through projectors casting images on the walls, floor and/or ceiling that change in line with a user's movement to maintain a realistic perspective. The first CAVE was conceptualized and built by the University of Illinois at Chicago, but the term is now used colloquially to describe any similar VR system.

**Chaperone**   Safeguarding feature for SteamVR headsets to warn users that they are reaching the boundary of their predefined area of use.

**computer vision**   A field within artificial intelligence and computer science aimed at giving computer systems the ability to understand and react to physical objects and environments that they can 'see'.

**constellation**   An outside-in positional tracking system for VR developed by Oculus.

**cyber sickness**   Physiological discomfort that some users experience when using VR and other digital technologies.

**digital eyewear**   Optical see-through AR head-mounted displays.

**DOP – director of photography**   Part of the crew on a 360 production that operates the camera and oversees the technical aspects of the production.

**eye tracking**   Camera-based technology to track eye movements and thereby determine what users are looking at within a virtual or physical environment.

**FOV – field of view**   How much of a digital environment you are able to see. Sometimes split into horizontal and vertical values.

**game engine**   A software package of visual development tools used to build 2D or 3D applications, including XR. The term 'game' is a misnomer nowadays as these tools are often used for non-gaming applications as well.

**goggles**   Colloquial term to describe an XR head-mounted display.

**Google Cardboard**   See 'Cardboard'.

**GPS – global positioning system**   A satellite-based navigation system used to pinpoint the location of a device.

**Guardian**   Safeguarding feature for Oculus VR headsets to warn users that they are reaching the boundary of their predefined area of use.

**hand tracking**   A technology system usually composed of cameras and infrared LEDs that is used to detect and instantaneously recreate hand and finger movements in VR.

**haptics**   The technology responsible for delivering feedback to users that can be felt through the sense of touch.

**HMD – head-mounted display**   Any wearable XR device that sits on the head.

**holographic video**   See 'volumetric video'.

**HUD – head-up display**   A transparent display of information presented to a user in their regular field of view.

**inside-out tracking**   A self-contained system of positional tracking used in standalone headsets that constantly processes information about the changing view of its environment to determine its movement within that environment.

**IoT – internet of things**   The concept of connecting devices to the internet, enabling them to transmit and receive data. Sometimes used as an adjective to describe such devices as well.

**IPD – interpupillary distance**   The distance between a user's eyes, measured from the centre of each pupil in millimetres.

**latency**   The delay between a command being sent and a response arriving.

**Lighthouse**   An outside-in positional tracking system for virtual reality developed by Valve.

**locomotion**   The act of moving within a virtual reality environment.

**marker**   A static image that acts as a visual cue to trigger the start of an AR experience.

**markerless**   A form of AR tracking that doesn't rely on visual markers – instead, the AR device's sensors map the physical environment, allowing a user to anchor the AR experience to a certain point within the environment.

**mobile device**   Catch-all term for mobile phones, tablets and similar handheld devices.

**monoscopic**    In relation to 360 media, content where the same image is sent to both eyes.

**motion sickness**    Physiological discomfort experienced by some users that is triggered by movement.

**OST – optical see-through**    A type of AR in head-mounted displays with a transparent visor which is used to display digital elements overlaid on the physical world. It is an alternative to video see-through (VST) AR.

**outside-in tracking**    A system of positional tracking that requires an external system to function.

**pass-through**    See 'VST – video see-through'.

**photogrammetry**    A technological process in which photos of a physical item or location are taken from different angles and then processed by a computer system to reconstruct that physical item or location as a digital 3D model.

**POI – point of interest**    A significant part of a 360 scene that is meant to capture a viewer's attention.

**positional tracking**    Computational process of regularly tracking the position of a headset, controller or other device.

**POV – point of view**    The perspective of a user in a VR experience.

**presence**    Used to describe a sense of full immersion in a virtual environment.

**projection mapping**    A form of AR that uses a projector to display information directly onto physical objects and environments.

**real time**    A processing delay so minuscule that it is perceived by a user as instantaneous.

**recce**    Short for 'reconnaissance', this is a task performed by a 360 production crew whereby they will visit a location in advance in preparation for filming.

**refresh rate**    How frequently a digital display is updated every second, measured in hertz (Hz).

**room scale**    Used to describe 6 DoF VR content.

**SAR – spatial augmented reality**    See 'projection mapping'.

**SBS – side by side**    A media format which displays two adjacent images or videos, each of which is sent to a different eye when viewing through a VR device.

**SDE – screen-door effect**    A visual artifact noticeable by some users in some VR headsets where the individual pixels of the screen can be discerned, creating the effect of looking through screen-door netting.

**SDK – software development kit**    A single collection of software tools relating to a specific hardware or software platform which allows developers to build applications for that platform.

**simulator sickness**    Physiological discomfort that some users experience when using physical simulator systems.

**SLAM – simultaneous localization and mapping**    Real-time visual processing of a device's surroundings to build a map of the environment while determining its location within that environment.

**smart glasses**    An AR head-mounted display worn by a user like a pair of glasses and similar in form to glasses.

**standalone**    A self-contained type of XR headset that doesn't need any other hardware to run.

**SteamVR**    A set of tools and technologies for VR headsets that provides a common system for tracking and other functionality.

**stereoscopic**    In relation to 360 media, content where a slightly different image is sent to each eye in an effort to mimic the slightly different view each eye receives in reality.

**tethered**    A type of XR headset that needs to be connected to an external computing system to run.

**uncanny valley**    A concept describing greater human affinity for robots that act and look more like humans up to a certain point after which they are seen as creepy or unsettling.

**Unity**    One of the popular game engines used to develop 3D applications (including XR experiences).

**Unreal**    One of the popular game engines used to develop 3D applications (including XR experiences).

**VFX – visual effects**    Imagery that is created or manipulated after a 360 production has been filmed.

**volumetric video**    A technology in which people and physical objects are recorded as a three-dimensional video.

**VR sickness**    A form of cyber sickness specifically connected to VR.

**VR180**    A video format created by Google in which a 180-degree field of view is captured and viewable on both VR headsets and flat screens.

**VST – video see-through**    A type of AR available in some VR head-mounted displays where the video feed from the device's camera is combined with digital elements before being presented to the user to create the AR effect. It is an alternative to optical see-through (OST) AR.

**WebAR/WebVR/WebXR**    Technology which allows AR/VR/XR experiences to be run in a web browser (ie without the need for a dedicated application).

# INDEX

Bold page numbers indicate figures, *italic* numbers indicate tables.

CPSIA information can be obtained
at www.ICGtesting.com
Printed in the USA
LVHW051405161220
674185LV00004B/7